Pathways from Ethnic Conflict

The book begins with an agenda-setting introduction which provides an overview of the central question being addressed, such as the circumstances associated with the move towards a political settlement, the parameters of this settlement and the factors that have assisted in bringing it about. The remaining contributions focus on a range of cases selected for their diversity and their capacity to highlight the full gamut of political approaches to conflict resolution. The cases vary in:

- the intensity of the conflict (from Belgium, where it is potential rather than actual, to Sri Lanka, where it has come to a recent violent conclusion);
- the geopolitical relationship between the competing groups (from Cyprus, where they are sharply segregated geographically, to Northern Ireland, where they are intermingled);
- the extent to which a stable constitutional accommodation has been reached (ranging from the Basque Country, with a large range of unresolved problems, to South Africa, which has achieved a significant level of institutional stability).

This book ranges over the world's major geopolitical zones, including Asia, the Middle East, Africa and Europe and will be of interest to practitioners in the field of international security.

This book was published as a special issue of *Nationalism and Ethnic Politics*.

John Coakley is a Professor in the School of Politics and International Relations, University College Dublin. He is contributing editor or co-editor of *Politics in the Republic of Ireland* (5th ed., London: Routledge, 2010), *Crossing the Border: New Relationships between Northern Ireland and the Republic of Ireland* (Dublin: Irish Academic Press, 2007), *Renovation or Revolution? New Territorial Politics in Ireland and the United Kingdom* (Dublin: University College of Dublin Press, 2005), and *The Territorial Management of Ethnic Conflict* (2nd ed., Portland, OR: Frank Cass, 2003).

Nationalism and Ethnicity / Routledge Studies in Nationalism and Ethnicity

Formerly known as Cass Series: Nationalism and Ethnicity, ISSN 1462-9755

Series Editor: William Safran, University of Colorado at Boulder

This new series draws attention to some of the most exciting issues in current world political debate: nation-building, autonomy and self-determination; ethnic identity, conflict and accommodation; pluralism, multiculturalism and the politics of language; ethnonationalism, irredentism and separatism; and immigration, naturalization and citizenship. The series will include monographs as well as edited volumes, and through the use of case studies and comparative analyses will bring together some of the best work to be found in the field.

Nationalism and Ethnicity

Ethnicity and Citizenship
The Canadian Case
Edited by Jean Laponce and William Safran

Nationalism and Ethnoregional Identities in China
Edited by William Safran

Identity and Territorial Autonomy in Plural Societies
Edited by William Safran and Ramon Maíz

Ideology, Legitimacy and the New State
Yugoslavia, Serbia and Croatia
Siniša Malešević

Diasporas and Ethnic Migrants
Germany, Israel and Russia in Comparative Perspective
Rainer Munz and Rainer Ohliger

Ethnic Groups in Motion
Economic Competition and Migration in Multiethnic States
Milica Z. Bookman

Post-Cold War Identity Politics
Northern and Baltic Experiences
Edited by Marko Lehti and David J. Smith

Welfare, Ethnicity and Altruism
New Findings and Evolutionary Theory
Edited by Frank Salter

Routledge Studies in Nationalism and Ethnicity

Ethnic Violence and the Societal Security Dilemma
Paul Roe

Nationalism in a Global Era
The Persistence of Nations
Edited by Mitchell Young, Eric Zuelow and Andreas Sturm

Religious Nationalism in Modern Europe
If God be for Us
Philip W. Barker

Nationalism and Democracy
Dichotomies, Complementarities, Oppositions
Edited by André Lecours and Luis Moreno

Pathways from Ethnic Conflict
Institutional Redesign in Divided Societies
Edited by John Coakley

Political Liberalism and Plurinational Democracies
Edited by Ferran Requejo and Miquel Caminal

Pathways from Ethnic Conflict

Institutional Redesign in Divided Societies

Edited by John Coakley

Routledge
Taylor & Francis Group
LONDON AND NEW YORK

First published 2010 by Routledge
2 Park Square, Milton Park, Abingdon, Oxon, OX14 4RN

Simultaneously published in the USA and Canada
by Routledge
711 Third Avenue, New York, NY 10017

Routledge is an imprint of the Taylor & Francis Group, an informa business

First issued in paperback 2011
© 2010 Taylor & Francis

This book is a reproduction of *Nationalism and Ethnic Politics*, vol. 15, issues 3 & 4. The Publisher requests to those authors who may be citing this book to state, also, the bibliographical details of the special issue on which the book was based

Typeset in Garamond by Value Chain, India

British Library Cataloguing in Publication Data
A catalogue record for this book is available from the British Library

ISBN13: 978-0-415-55402-2 (hbk)
ISBN13: 978-0-415-51864-2 (pbk)

CONTENTS

List of Tables

List of Figures

Notes on Contributors

Pierre Baudewyns is Research Assistant at the Pôle Interuniversitaire sur l'Opinion publique et la Politique (PIOP) at the Université catholique de Louvain. He has published several articles on elections and political behaviour in Belgium. He is working on survey methodology and public opinion within the Belgian regions.

Roberto Belloni is Associate Professor of International Relations at the University of Trento, Italy. He has published extensively on issues pertaining to democratization and peacebuilding in deeply divided societies, with particular reference to the Balkans. His recent work includes the book *State Building and International Intervention in Bosnia* (London: Routledge, 2007).

John Coakley is a Professor in the School of Politics and International Relations, University College Dublin. He is contributing editor or co-editor of *Politics in the Republic of Ireland* (5th ed., London: Routledge, 2010), *Crossing the Border: New Relationships between Northern Ireland and the Republic of Ireland* (Dublin: Irish Academic Press, 2007), *Renovation or Revolution? New Territorial Politics in Ireland and the United Kingdom* (Dublin: University College of Dublin Press, 2005), and *The Territorial Management of Ethnic Conflict* (2nd ed., Portland, OR: Frank Cass, 2003).

Lieven De Winter is Senior Professor at the Université Catholique de Louvain, where he is director of the Centre de Politique Comparée and codirector of the Pôle Interuniversitaire sur l'Opinion publique et la Politique (PIOP). He is editor or coeditor of *Non-state wide Parties in Europe* (Barcelona: ICPS, 1995), *Regionalist Parties in Western Europe* (Routledge, 1998), *Autonomist Parties in Europe* (ICPS, 2006), *Elections: le reflux? Comportements et attitudes lors des élections en Belgique* (Bruxelles: De Boeck, 2007), and *The Politics of Belgium* (London: Routledge 2009). He is author of numerous journal articles and book chapters on political parties, legislatures and cabinets, public opinion, and Belgian politics.

Adrian Guelke is Professor of Comparative Politics and director of the Centre for the Study of Ethnic Conflict in the School of Politics, International Studies and Philosophy at Queen's University, Belfast. Recent publications include *The New Age of Terrorism* (London: I. B. Tauris, 2009), *Terrorism and Global Disorder* (London: I. B. Tauris, 2006), and *Rethinking the Rise and Fall of Apartheid* (New York: Palgrave

Macmillan, 2005). He is the chair of the International Political Science Association's research committee on politics and ethnicity.

Simon Haddad is lecturer in the Department of Political Studies and Public Administration at the American University of Beirut and is the author of *The Palestinian Impasse: The Politics of Refugee Integration* (Sussex, UK: Sussex Academic Press, 2003) and of various articles in academic journals such as *Security Dialogue*, *Studies in Conflict and Terrorism*, and *Journal of Conflict Resolution*.

Joseph S. Joseph is Jean Monnet Professor of International Relations and European Affairs at the University of Cyprus. He received his BA from Panteion University (Greece), MA from the University of Stockholm (Sweden), and PhD from Miami University (USA). He was a postdoctoral fellow at Harvard and taught at the University of Alabama, Gustavus Adolphus College (Minnesota) and Miami University. His publications include: *Turkey and the European Union: Internal Dynamics and External Challenges* (ed., New York: Palgrave, 2006); *Cyprus: Ethnic Conflict and International Politics, from Independence to the Threshold of the European Union* (New York: St. Martin's Press/ Macmillan, 1997). He is currently serving as Ambassador of Cyprus to Greece.

Francisco J. Llera is Professor (1992) and Director of the Department of Political and Administration Sciences in the University of the Basque Country (2004-07), where he founded and currently directs the *Euskobarometro* research team (www. ehu.es/euskobarometro). He has been chairperson of the Spanish Association of Political and Administration Sciences (2004-09), Spanish Federation of Sociology (1991-95) and Basque Sociological Association (1975-80) and a member of the European Academy (2002) and of the Executive Committee of the International Political Science Association (2009). He has published several books, chapters and articles on elections and political behaviour, terrorism and political violence, regional identity and selfgovernment, and public opinion in Spain.

S. W. R. de A. Samarasinghe is on the faculty of the Payson Center for International Development (payson.tulane.edu) at Tulane University, New Orleans, USA, and is Executive Chairman of Global Vision—Centre for Knowledge Advancement, Kandy, Sri Lanka (www.gvglobalvision.org). He was Takemi Fellow at Harvard University (1985-86) and Cornell Professor at Swarthmore College, Pennsylvania (1989-90). He has been consultant to major international development agencies including World Bank, USAID and UN. He has published extensively on economic development, corruption and democratization in Sri Lanka and South Asia, and on ethnic conflict in Sri Lanka and elsewhere.

Jennifer Todd is a Professor in the School of Politics and International Relations, University College Dublin. She is coauthor of *Dynamics of Conflict in Northern Ireland* (Cambridge, UK: Cambridge University Press, 1996) and has published widely on Northern Ireland politics, and on ethnicity, identity, and identity change, in *Political Studies*, *Archives Européennes de Sociologie*, *Theory and Society*, and *Nations and Nationalism*. She is currently finishing a new book on the Northern Ireland conflict and settlement.

Preface

This book is one of the most substantial contributions to the Studies in Nationalism and Ethnicity. Professor John Coakley, the editor, brings together a number of well documented case studies from Europe, the Middle East, Africa, and South Asia that explore different varieties of contemporary ethnic conflicts and solutions. In his Introduction, he points out the determining variables of ethnic conflict, such as language, religion, race, relative political and economic deprivations, collective memory, and outside intervention. Reminding us once again of the staying power of ethnic minorities, he explores commonalities and differences in the history of the conflicts, the types and degrees of ethnic and other fractionalizations, and the proximate causes of ethnic violence. He presents a comparative statistical portrait of ethnic divisions while adverting to the controversies about statistics; and in a concluding summary, calls attention to the multiform methods of mobilization, to the range of ethnic demands from cultural and territorial autonomy to constitutional engineering to separatism, to the varied paths to the settlement of conflicts and their durability, and to the conclusions to be drawn from them.

The individual chapters illustrate the diversities of history, political context, the relative weight of ethnic minorities, and the extent of external involvement, all of which help to explain the variety of processes and the range of results from the seemingly hopeless case of Belgium to the relatively peaceful and successful outcomes in Spain and South Africa. Each case is different: language is the dominant divisive element in Belgium and Spain; religion in Bosnia, Lebanon, and Northern Ireland; race in South Africa; and a mix of factors in Cyprus and Sri Lanka. Spain provides an interesting example of the relationship between constitutional revisions and regionally differentiated combinations of national and ethnic identities; South Africa, of ethnoracial reconciliation and nation-building; and several of the remaining case studies, of still simmering conflicts and the role of third party facilitations (or, in some cases, complications) in the pursuit of peace.

William Safran
February 2010

Foreword

Gudmund Hernes

President, International Social Science Council

A common theme runs through conceptions of the development of the modern world: that it is becoming *one* world, with national institutions more alike and global institutions more shared, with citizens increasingly getting the same liberties and developing similar mindsets. According to this view, the driving force towards homogenization and integration is an economic system based on capitalist principles, nation states with similar constitutions, and citizens moving towards universal human rights. Moreover, in this view, local cultures would be supplanted by a cosmopolitan one – indeed, this process could be hastened by constructing a joint language with elements taken from many different national languages, such as Esperanto.

The founding fathers of social science recounted different aspects of this story. Marx, for example, in *The Communist Manifesto,* described how inexorable forces of competition would destroy national industries and even promote a uniform world culture:

> [Old established national industries] are dislodged by new industries, whose introduction becomes a life and death question for all civilized nations, by industries that no longer work up indigenous raw material, but raw material drawn from the remotest zones; industries whose products are consumed, not only at home, but in every quarter of the globe. In place of the old wants, satisfied by the production of the country, we find new wants, requiring for their satisfaction the products of distant lands and climes. In place of the old local and national seclusion and self-sufficiency, we have intercourse in every direction, universal inter-dependence of nations. And as in material, so also in intellectual production. The intellectual creations of individual nations become common property. National one-sidedness and narrow-mindedness become more and more impossible, and from the numerous national and local literatures, there arises a world literature.

Max Weber told the story of how legal-rational systems and modern bureaucracies would increasingly replace traditional and local models of social organization. Other examples are easily found. The most recent grand statement to this effect is probably to be found in Francis Fukuyama's *The End of History and the Last Man* (1992), where he described the coming period as "the end point of mankind's ideological evolution and the universalization of Western liberal democracy as the final form of human government."

Clearly this is not the whole story – substantial impediments lay on the path towards global markets, universal political arrangements, and a cosmopolitan mono-culture. The counter-story is that of ethnic divisions and fractionalization. For social development has not been a one-way street. Not only have ethnic divisions survived in modern states; in many cases they have become more pronounced, more disruptive and more potent. Millions in every continent have found their identity in loyalties other than national alignments. The bases for these ethnic divisions vary (the lines of ethnic demarcations can be religious, linguistic, racial or economic), and are often overlapping and mutually reinforcing. Whatever their source, ethnic divisions remain politically trenchant, frequently trumping national allegiances and making states more fragile. Ethnic identities express themselves as separatism, factionalism and sometimes irredentism. They may also become more pronounced due to modern migration; immigration and intermingling may not always result in a melting pot.

How should ethnic divisions be analyzed? A very good answer is provided in this volume. It samples a wide range of cases where ethnicity manifests itself in multiple ways. In these cases, the authors look for hidden commonalities and more general latent structures in the varying expressions. For there is information in variation – and it makes for exciting reading. The result not only has academic interest; it is pertinent for policy makers as well.

In the early 1990s the International Social Science Council (ISSC), the global body which for more than 50 years has been acting as a shared forum for international disciplinary associations and, more recently, national research councils, developed an important program in the area of "Conflict early warning systems". This sought to learn from the experience of successful efforts at reconciliation between groups and states with a view to promoting a less violent world.

The present book emerges from a similar ISSC program, "Research in ethnic conflict: approaches to peace" (RECAP). In particular, it reflects the outcome of a roundtable meeting in Dublin sponsored by the ISSC in December 2008. The book grew out of papers presented at that meeting, and by associated debates on the issues raised there.

In addition to the analysis of the sources and consequences of ethnic conflict the book also addresses the manner in which conflicts are resolved, and the kinds of international mediation that can play a role, in addition to domestic factors, in reducing differences between ethnic groups.

It is this combination of intrinsic interest and practical relevance which makes this book at the same time disturbing and stimulating reading.

1

Comparing Ethnic Conflicts:
Common Patterns, Shared Challenges

JOHN COAKLEY
University College Dublin

Notwithstanding predictions over the past century and a half that minorities defined in ethnic, linguistic, or cultural terms would gradually reconcile themselves to coexistence in states dominated by metropolitan cultures, difficulties arising from the mobilization of minority communities continue to be pronounced at the beginning of the twenty-first century. This article provides an overview of the extent of ethnic division in modern states, describes characteristic patterns of ethnic mobilization and focuses on a smaller set of illustrative cases that reveal many of these patterns. In this, it defines the context for a set of case studies that follow: Belgium, Spain, Northern Ireland, Bosnia and Herzegovina, Cyprus, Lebanon, South Africa, and Sri Lanka.

INTRODUCTION

The failure of minorities defined in ethnic, linguistic, or cultural terms to conform to the predictions of observers and to fade quietly away in an increasingly cosmopolitan world is one of the better-known illustrations of the capacity of social analysts to "get it wrong" in their expectations about human development. Whatever the language used or the paradigm in which it is embedded, the list of failures is impressive, ranging from left-wing political activism in the nineteenth century to conservative social theory in the twentieth. Thus it was that early Marxist predictions that "ethnic trash" (to use Engels's term) would be consigned to the dustbin of history with the advent of advanced capitalism collapsed in the face of ethnonational rebellion that blew the Habsburg and Ottoman empires apart and that helped transform the Russian Empire into a multinational Soviet Union.[1] But the predictions of the "politics of development" school in the mid-twentieth century that ethnic particularism would inevitably fall victim to the progressive forces of "nation-building" in the course of the modernization process also fell victim to historical realities, with widespread ethnonational resurgence in the 1970s and 1980s not just challenging existing state structures but in some cases leading to their collapse.[2]

We know now that these expectations were unjustified, though we know less about *why* they were unjustified. This introductory chapter seeks not to explore the reasons for the continued vitality of ethnic protest but rather to provide an introduction to the kinds of issues that arise when ethnonational consciousness is mobilized politically—in particular those issues that have implications for the organization of the state. The chapter falls into three parts. The first seeks to describe the broad parameters of the problem by highlighting the global character of ethnic diversity. The second generalizes about patterns of mobilization and the goals of ethnic protest movements. The third narrows the focus to a range of illustrative cases, introducing the more detailed analyses that feature later in this volume.

ETHNIC DIVISIONS

The volume of material that deals with ethnonational division within the countries of the world is huge and of well-established vintage. In its initial phase, it focused on the "old world" or, more specifically, on Europe.[3] More recently, it has been global in reach and has been based on accumulated research deriving from a range of approaches. Broadly speaking, our basic data in this area now derive from three types of source. First, a considerable number of handbooks of various kinds seek to cover the globe comprehensively, systematically presenting a wide range of political and nonpolitical material, including data on ethnonational divisions.[4] Second, a great deal of scholarly activity has been directed specifically at the issue of ethnonational minorities and has generated several important cross-national surveys.[5] Third, certain activist groups have a vested interest in describing the ethnonational breakdown of the countries of the world and have also been wide-ranging in coverage.[6]

This wealth of data, qualitative and quantitative, places researchers under some pressure to reduce the complex global picture to a more concise summary of the position. Although this is of obvious interest to political scientists, efforts to measure ethnic fractionalization have been a particular focus of attention within economics, because of its perceived implications for economic development. As regards measurement, there seems to have been a high degree of convergence in this area, with remaining differences between specialists attributable to variations in data sources and in the definition of ethnonational division. The generally accepted index, which we may identify with the long-established Simpson index in ecology (or the Herfindahl index in economics), defines ethnonational fractionalization as one minus the sum of the squared proportionate shares of each ethnonational group. This ranges from a value close to one (maximum fractionalization) to zero (no fractionalization).

Already in the 1950s, this index was being applied in sociolinguistics: Joseph Greenberg devised a set of indices of *linguistic diversity*, the first and simplest of which was identical to the Simpson index (the others included weightings to take account of such factors as interlanguage distance and personal bi- or multilingualism).[7] This was applied by other scholars to provide a hard estimate of mother-tongue diversity over time in 35 countries, and to illustrate the wider applicability of such indices.[8] This approach was also proposed as a way of measuring political fractionalization, and it has been used to summarize a wide range of data in major cross-national data collections, such as that of Taylor and Hudson, where the fractionalization index has been applied to electoral, linguistic, and ethnic data.[9]

The dominant position occupied by the Simpson index is illustrated in a number of recent applications. We may consider four of these, each sharing three characteristics: agreement on the centrality of the Simpson index as the obvious measure of fractionalization, on the sensitivity of this measure to matters of definition and classification, and on the difficulty of obtaining consistent empirical data. In the first of these, Anthony Annett computed three indices: of *ethnolinguistic fractionalization*, based on data listing the maximum number of groups; of *religious fractionalization*, based on major religions, but with Christianity broken into its several denominations; and a combined index of *ethnolinguistic and religious fractionalization* produced by merging these two.[10] Second, Philip Roeder calculated an index of *ethnolinguistic fractionalization* in three different ways: a first measure based on maximum differentiation, defining cultural and racial subgroups within linguistic groups as separate; a second one centered on an intermediate level of differentiation, defining cultural but not racial subgroups as separate; and a third one, based on minimum differentiation, where cultural and racial subgroups within ethnic groups defined by language are ignored.[11] James Fearon adopted a similar approach but distinguished between an index of *ethnic fractionalization* (based on a mixture of criteria) and an index of *cultural fractionalization* (which adjusts for linguistic adjacency, thus reducing the number of discrete groups in countries where some people speak closely related languages).[12] Alberto Alesina and his colleagues, rather than seeing one index as a modification of another, distinguished between three quite separate approaches: an *index of linguistic fractionalization*, an *index of religious fractionalization* (each of these with obvious defining criteria), and an *index of ethnic fractionalization* (which defines groups by reference to linguistic and racial criteria).[13]

The four approaches also differ in the data sources on which they are based, and on the period to which they refer. Annett relied on the source in which the World Christian Database originated, a major encyclopedia of religion that also reports a huge amount of ethnolinguistic data.[14] Roeder used several comparative Soviet sources and the *Europa World Yearbook* and calculated his measures separately for two years, 1961 and 1985. Fearon used the CIA *World Factbook*, *Encyclopedia Brittanica*, the Library of Congress *Country Studies*, and the Ethnologue and Minorities at Risk (MAR) databases (described below), among other works, and his data referred to the 1990s. Alesina and his colleagues relied on *Encyclopedia Britannica*, but for their index of ethnic fractionalization they also used the CIA *World Factbook*, publications of the Minority Rights Group and other sources including national population censuses; their data referred to the period around 2000.

For some analysts of conflict, there are problems with any index like the parent of those just discussed, generally described as the ethnolinguistic fractionalization (ELF) index—in particular, it does not consider the relative power of the competing groups. In an effort to rectify this, specifically in the case of Africa, an alternative index of *politically relevant ethnic groups* (PREG) has been devised. This excludes all groups in respect of which there is no evidence of an autonomous political presence and bases the value of the index only on the remaining groups.[15] In a variant, other African specialists have tried to expand the range of politically relevant groups by considering the impact of crosscutting cleavages and other divisions, resulting in a more inclusive approach; they labelled the result the index of *ethnopolitical group fragmentation*.[16] The logic of this approach has been taken further in one important study of the impact of ethnic divisions on nationalist insurgencies: it has suggested a new index, N^*, which takes account not just of the diversity of groups but also of the question of which groups are in power and which are excluded.[17]

Since it is proposed in this chapter to use a concentration or diversity index not as an explanatory variable but rather as a simple descriptive and comparative measure, a straightforward approach will suffice for further illustrative purposes. We may examine more closely the index of ethnolinguistic fractionalization elaborated by Roeder; this is based on data referring to the mid-1980s covering a very wide range of cases using mainly data from specialists in the area (Soviet ethnographers).[18] This approach to measurement of course allows us to score countries and to rank them in respect of their degree of ethnonational fractionalization. We may, however, also need to recognise cut-off points that are of potential political significance. One way of doing this would be to use a basic arithmetical procedure to convert the fractionalization index into a measure of the "effective number of ethnic groups," analogous to the well-known index in the literature on party systems, the "effective number of parties."[19] The outcome of such a conversion is reported in Table 1.

It should be noted that the label "effective number" is as misleading in respect of ethnic groups as it is in relation to parties: it does not in any

TABLE 1 Approximate Distribution of States by Level of Ethnolinguistic Fractionalization, c. 1985

Level of fractionalization	Range of ELF index	"Effective number of ethnic groups"	No. of countries
None (homogeneous society)	less than 0.10	1	22
Low	0.10–0.50	1–2	69
Medium	0.50–0.67	2–3	30
High	0.67–0.75	3–4	16
Very high	more than 0.75	4+	32
All countries			169

Note. "ELF" refers to the index of ethnolinguistic fractionalization, measuring the extent of diversity (D, as defined in note 19). Microstates (with populations less than 100,000 in 2005) and dependencies are excluded.

Source: Based on Philip G. Roeder, Ethnolinguistic Fractionalization (ELF) Indices, 1961 and 1985 (2001); available weber.ucsd.edu/~proeder/elf.htm.

way approximate the number of groups (or parties), or even the number of relevant ones: it is simply an index, and the unfortunate labeling has been retained here only to preserve the useful analogy with party systems, where this terminology is so widely accepted. It does, however, assist in giving us an intuitive impression of what the implications of a particular level of diversity actually are: the number of competitors in interethnic relations can be at least as important as the number of competing units in a party system. It must continually be borne in mind, however, that while it is difficult enough to measure parties in this way, the challenge is even greater in respect of ethnic groups, whose boundaries (and, indeed, whose very existence) tend to be much more fluid. As Table 1 shows, in any event, the number of countries with a very high level of ethnic fractionalization as measured in this way (where the index is at least .50) amounts to almost half of all countries (78 out of 169). In such cases, the "effective number of ethnic groups" is at least two; there are two groups of equal size or, more likely, three or more significant groups of varying sizes.

ETHNIC MOBILIZATION

Ethnic division need not of itself be politically significant. Indeed, we need to go much further than determining *whether* a country is ethnically divided, and, if so, to what extent. We need to know *how* it is so divided—how deep the divisions are, and how far they have spilled over into the political domain. Here, too, we are obstructed by ambiguous or clashing criteria, so that even identifying the universe of cases may be quite a challenge.

This will become clear if we consider a number of cross-national surveys. For example, Rudolph's *Encyclopedia of Modern Ethnic Conflicts* analyzes 37 such conflicts spread over 25 states or regions, extending from classic historical conflicts (such as the "Irish question" in the pre-1922 United Kingdom) to well-known contemporary ones (such as the issue of Corsica within France).[20] Levinson's *Encyclopaedia of Ethnic Relations* identifies 41 contemporary cases divided between five types, defined in respect of group goals: separation, autonomy, conquest, survival, and irredentism, with cases ranging from the separatist Basques in Spain to the irredentist Armenians in Azerbaijan.[21] A further classification, based on systematic and detailed analysis of a large number of cases as part of a major *Ethnic Conflicts Research Project*, identifies 80 conflicts continuing during the period 1995–96, spread over seven categories, including ethnonationalist conflicts, interethnic conflicts, decolonization wars, and cases of genocide (which between them accounted for the great majority of cases), and three categories where the ethnic dimension was weak or nonexistent: interstate wars, gang wars, and antiregime wars.[22]

Yet another perspective on ethnic conflict is represented by those whose starting point is not the phenomenon of ethnicity but the reality of conflict: the key is provided not by ethnocultural difference but by violent struggle. A wide range of studies seeks to generalize about the character of such divisions, in which ethnic conflicts commonly feature. Formidable databases have been constructed to summarize such conflicts (which by no means confine themselves to internal wars; interstate wars may also be included). Examples are the International Peace Research Institute in Oslo (PRIO), which has jointly prepared a large dataset on armed conflict since 1945 (accounted for mainly by internal conflicts), and the Heidelberg Institute for International Conflict Research, which maintains a similar database on national and international conflicts since 1945.[23]

These contrasting but overlapping perspectives on ethnic conflict help greatly in identifying all potential cases. The varying systems of classification and alternative terminologies in the survey works described above should not surprise us: none can claim to be comprehensive or "objective" nor do any of these collections even try to make such a claim. The sheer complexity of the issue emerges clearly from qualitative studies, such as a well-known French encyclopedia of internal conflict, which deals with civil wars and political violence of varying degrees of intensity, finding examples in most of the countries of the world.[24] A possible approach is to start with one major effort to scan the globe for actual or potential instances of ethnic conflict that combines qualitative documentation with efforts at measurement, the *Minorities at Risk* (MAR) project, which identifies more than 300 such groups across the world.[25]

Developed over several decades by Ted Robert Gurr and his colleagues, the MAR project sets a low threshold of inclusion, focusing on minorities that have achieved a minimum degree of political mobilization. It makes a preliminary distinction within such groups between "national peoples" (regionally concentrated groups that no longer enjoy autonomy but are culturally distinct) and "minority peoples" (a residual category, commonly made up of immigrants). Within the first group, MAR defines two categories. The first is that of *ethnonationalist groups* (relatively large groups mobilized behind demands for political autonomy, such as the Basques in Spain) and *indigenous peoples* (economically and politically marginalized groups descended from the original population, such as the Maori in New Zealand). These account for about 40% of the 315 minorities that are included in the 2005 edition of the MAR dataset (which identifies 55 ethnonationalist groups and 73 indigenous peoples). The remaining 60% are divided between four other categories: *ethnoclasses* (ethnically or culturally distinct minorities occupying a characteristic economic niche, such as the Roma in Italy, 46 in all); *communal contenders* (other cultural minorities seeking to participate in state power, such as the confessional groups in Lebanon, numbering 81); *militant sects* (minorities aiming primarily to defend their religious beliefs, such as the Muslims in Greece, totaling 16); and *national minorities* (fragments of an external population that controls an adjacent state, such as the Hungarians in Slovakia, 44 in all).[26]

Although no dataset like MAR can be perfect, it does provide a plausible starting point for generalizing about societies where the capacity for ethnic rebellion is potentially threatening for the state. There may, of course, be problems with borderline cases. Thus, the dataset may be too inclusive in respect of "militant sects." This category includes such groups as Shia Muslims in Iraq and Sanjak Muslims in Yugoslavia, but also the Copts in Egypt and the Muslims in Greece, despite their modest level of mobilization. On the other hand, there are respects in which the dataset is rather exclusive, resulting in some surprising omissions from the list—ones that loom large in other sources, such as the Ethnologue list of complex multilingual societies. Although India and Switzerland are included in the MAR dataset, for instance, this is not because of their remarkable linguistic diversity, but because of certain minorities that have been visible in recent times (such as Sikhs and Kashmiris in the former, and foreign workers and Jurassians in the latter). While this chapter uses the MAR dataset, then, in providing a general statistical overview, care needs to be taken about relying on it in specific cases, and about difficult classification issues.

In using the MAR dataset to provide a general overview of minorities globally, the most interesting question has to do with the manner in which the minority is differentiated from the rest of the population. The dataset codes all minorities on their distinctiveness in respect of four features: language, group customs (in such areas as marriage, the family, and dress codes), religion, and race (or physical appearance). Out of 268 cases coded in the 2009 release, no external difference was reported in 21 cases, and group customs constituted the exclusive criterion only in a further two. Leaving customs aside, and focusing on the relative importance of language, religion, and race, language emerges as overwhelmingly the most prominent indicator, present in 81%

of cases (though language alone was coded as a differentiating factor in just 20% of cases). Religion was present as a source of differentiation in 49% of cases (though as a sole source in only 6%), and race was a factor in 46% of cases (but as the sole factor in only 4%).[27]

If we move, then, from the domain of statistical summary through that of comparative description to that of actual cases of ethnonational conflict, what picture emerges? There is no such thing as an ideal-type "ethnonational conflict," but common elements in the evolution of such conflicts over time are apparent. Broadly speaking, such conflicts tend to have their origin in pressure on the part of groups that are (or at least feel themselves to be) marginalized. Particularly in the past, and in transitional societies, minorities may be confronted by formidable barriers that use quasi-objective criteria such as religion and race to limit their participation in political life. For such groups, the demand for *individual rights*, based on the concept of universal equality before the law, is critical. But whether or not the concession of such rights is an issue, the leaders of minority groups may raise further fundamental demands regarding their status: they wish their collective identity to be recognized, whether in the domain of cultural or linguistic regime reform, or through the concession of a measure of political autonomy. In such cases, the issue is one of *group rights* rather than of individual rights: the minority wishes its separate identity to be formally acknowledged. In addition to groups that address primarily one or other of these sets of demands (liberation from a regime of inequality, or establishment of a regime that formalizes difference), in many instances groups will cycle through these demands in two phases. Francophone Canada is one example, and nineteenth-century Europe offers many examples, with early calls for universal political and civil rights giving way to later campaigns for cultural rights, territorial autonomy, or independence, as in the case of the Finns, Estonians, Latvians, Czechs, Irish, and others.[28]

CASE STUDIES OF ETHNIC CONFLICT

In looking further at specific instances of ethnonational conflict, it is worth recalling the discussion above that identified religion, language, and race as three of the underlying factors that help to account for the nature of conflicting patterns of identity. In selecting cases, it makes sense to ensure that these characteristics are represented. In the rest of this chapter and in those that follow, we thus consider two cases where the basis of the conflict appears to be primarily linguistic (Belgium and Spain); three where it is primarily religious (Northern Ireland, Bosnia, and Lebanon), two where these two criteria reinforce each other (Cyprus and Sri Lanka), and one where the predominant criterion has been race (South Africa). Of course, this definition of these categories oversimplifies, as will be seen below. It nevertheless gives us a set of eight cases that span the regions of the globe (Europe, Middle East, Africa, and South Asia). The cases range from ones where groups making reform demands are very small as a proportion of the population (Spain) to those where they are very large (South Africa), from cases where the outcome emerges from a peaceful struggle (Belgium) to ones where it follows from a violent conflict (Sri Lanka), and from countries where the ultimate settlement was decided on the basis of peaceful negotiation to those where armed conflict decided the issue (again, Belgium and Sri Lanka represent the poles). Following a general description of these cases, we consider the relationship between dominant and subordinate groups within each and then look at the overall significance of the ethnic dimension.

Sources of Ethnic Dissent

A general summary of the main ethnic divisions in the eight cases mentioned is provided in Table 2, which aims to present the position at two points in time: around the middle of the twentieth century and at the century's end. In all cases, the aim is to refer to the resident population, not the citizen population (there can be a very big difference between ethnic distributions depending on which of these criteria is used). Indeed, the contrast between these two dates is illustrative of the very significant effects of the transition that took place in the second half of the twentieth century, arising from renewed patterns of nationalist mobilization. The mid-twentieth century figures are relatively uncontroversial. Nevertheless, problems arise in certain cases. For example, Table 2 adjusts the officially reported Belgian data for all three groups, since the original report follows the unusual practice of dividing the population into four linguistic groups, not three, the fourth group being those not speaking any of these languages (4.6%), made up mainly of infants, most of whom would grow up to be Dutch speakers. As a consequence, the official census report lists Dutch speakers as comprising 52.6% of the population, rather than the 55.1% reported here (the latter offers a truer statement of the size of the Dutch-speaking majority).

For the more recent period, the problems are much greater. In Belgium, no census data on language have been reported at all since the 1947 census, notwithstanding the great potential significance of language as a public policy issue (in determining the language regime within municipal administrations, for instance). Since, however, the language groups are geographically polarized, it is possible to use regional populations as a surrogate mechanism for estimating language use, making appropriate adjustments for the population of Brussels, a bilingual city.[29] For similar reasons, no official information has been made available on Lebanon's religious denominations since 1932—again, notwithstanding (or perhaps, as in Belgium, because of!) their crucial public policy significance. Here, crude estimates have been used: figures produced by a reputable Beirut research firm have been adjusted to

J. Coakley

TABLE 2 Ethnonational Divisions in Selected States, c. 1950 and c. 2000

Group	Percentage of population		Comment
	Early (year)	Recent (year)	
Belgium	(1947)	(2008)	For 2008, based on populations of regions;
Dutch speakers	55.1	58.7	adjustment for Brussels (90% French)
French speakers	44.0	40.6	
German speakers	1.0	0.7	
Population (000s)	8,515	10,667	
Spain	(1950)	(2001)	Based on population of autonomous
Spanish etc.	75.4	72.8	communities
Catalans	11.5	15.5	
Galicians	9.3	6.6	
Basques	3.8	5.1	
Population (000s)	28,118	40,847	
Northern Ireland	(1951)	(2001)	2001 data refer to religious background,
Protestants	63.9	53.1	not current affiliation
Catholics	34.4	43.8	
Others	1.8	3.1	
Population (000s)	1,371	1,685	
Bosnia	(1961)	(1991)	No reliable data after 1991
Bosniaks/Muslims	25.7	43.5	
Serbs	42.9	31.2	
Croats	21.7	17.4	
Yugoslavs	8.4	5.6	
Others	1.3	2.3	
Population (000s)	3,278	4,377	
Cyprus	(1960)	(2006)	No reliable data after 1960; "Turks"
Greeks	77.0	62.5	include settlers from Turkey
Turks	18.3	24.8	
Others	4.7	12.9	
Population (000s)	574	1,044	
Lebanon	(1932)	(2007)	No reliable data after 1932; "Others"
Maronite	28.7	*20*	include Palestinians in 2007;
Sunni Muslim	22.4	*25*	2007 data in italics are estimated.
Shia Muslim	19.5	*25*	
Greek Orthodox	9.7	*7*	
Druze	6.7	*5*	
Greek Catholic	5.9	*4*	
Others	6.9	*14*	
Population (000s)	793	3,926	
South Africa	(1951)	(2001)	
Black African	67.5	79.0	
Coloured	8.7	8.9	
Indian or Asian	2.9	2.5	
White	20.9	9.6	
Population (000s)	12,646	44,820	

TABLE 2 Ethnonational Divisions in Selected States, c. 1950 and c. 2000 *(Continued)*

Group	Percentage of population		Comment
	Early (year)	Recent (year)	
Sri Lanka	(1946)	(1981)	No reliable data after 1981
Sinhalese	69.4	74.0	
Sri Lanka Tamils	11.0	12.7	
Indian Tamils	11.7	5.5	
Moors/Muslims	5.6	7.1	
Others	2.3	0.8	
Population (000s)	6,657	14,847	

Source: **Belgium**: *Recensement général de la population . . .* 1947 (Brussels: Institut National de Statistique, 1949–53) and *Europa World Yearbook, 2009*; **Spain**: *Historical Population Series* and *Population and Housing Census 2001*; www.ine.es; **Northern Ireland**: *Ulster Year Book 1956* (Belfast: HMSO, 1956) and *2001 Census Output*; www.nisra.gov.uk; **Bosnia**: *Statistical Yearbook 2008* (Sarajevo: Federal Office of Statistics, 2008), www.fzs.ba; **Cyprus**: *Demographic Report 2006* (Lefkosia: Statistical Service, 2007), www.pio.gov.cy/mof/cystat/statistics.nsf; TNRC census 2006, nufussayimi.devplan.org; **Lebanon**: J. Ballita, *Éléments de statistiques générales sur la population* (Beirut: Bureau de Statistique, 1943); US State Department, Bureau of Democracy, Human Rights and Labor, *Lebanon: International Religious Freedom Report 2007*; www.state.gov/g/drl/rls/irf/2007/; CIA, *World Factbook* 2007; **South Africa**: *Statesman's Yearbook*, 1964; Statistics South Africa, Census 2001, www.statssa.gov.za; **Sri Lanka**: *Statistical Abstract 2008*, www.statistics.gov.lk.

take account of the Palestinian population of about 10% (included here with "others"). This results in a reduction in the relative size of all of the other Lebanese groups, and it leads in particular to the appearance of a significant decline in the proportion of Christians.[30]

In a further three cases, war and its aftermath has discouraged data gathering of this kind. Thus, ethnic rivalries in Bosnia following the war of 1992–95 and the associated massive population displacement have promoted conflicting perspectives on the desirability of a census, since the political and territorial stakes are high. In Cyprus, de facto partition has left the island without any administration capable of managing an island-wide census. Although the statistics office of the Republic of Cyprus seeks to report on the population of the entire island, its estimates for Northern Cyprus clash with those of the administration there, with important differences in particular over the issue of the large number of Turkish settlers in the North. Thus, if we use the figures produced by the northern administration (as in Table 2) the Turkish population amounts to 24.8% of that of the island; the southern statistics office estimates a figure of 10.2%.[31] In Sri Lanka, similarly, the warlike conditions that prevailed from 1983 to 2009 left the government in Colombo in a weak position to conduct a state-wide census; the census of 2001 reports a Sri Lanka Tamil population of only 4.3% (though the official report points out that this includes only the 18 of the island's 25 districts where it was possible to conduct the census).[32]

But even the remaining three cases are not unproblematic. In Northern Ireland since 1971, considerable numbers of people have been refusing to state their religion, or indicating that they have none. Since the religion question in the census is designed not to sound out beliefs but to measure community affiliation, an alternative mechanism is now used: people are asked an additional question about the religion in which they were brought up, creating a new variable called "community background," the one reported here. In Spain, for both periods, clear-cut, state-wide information on ethnonational background and linguistic status is not available. The data here report the position only in the three most distinctive autonomous communities (Catalonia, Galicia, and the Basque Country), grouping all others as "Spanish etc."—a crude oversimplification, but in the circumstances a necessary one. In South Africa, the data reported here may be adequate for their primary comparative purpose, but they do not report the significant language differences (within both the White and the African populations) that, in South Africa as elsewhere, are of very considerable potential political impact.

Distinctive Patterns

Notwithstanding difficulties in seeking to measure the differences conventionally seen as being politically relevant in the eight countries considered here, some obviously significant findings emerge from Table 2. These are highlighted in Figure 1, which seeks to report the changing position of the traditionally ruling or dominant group in each case. There are some problems with this approach. In most cases, the identity of the ruling group is clear, whether it is very large (as in Spain) or very small (as in South Africa). But it should be noted that in Cyprus and Lebanon these groups (the Greeks and Maronite Christians, respectively) were constrained to share power with other groups; in Bosnia it is misleading to refer to the ethnic Muslim (now Bosniak) population as a "ruling group"—they exchanged their status as part of a Serb-dominated Yugoslavia for a power-sharing arrangement in independent Bosnia; and in Belgium treating the Francophone population as a "ruling group" was unproblematic in the past but now raises serious issues of accuracy of description.

Nevertheless, some relatively clear patterns emerge. First, it appears that certain dominant groups are "winners," in that they have been increasing as a proportion of the population: the Sinhalese population of Sri Lanka seems to have increased in relative size in the second half of the twentieth century. The ethnic Muslim population of Bosnia, too, has increased dramatically, but this group cannot, of course, be described as a dominant one. Indeed, in 1961 it did not constitute even a plurality of the population of Bosnia; it was significantly smaller than the Serbian population. The big change in the demographic relationship between these groups took place between 1961 and 1971: Muslims became a plurality of the population in the latter year,

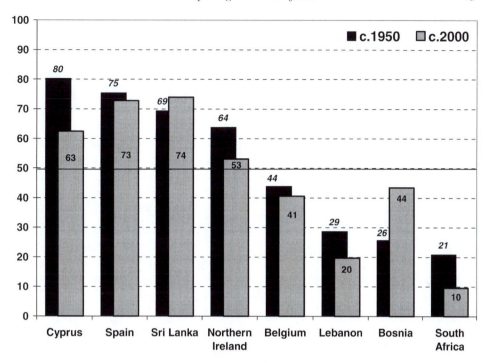

FIGURE 1 Relative Size of Traditional Ruling or Plurality Group, Selected States, c. 1950 and c. 2000. Source: Derived from data in Table 2.

when more than half a million additional people so labeled themselves. By contrast, in 1971 Serbs were more than 200,000 fewer than ten years earlier, and Yugoslavs a quarter of a million fewer.[33] This suggests that many people from a Muslim background who might earlier have described themselves as Yugoslavs, or even as Serbs, now switched designation.

In three other cases, groups that had big majorities saw this position erode. In Spain, the population of the core "Spanish" areas fell back slightly. This was driven by rapid population rise in two of the more economically advanced autonomous communities, Catalonia and the Basque Country (but not in the third, Galicia, whose share of Spain's population has been declining). However, the headline figures tell us little about the extent to which (if at all) this might have represented demographic advance on the part of Catalans and Basques (rather than simply of people living in those regions, many of whom might not identify with the regional culture). The figures for Cyprus are more difficult to interpret, since they are substantially influenced by the influx of settlers from Turkey in the northern part of the island. To the extent that these become permanent residents, the long-standing ratio of Turks to Greeks (which had declined steadily from 1881, when Muslims comprised 24.4% of the population, to 1946, when they made up 17.9%) is likely to be disturbed by this.[34] In Northern Ireland, too, the long-dominant Protestant community now constitutes only a bare majority of the population and is already outnumbered by Catholics among those aged under 25—a development with potentially significant long-term political implications.

Finally, there are three cases where a once-dominant community has shrunk further as a share of the population. Although they never constituted a majority of the Belgian population, French-speakers there had occupied all positions of prestige in Belgian society in the nineteenth century and continued to dominate its political system until well into the twentieth century. The overall pattern, however, has been one of decline on the part of this group, with Brussels (where the number and proportion of French speakers has steadily grown, for a variety of reasons) as the major exception. The position of Maronite Christians in Lebanon has been similarly weakened: once the dominant component of the Christian population, which accounted for 55% of the population in 1932, they are now a much smaller proportion, and the broader Christian group of which they are a part probably amounts to only about a third of the population. Finally, the White population of South Africa has not just seen its political power evaporate but its demographic position has also weakened greatly. Once a small minority of 21%, it is now a much smaller one of 10%. The deep racial cleavages reported here have overshadowed linguistic divisions that might elsewhere pose an existential challenge to the state: 59% of the white population speak Afrikaans (as do most Coloreds); 39% speak English (as do almost all Indians/Asians); and the African population speak a range of languages, with the five biggest accounting for 85% of all (and Zulu and Xhosa accounting for a majority of all Africans).[35]

Profiling the Cases

The dynamics of ethnonational competition analyzed in the eight case studies that follow are not just artefacts arising from the cultural realities described above (the patterns of division along linguistic, religious, racial, and more generally ethnonational lines). Nor do they gain their momentum simply from changes in ethnodemographic realities, however politically traumatic these might sometimes be. Instead, existing intercultural relationships are colored by profound underlying socioeconomic factors, such as structural advantage (associated with a drive to protect privilege) or structural disadvantage (leading to a potentially destabilizing sense of injustice). They are also influenced by geographical factors (such as patterns of territorial concentration, or of dispersion), which determine the options for collective action. These realities, with other considerations, domestic and international, set the stage for particular patterns of political mobilization—patterns that may in certain circumstances spill over into armed violence. This interplay between ethnocultural balance, socioeconomic reality, and political mobilization varies considerably from case to case, and this is documented in the chapters that follow.

First, there are circumstances where the resources available to the two sides are so uneven that the ultimate victory of one side seems assured. Thus, the numerical superiority of the Sinhalese in Sri Lanka and of the dominant population group in Spain is so great that the governments in these two cases have been able to fight an unequal battle against Tamil and Basque rebels, respectively. In each case, they have sought in the past to undermine dissent in these areas by making concessions at the level of territorial government. But in one case ultimate military victory was much more decisive than in the other, at least for the present: the defeat of the last remnants of the Tamil rebels in May 2009 gave the Sri Lankan government the fullest measure of real authority it had enjoyed for decades over the territory of the island, as Stanley Samarasinghe shows. However, relying on military victory to resolve long-term political problems is a dangerous strategy, and in Spain, where the authority of the central government has never been as effectively challenged as in Sri Lanka (at least, since the Spanish civil war of 1936–39), imaginative political solutions have been pursued more vigorously, more proactively, and apparently to good effect, as Francisco Llera's chapter makes clear.

Second, there are cases where the two sides are evenly balanced, and relations between the two communities are disturbed by patterns of asymmetrical demographic and socioeconomic change, but where bloc leaders were nevertheless able to negotiate a settlement. In Belgium and Northern Ireland the Francophone population and the Protestant community, respectively, have seen their size reduced, their once-unassailable position of cultural dominance eroded, and their traditional position of economic dominance being reversed. The Belgians were able to renegotiate political relationships in an evolutionary way, as Lieven De Winter and Pierre Baudewyns show, with a series of painfully agreed constitutional amendments over three decades managing to keep the lid on potential unrest. In Northern Ireland, it took several decades of civil unrest and paramilitary conflict before the two sides were able to negotiate a settlement, as described by Jennifer Todd. In many respects this emulated the Belgian model, but the route to that outcome was over a bloodier path and required very substantial external intervention. Indeed, this conflict had never been an exclusively domestic one: it formed part of a broader, longer conflict between Great Britain and Ireland, reflected in the reality of British involvement as the ultimate source of sovereignty, and clashing claims by the Irish government.

Third, it is clear that the outcome of internal war is not always an exhausted stalemate, as in Northern Ireland, or a comprehensive victory for one side, as in Sri Lanka: both sides may win victories at regional levels. Thus it was that ethnically mixed Bosnia and Herzegovina ended up being partitioned in 1995 between a Serb-controlled area and one controlled by a forced Bosniak-Croat marriage, with only small minorities on the "wrong" side of the new border, resulting in the political challenge analyzed by Roberto Belloni. Cyprus, similarly, where all districts were ethnically mixed in 1960, was partitioned between a Turkish north and a Greek south in 1974, as part of a process described by Joseph S. Joseph. In each case, external military intervention was critical in reinforcing the position of the weaker side, but the efforts of outside powers to stitch the pieces together afterwards enjoyed uneven success: the Dayton Agreement (1995) brought a semblance of political unity back to Bosnia, but the Annan Plan (2004) enjoyed no comparable success in Cyprus.

Finally, two other cases illustrate the capacity of minorities to fight with determination to protect their position against the incoming tide of majority rule. In South Africa, as Adrian Guelke points out, the white minority that completely dominated government and economic life chose the option of surrender before this was absolutely necessary and may thereby have helped to protect its own longer term interests by negotiating from a position of strength and accepting the inevitability of majority democratic rule. In Lebanon, whose patterns of group coexistence and governmental post-sharing are examined closely by Simon Haddad, the issue was not so much one of protecting minority rule as of groups (such as the Maronite Christians) attempting to maximize their influence. But here, too, external intervention and the role of Syria and Israel brought about a new pattern of alignments in which the old confessional loyalties were compromised.

CONCLUSION

The complex world of ethnic diversity described in this chapter draws our attention to the fact that diversity of itself is unproblematic: in most societies, most groups coexist relatively peacefully and make few group-specific demands on each other or on the state. But the mere existence of an ethnic group that exceeds a certain critical mass in respect of population, especially if it reaches a modest level of territorial concentration, may result in an enhanced sense of identity, an escalation of calls for political change, and a cycle of demands, concessions, and refusals in its relationship with the state. Ethnic mobilization may confine itself to conventional activities and may operate within the limits of the constitution; but it may also take the form of armed rebellion and direct action against the state.

The chapters that follow revisit these issues in the eight cases already discussed above. In each case, the author begins by looking at the historical evolution of the problem as it had emerged by the end of the twentieth century. This is followed by an examination of the manner in which the groups involved in the conflict were mobilized politically, identifying their primary organizations, and describing their preferred long-term institutional and constitutional arrangements. Each chapter concludes with an outline of the parameters of a settlement, whether this lies in the future, is being currently negotiated or has already been achieved (though not necessarily on a stable basis).

Our collective concern, then, is to use these case studies to explore the diversity that lies behind a range of representative conflicts of an ethnic character and to generalize about the paths that ethnic leaders have taken to bring these conflicts to some kind of a resolution (whether successfully or otherwise). The case studies allow us to address a number of important questions. How deeply embedded was the conflict in the societal structure and to what extent was it aggravated or mitigated by patterns of stability or change in this? In what form were the interests of the competing groups mobilized, and how far was the process of intergroup negotiation influenced by external actors? Are there general features that are shared in the settlements arising in these cases, to the extent, that is, that a settlement has been arrived at, at all? These matters are discussed in the individual chapters that follow, and we return in the last chapter to the comparative perspective, addressing the question that lies at the core of this collection: allowing for the specific ethnic balance in individual cases, are there any common elements in the pathway out of ethnic conflict, and towards what kind of ultimate settlement does this pathway lead?

ACKNOWLEDGMENT

This chapter and most of those that follow are based on papers presented initially at a roundtable meeting "Recent Advances in Research on Ethnic Conflict Resolution" sponsored by the International Social Science Council under its programme Research on Ethnic Conflict: Approaches to Peace, organized by the Institute for British-Isles Studies, University College Dublin, 5 Dec. 2008. I am indebted to Roberto Belloni, Lieven De Winter, Adrian Guelke, Joseph S. Joseph, Stanley Samarasinghe, Thomas Sattler, Tobias Theiler, and Jennifer Todd for comments on an earlier draft.

NOTES

1. See Charles C. Herod, *The Nation in the History of Marxian Thought: The Concept of Nations with History and Nations without History* (The Hague, The Netherlands: Martinus Nijhoff, 1976); Walker Connor, *The National Question in Marxist-Leninist Theory and Strategy* (Princeton, NJ: Princeton University Press, 1984); Roman Rosdolsky, *Engels and the "Nonhistoric" Peoples: The National Question in the Revolution of 1848*, translated and edited by John-Paul Himka (London: Critique Books, 1986); Ronaldo Munck, *The Difficult Dialogue: Marxism and Nationalism* (London: Zed Books, 1986).

2. The outstanding corpus of literature in this area is the series *Studies in Political Development*, sponsored by the US Social Science Research Council, in which nine volumes appeared between 1963 and 1978. Though there was a great deal of variation from one contributor to another, the dominant perspective on the progressive character of the "nation-building" enterprise is summarized in, for example, Lucian W. Pye, "Introduction: Political Culture and Political Development," in Lucian W. Pye and Sidney Verba (eds.), *Political Culture and Political Development* (Princeton, NJ: Princeton University Press, 1965), pp. 3–26. For an overview, see Howard J. Wiarda, "Rethinking Political Development: A Look Backward over Thirty Years, and a Look Ahead," *Comparative Studies in International Development*, Vol. 24, No. 4 (1989), pp. 65–82.

3. For early examples, see Jan Auerhan, *Die sprachlichen Minderheiten in Europa* (Berlin: Hensel, 1926); Ewald Ammende (ed.), *Die Nationalitaten in den Staaten Europas: Sammlung von Lageberichten* (Wien: Wilhelm Braumüller, 1931); Wilhelm Winkler, *Statistisches Handbuch der Europäischen Nationalitaten* (Wien: Wilhelm Braumüller, 1931); and Otto Junghahn, *National Minorities in Europe* (New York:

Covici, Friede, Inc., 1932). A later wave is represented by Manfred Straka, *Handbuch der europäischen Volksgruppen* (Wien, Stuttgart: Wilhelm Braumüller, 1970); Meic Stephens, *Linguistic Minorities in Western Europe* (Llandysul: Gomer Press, 1976); and Jochen Blaschke (ed.), *Handbuch der westeuropäischen Regionalbewegungen* (Frankfurt-am-Main: Syndikat, 1980).

4. The *Europa World Yearbook* (1959–), the *Statesman's Yearbook* (1864–), and the CIA's *World Factbook* (1975–) are among the more widely used examples.

5. Reflecting the multinational character of their state, a large volume of work has been conducted by Soviet scholars, including most notably S. I. Bruk and V. S. Apenchenko (eds.), *Atlas Narodov Mira* [Atlas of the Peoples of the World] (Moscow: Institut Etnografii, Akademiya Nauk SSSR, 1964). Other examples include David Levinson (ed.), *Ethnic Relations: A Cross-Cultural Encyclopedia* (Santa Barbara, CA: ABC Clio, 1994); and Joseph R. Rudolph, Jr. (ed.), *Encyclopedia of Modern Ethnic Conflicts* (Westport, CT: Greenwood Press, 2003).

6. Examples are the Minority Rights Group (see www.minorityrights.org), the Summer Institute of Linguistics, a Christian organization that maintains a vast database on languages and language use (see www.ethnologue.com), and the Center for the Study of Global Christianity at Gordon-Conwell Theological Seminary, which maintains an enormous database on religions and ethnolinguistic groups, the World Christian Database (see www.worldchristiandatabase.org/wcd).

7. Joseph H. Greenberg, "The Measurement of Linguistic Diversity," *Language,* Vol. 32, No. 1 (1956), pp. 109–15.

8. Stanley Lieberson, Guy Dalto, and Mary Ellen Johnston, "The Course of Mother-Tongue Diversity in Nations," *American Journal of Sociology,* Vol. 81, No. 1 (1975), pp. 34–61; Stanley Lieberson, "An Extension of Greenberg's Linguistic Diversity Measures," *Language,* Vol. 40, No. 4 (1964), pp. 526–531.

9. Douglas W. Rae and Michael Taylor, *The Analysis of Political Cleavages* (London: Yale University Press, 1970), pp. 22–44; Charles Lewis Taylor and Michael C. Hudson, *World Handbook of Political and Social Indicators,* 2nd ed. (New Haven, CT: Yale University Press, 1972), pp. 21, 216. Like many of their successors, Taylor and Hudson used the Soviet collection (Bruk and Apenchenko, *Atlas*) as their starting point. The same index was also used as a control variable by economists analyzing the impact of corruption on economic growth and in analyzing the impact of ethnic diversity on economic growth in Africa; see Paolo Mauro, "Corruption and Growth," *Quarterly Journal of Economics*, Vol. 110, No. 3 (1995), pp. 681–712, and William Easterly and Ross Levine, "Africa's Growth Tragedy: Policies and Ethnic Divisions," *Quarterly Journal of Economics*, Vol. 112, No. 4 (1997), pp. 1203–50. For a more critical assessment of the quality of the Soviet data, see Benjamin Reilly, "Democracy, Ethnic Fragmentation, and Internal Conflict: Confused Theories, Faulty Data, and the 'Crucial Case' of Papua New Guinea," *International Security*, Vol. 25, No. 3 (2000–01), pp. 162–85.

10. Anthony Annett, "Social Fractionalisation, Political Instability, and the Size of Government", *IMF Staff Papers*, Vol. 48, No. 3 (2001), pp. 561–92.

11. Philip G Roeder, *Ethnolinguistic Fractionalisation (ELF) Indices, 1961 and 1985* (2001); available weber.ucsd.edu/~proeder/elf.htm (accessed 30 Oct. 2009)

12. James D. Fearon, "Ethnic and Cultural Diversity by Country," *Journal of Economic Growth,* Vol. 8, No. 2 (2003), pp. 195–222.

13. Alberto Alesina, Arnaud Devleeschauwer, William Easterly, Sergio Kurlat, and Romain Warcziarg, "Fractionalization," *Journal of Economic Growth,* Vol. 8, No. 2 (2003), pp. 155–94.

14. David B. Barrett (ed.), *World Christian Encyclopedia: A Comparative Study of Churches and Religions in the Modern World AD 1900–2000* (Oxford, UK: Oxford University Press, 1982).

15. Daniel N. Posner, "Measuring Ethic Fractionalisation in Africa," *American Journal of Political Science*, Vol. 48, No. 4 (2004), pp. 849–63.

16. Shaheen Mozaffar, James R. Scarritt, and Glen Galaich, "Electoral Institutions, Ethnopolitical Cleavages, and Party Systems in Africa's Emerging Democracies," *American Political Science Review*, Vol. 97, No. 3 (2003), pp. 379–90.

17. Lars-Erik Cederman and Luc Girardin, "Beyond Fractionalisation: Mapping Ethnicity onto Nationalist Insurgencies," *American Political Science Review*, Vol. 101, No. 1 (2007), pp. 173–85.

18. Roeder, "Ethnolinguistic Fractionalisation Indices."

19. The index of concentration may be defined as follows: $C = \Sigma_{i=1,z} \; p_i^2$, where z = the number of groups and p = the proportional size of each. This may easily be converted into an index of diversity $(D = 1 - C)$, and it may equally easily be converted into an "index of the effective number of ethnic groups" $(E = 1/C)$. On the analogous measure of party fractionalization, see Markku Laakso and Rein Taagepera, "'Effective Number of Parties': A Measure with Application to West Europe," *Comparative Political Studies,* Vol. 12, No. 1 (1979), pp. 3–27.

20. Rudolph, *Encyclopedia*.

21. Levinson, *Ethnic Relations*, pp. 62–70.

22. Christian P. Scherrer, "Towards a Comprehensive Analysis of Ethnicity and Mass Violence: Types, Dynamics, Characteristics and Trends," in Håkon Wiberg and Christian P. Scherrer (eds.), *Ethnicity and Intra-State Conflict* (Aldershot, UK: Ashgate, 1999), pp. 52–88.

23. The PRIO database is produced jointly with the Uppsala Conflict Data Program; see www.prio.no/CSCW/. Updates are published annually in the *Journal of Peace Research*. As well as its "Cosimo" database on conflict, the Heidelberg Institute for International Conflict Research publishes an annual *Conflict Barometer*; see www.hiik.de [accessed 30 Oct. 2009].

24. Jean-Marc Balencie and Arnaud de La Grange (eds.), *Les Nouveaux Mondes rebelles,* 4th ed. (Paris: Éditions Michalon, 2005). Some of the other more quantitative overviews discussed in this chapter are accompanied by detailed qualitative information, and this is exceptionally extensive in the case of the Minorities at Risk and Ethnologue projects; see www.cidcm.umd.edu/mar/data.asp#qualitative and www.ethnologue.com/web.asp [accessed 30 Oct. 2009].

25. The MAR dataset, with 315 cases in its 2005 edition, is in general more inclusive than other efforts to explore the range of minorities that may be detected worldwide, such as the Minority Rights Group, *World Directory of Minorities* (Harlow, UK: Longman, 1990), which lists 170. The new MAR dataset release of 2009 covers 284 cases; see www.cidcm.umd.edu/mar/ [accessed 30 Oct. 2009].

26. For an elaboration of the first five of these categories, see Ted Robert Gurr, with Barbara Harff, Monty G. Marshall, and James R. Scarritt, *Minorities at Risk: A Global View of Ethnopolitical Conflicts* (Washington, DC: United States Institute of Peace, 1993), pp. 15–23; the sixth was added in the 2005 edition of the dataset.

27. Derived from the 2009 edition of the MAR dataset.

28. These points are developed further in John Coakley, "Introduction: The Challenge," in John Coakley (ed.), *The Territorial Management of Ethnic Conflict*, 2nd ed. (London: Frank Cass, 2003), pp. 1–22. Similarities in the positions of the nationalist movements mentioned are described in John Coakley, "Independence Movements and National Minorities: Some Parallels in the European Experience," *European Journal of Political Research,* Vol. 8, No. 2 (1980), pp. 215–47; and John Coakley, "National Minorities and the Government of Divided Societies: A Comparative Analysis of some European Evidence," *European Journal of Political Research,* Vol. 18, No. 4 (1990), pp. 437–56.

29. However, the European Social Survey, rounds 1–4, 2002–08, contained 340 respondents in the Brussels region speaking either French or Dutch; of these, 90% were French speakers and 10% Dutch speakers, and these proportions were used here (computed from European Social Survey; data available ess.nsd.uib.no [accessed 30 Oct. 2009]). These data should be treated with caution due to the complexity of the Brussels region.

30. The 2007 data, reported by the US State Department's Bureau of Democracy, Human Rights and Labour, were prepared by Information International, Beirut (see www.information-international.com). It should be noted that many Christians oppose the taking of a census confined to Lebanon itself, arguing that the diaspora (where they are relatively better represented) should be included.

31. Computed from *Demographic Report 2006* (Lefkosia: Statistical Service, 2007), www.pio.gov. cy/mof/cystat/statistics.nsf; TNRC census 2006, nufussayimi.devplan.org. [accessed 30 Oct. 2009]

32. Sri Lanka, *Statistical Abstract 2008*, www.statistics.gov.lk [accessed 30 Oct. 2009].

33. Computed from Bosnia and Hercegovina, *Statistical Yearbook 2008* (Sarajevo: Federal Office of Statistics, 2008), p. 66.

34. Republic of Cyprus, *Demographic Report 2006* (Lefkosia: Statistical Service, 2007), p. 32; available www.pio.gov.cy/mof/cystat/statistics.nsf/ [accessed 30 Oct. 2009].

35. Computed from Statistics South Africa, Census 2001; www.statssa.gov.za [accessed 30 Oct. 2009].

2

Belgium: Towards the Breakdown of a Nation-State in the Heart of Europe?

LIEVEN DE WINTER and PIERRE BAUDEWYNS
Université Catholique de Louvain

Due to reversal of the center-periphery cleavage between Flemish and Francophones by the 1960s, the Belgian unitary state was transformed gradually into a fully fledged federal state. In spite of this empowerment of the regions and communities, the aftermath of the June 2007 general elections showed that Belgium was moving into a crucial, and maybe final, phase of its community conflict. Conflicts over socioeconomic autonomy have replaced the original language issues, essentially opposing on the one hand the Franco-phones in Wallonia and Brussels unanimously defending the in-stitutional status quo of the current federal state, and on the other hand most Flemish political elites calling for radical autonomy, and some even for independence. In the near future, undoubtedly more policy competences will be devolved, but this "lighter but fitter Belgium" outcome may not satisfy Flemish elites.

INTRODUCTION

The aftermath of the June 2007 general elections showed that Belgium was moving into a crucial, and maybe final, phase of its community conflict. Due to profound differences between Dutch and French speakers on the future shape of the Belgian federation, it took 193 days to form an in-terim government (Verhofstadt III). In the following 12 months, two new governments were formed. Apart from the three separatist Flemish parties, some mainstream Flemish parties also threatened to blow Belgium up if the Francophones would not give in, and these threats were widely en-dorsed by the Flemish media. In the Francophone media, strategies were discussed as to how the Francophones should react in such a regime crisis, and whether a left-over Belgium (Wallonia and Brussels) would be viable. Even foreign correspondents stationed in Brussels, who usually only report on EU and NATO issues, started to write about the potential demise of the country.

For long-term observers this big escalation of the Belgian community conflict is a paradox. This was certainly not the first major clash between north and south, but past crises had been quite successfully accommodated in the traditional consociational way.[1] The unitary state was transformed comparatively rapidly into a fully fledged federal state.[2] This radical transformation was achieved by entirely peaceful and constitutional means, in spite of some periods of heated mass mobilization by both camps. What happened to the almost genetic sense of compromise of the Belgians? In addition, in spite of the fact that the center-periphery cleavage between Flemish and Francophones had been reversed by the 1960s, the Flemish conquest of the Belgian state did not deradicalize Flemish calls for further self-government, thus challenging the claims that devolution may reduce such calls.[3] Finally, the deep community conflict in the "heart of Europe," in an interface zone between "Latin" and "Germanic" cultures, seems anachronistic given the dominant post nation-state *Zeitgeist* induced by European integration and globalization. The heated conflict currently driven by socioeconomic differences in a relatively rich area of the EU certainly challenges integrationist calls for an "ever closer union of peoples of Europe" (preamble of the European Draft Constitution).

For the analysis of the emergence and success of a minority nationalist movement in respect of the center-periphery cleavage, the Belgian case is particularly interesting, because the geographical positions of center and periphery have been objectively reversed over time (see below).[4] The former periphery (Flanders) still mobilizes as "classic" minority nationalist movements do, while by now also the former center acts as a threatened minority within the new *Etat belgo-flamand*.[5] In most other common cases of regionalism, the center-periphery characteristics have remained relatively stable, and minority nationalist movements have not managed to reverse them. In subjective terms, the new center, Flanders, still behaves like a minority and accordingly mobilizes against the central state for more autonomy, while the old center has been considerably weakened over the past decades, due to the emergence of a federal state, with wide competences devolved to the substate level (regions and communities).[6] In spite of the radical empowerment of the Flemish community, new demands were voiced after the full federalization of the country, including calls for "post-federal" options, such as confederalism and full independence.

Given the complexity and changing nature of the community conflict in Belgium, for analytical clarity we will divide our presentation into three phases, and for each phase we identify the factors that fuelled the conflict, its main actors, and major accommodation policies.[7] These phases are:

- The period of the struggle for Flemish linguistic emancipation, from Belgian independence in 1830 until the linguistic laws of 1963;
- The institutionalization of demands for cultural and economic self-government leading to the emergence of the federal state, 1963–95;
- The period "beyond federalism" from 1995 onwards.

FLEMISH LINGUISTIC EMANCIPATION, 1830–1963

Genesis of the Community Problem

The Belgian state was created in 1830 after breaking away from the Netherlands, with which it had been merged by the Vienna Congress in 1815. Most provinces that would constitute the new state had been governed for four centuries—indeed, since the late middle ages—as a common ensemble by foreign rulers (Spanish, Austrian, and French). The linguistic fault line between the Belgian provinces—running from east to west, separating the Germanic and Roman dialect-speaking tribes—emerged around the fourth century and was consolidated by the tenth century.

From its creation, the Belgian state was ethnically mixed, with a Flemish-speaking community in the north (without a standardized language), and a French-speaking Walloon community in the south.[8] From the Middle Ages until the seventeenth century, Flanders was a very prosperous region, but it then declined in economic and cultural terms, and by 1830 it had practically no domestic elites that identified with Flemish culture. In fact, the Belgian independence movement resulted from an alliance between different groups of the French-speaking elites from the south as well as from the north: aristocracy, gentry, local notables, and an emergent industrial bourgeoisie in the growing urban centers.

Hence, when Belgium gained independence in 1830 the hegemony of French culture in the new state was very strong. Flanders was a poor agricultural region (with the exception of the commercial role of the port of Antwerp), while Wallonia became the first industrialized region of the continent. In spite of the fact that the Flemish always constituted a demographic majority (ranging from 57% at independence to 60% today), the official language of the state (used in administration, military affairs, politics, the legal system, education, and the media) was French, and this extended also to Flanders.[9] Brussels was chosen as the administrative and political capital.[10] Soon it also became the country's financial center. As a result of French hegemony in cultural, economic, and political life, Brussels—formerly a Flemish city situated inside Flemish "territory"—slowly became a predominantly French-speaking city and the center of the new state.[11]

To conclude, at the birth of the Belgian state the "center" was French speaking, in political, administrative/military, economic, and cultural terms.[12] Flanders was clearly peripheral in all these domains, while Wallonia was associated through its industrial development and language with Brussels, the political, administrative, financial, and cultural capital. Yet, this center-periphery definition gradually changed, and by now has been almost completely reversed, due to the mobilization of the so-called Flemish Movement, as well as socioeconomic structural changes.

Mobilizing the Flemish Periphery

In Flanders, opposition to the Francophone dominance of the Belgian state and society had grown already by the 1840s, with calls for the recognition of the Flemish language. The main actors within the Flemish movement were not party politicians, but rather cultural elites: intellectuals, the literate middle classes, and the lower clergy. Around 1840, the first Flemish cultural associations were created. The most important of these were linked to the three pillars that were to emerge later (the first integrated pillar was the Socialist one, a model copied in due course by the Catholics and Liberals), but some large nonpartisan overarching movements also emerged. Until the First World War, their aim was to have the Flemish community and its language fully recognized as constituent parts of the Belgian nation-state and "fatherland."[13] Only after the First World War did some factions of the Flemish movement start to voice separatist or even irredentist demands.

The emergence of genuine Flemish nationalist parties after the First World War further radicalized the center-periphery conflict. In 1919, universal male suffrage with proportional representation was introduced, and this facilitated the emergence of new parties. At the first postwar elections held under universal male suffrage (1919), the *Frontpartij* (the first genuine Flemish nationalist party) won five seats in parliament, with 5.2% of the Flemish vote.[14] The program of the *Frontpartij* became more radical during the 1920s and 1930s, causing the more moderate nationalists to leave this party and to advocate—with some success—the Flemish cause within the traditional political "families" (Catholics, Socialists, and Liberals).

In the 1930s, the main Flemish nationalist party was the *Vlaams Nationaal Verbond* (VNV, Flemish National Union), a radical separatist party that was more explicitly Catholic and that also sympathized with national socialist ideology. At the 1936 general election, it captured 10% of the Flemish vote but already at the following elections in 1939 suffered a decline. Eventually, the VNV collaborated with the Nazis, who recognized it as the only representative of the Flemish population.[15] Hence, as during the First World War, German occupation was seen by a minority of Flemish nationalists as a window of opportunity to push through more demands for autonomy against the Belgian state. These excesses and open collaboration with the enemy, together with a revival of Belgian patriotism, led to severe legal repression, delegitimized the Flemish movement and would thus seriously compromise the political reemergence of the Flemish nationalist movement and parties in the postwar period.[16] With the disappearance of relevant Flemish nation-alist parties after the Second World War, the Flemish movement continued its struggle for linguistic protection mainly through the traditional statewide parties.[17]

Policies of Accommodation

At the level of purely linguistic and cultural claims, during the 1856–98 period the Flemish language gradually earned full recognition. In 1856, the govern-ment set up a parliamentary commission to examine the "Flemish question," the first official recognition of the existence of two different cultural groups in Belgium. In the 1860s, the first Flemish-speaking members of parliament (MPs) were elected on the lists of the two state-wide and French-dominated parties, the Catholics and Liberals (before this, representatives of the Flemish constituencies were French-speaking notables). Initial reforms allowed the use of Flemish in court (1873), in the administration (1878), and in public schools (1883). A second wave of linguistic laws advanced the standing of Flemish in the army (1887) and the educational system (1895, except for higher education).[18] Finally, the so-called "law of equality" of 1898 treated the two languages equally regarding the promulgation of parliamentary laws and royal decrees issued by the government. This was followed by the abo-lition of French as a language for official communication in Flanders in 1932.

Even when the main linguistic demands of the Flemish movement were met (the linguistic division of the country into a Flemish monolingual Dutch-speaking area, a Walloon monolingual French-speaking area, and a bilingual capital), the borders between these three "language regimes" were flexible.[19] The linguistic status of a commune was decided on the basis of the results of the most recent census, and thus a commune could switch from one language regime to another due to an influx of French or Dutch speakers. These shifts of the "language border" were especially significant in and around Brussels, which became more and more a Francophone city, a French-speaking "is-land" in Flanders, gradually expanding into the Flemish countryside. Since 1932, the 27 communes on the language border with a linguistic minority of at least 30% of the local population have provided "facilities" in the minority language (Dutch or French) for the benefit of the minority.

From 1930 onwards, new linguistic laws adopted and confirmed the linguistic territoriality principle. The new linguistic issue would become the definition of the territorial zones to which the three language regimes were applicable. In 1962–63 the so-called "language laws" consolidated the lin-guistic borders to arrive at "linguistically homogeneous territories" (Flanders and Wallonia) and the bilingual territory of the capital, Brussels. The en-forcement of Dutch as the only official language in Flanders gradually extin-guished pockets of the French-speaking bourgeoisie (mainly in the cities of Ghent and Antwerp), who chose either to assimilate or to migrate, whether voluntarily or under strong popular pressure (as was the case of the Franco-phone sections of the Catholic University in the Flemish town of Leuven).

FROM SELF-GOVERNMENT TO FEDERATION, 1963–95

Decline of the Classical Center-Periphery Conflict

By the early 1960s, the postindependence center-periphery relationship had changed profoundly. Formally, the Dutch had reached an equal footing with the French, while in practice it took another decade for the state-wide administration to live up to the new regime, and in the Brussels region full bilingualism is still a problem.[20] Politically, from 1965 onwards, due to the reapportionment of parliamentary seats in that year and their growing demographic importance, Flemish MPs formed a majority in Parliament.[21] Economically, Flanders was in full expansion. After the Second World War, Flanders had managed to attract many new industries (small- and medium-sized enterprises as well as multinationals), while Wallonia's economy—based on the heavy coal and steel industry—started to decline slowly.[22] In addition, the Flemish elites, which slowly "conquered" the Belgian state after the Second World War, also managed to direct economic development policies towards further expansion of the Flanders economy.

Yet, in spite of having reversed their center-periphery position, the Flemish movement did not try to exploit this conquest of the Belgian state to steer it towards further promotion of Flemish interests (although such a "minimalist" strategy was advocated by some Flemish nationalist Christian Democrats). As a "normal" minority nationalist movement, it sought devolution of cultural competences (in education, culture, and the media) to the Flemish cultural community (*cultuurautonomie*). Later on, demands for socioeconomic self-government were added.

This widening of the self-government agenda was reinforced by the breakthrough of the Walloon movement that reacted against Flemish emancipation and the growing Flemish grip on the Belgian unitary state ("*l'Etat belgo-flamand*"). The first signs of Walloon mobilization go back to the 1880s but remained rather insignificant politically until the early 1960s (apart from a few short-lived moments of large popular support on the eve of the First World War and just after the Second World War). Triggered by the first successes of the Flemish movement, it started as a linguistic movement, defending French as Belgium's only official language (from 1880 onwards). Quickly, however, working class, republican, and autonomist demands were also added. After the failure of a long and violent general strike in the winter of 1960–61, Walloon militants—especially within the Socialist trade union—started to rally for economic regionalization.[23] The 1963 language laws also triggered a resistance movement of the French-speaking population in Brussels, who conceived the bilingual status of their region as advantageous to the Flemish, as they were more likely to be bilingual and were thus in a position to occupy disproportionately more public sector jobs in Brussels.

The combination of three different types of autonomy movements eventually led to the gradual acceptance by Belgium's hitherto unitarist elites of a certain degree of devolution, eventually leading to a *sui generis* type of "double federalism."

Mobilization of Flemish, Walloon, and Brussels Minorities

This acceptance of new realities was facilitated by the drastic redrawing of the party landscape, leading to a bifurcation—and record level of fragmentation—of the party system (see Table 1).[24] The "regionalization" of the national party system occurred in several waves.[25] First the ethnoregionalist parties broke through in the mid-1960s: the *Volksunie* (VU) in Flanders,[26] the *Rassemblement Wallon* (RW) in Wallonia,[27] and the *Front Démocratique des Francophones* (FDF) in the Brussels region.[28] By the early 1970s, these were able to capture respectively 20% of the Flemish and Walloon vote, and 40% of the Francophone vote in Brussels. Second, the growing saliency of the linguistic and regional cleavage, on which their success was based, became a deep source of division within the unitary Christian Democrat, Liberal, and Socialist parties, and each traditional party split into two organizationally and programmatically independent Flemish- and French-speaking branches (respectively in 1968, 1972, and 1978).[29] These parties split up because increasing internal divisions between Flemings and Francophones forced them to reach internal compromises with regard to regional and linguistic issues that no longer satisfied their respective electorates, as the ethnoregionalist parties offered more attractive, regionally tailored programs. Third, at the end of the 1970s, another wave of expansion of the party system occurred, through the emergence of the Flemish separatist and xenophobe *Vlaams Blok*[30] and the Green parties (*Agalev* in Flanders and *Ecolo* in the Francophone areas).[31]

Thus, since 1978 (when the last traditional party split) one can no longer strictly speak of a single-party system at the Belgian level. By now, there were two distinct party systems, a Flemish and a Francophone one. In the Flemish constituencies, only Flemish parties compete for votes, and as a rule they do not present any lists in the Walloon constituencies (and vice versa). Only in the large Brussels-Halle-Vilvoorde constituency, where these two party systems overlap, do Flemish as well as Francophone parties compete, at least potentially, for the same set of voters. These two party systems differ in terms of the type of party families that are predominant, their electoral evolution, and to some extent their cleavage structure.[32]

The bifurcation into two quasi-autonomous regional party systems fuelled the centrifugal tendencies in the Belgian polity. Thus, in Sartorian

TABLE 1 Belgium: General Election Results, 1946–2007

Year	CVP	PSC	BSP	PSB	PVV	PRL	PCB	FDF	RW	VU	Agalev	Ecolo	VB	FN	Other	Volatility	ENP
1946	42.5		31.6		8.9		12.3										2.9
1949	43.6		29.8		15.3		7.5			2.1						8.1	2.8
1950	47.7		34.5		11.2		4.8									8.9	2.5
1954	41.1		37.3		12.1		3.6			2.2						6.9	2.6
1958	46.5		35.8		11.0		1.9			2.0						5.0	2.5
1961	41.5		36.7		12.3		3.1			3.5						5.0	2.7
1965	34.5		28.3		21.6		4.6	1.3	0.9	6.7						15.8	3.6
1968	22.3	9.4	28.0			20.9	3.3	3.0	2.9	9.8						6.0	5.0
1971	21.9	8.2	27.2		9.5	7.2	3.0	5.4	5.8	11.1						6.9	5.9
1974	23.3	9.1	26.7		10.4	6.0	3.2	5.7	5.1	10.2						3.3	5.8
1977	26.2	9.8	27.0		8.5	7.8	2.1	4.7	2.4	10.0						6.4	5.2
1978	26.1	10.1	12.4	13.0	10.4	6.0	3.3	4.7	with FDF	7.0			1.4		0.9	6.2	6.8
1981	19.3	7.1	12.4	12.7	12.9	8.6	2.3	4.2	with FDF	9.8	2.3	2.2	1.1		2.7	14.4	7.7
1985	21.3	8.0	14.6	13.8	10.7	10.2	1.2	1.2	0.0	7.9	3.7	2.5	1.4		1.2	9.8	7.0
1987	19.5	8.0	14.9	15.7	11.5	9.4	0.8	1.2	0.0	8	4.5	2.6	1.9		0.1	4.3	7.2
1991	16.8	7.7	12.0	13.5	12.0	8.1	0.1	1.1	0.0	5.9	4.9	5.1	6.6	1.0	3.2	12.4	8.4
1995	17.2	7.7	12.6	11.9	13.1	*10.3				4.7	4.4	4.0	7.8	2.3	0.0	6.7	8.1
1999	14.1	5.9	9.5	10.2	14.3	*10.1				5.6	7.0	7.4	9.9	1.5	2.1	10.9	9.1
2003	13.3	5.5	*14.9	13.0	15.4	*11.4				3.1	2.5	3.1	11.7	2.0	1.2	12.7	7.0
2007	*18.5	6.1	*10.3	10.9	11.8	*12.5					4.0	5.1	12.0	2.0	4.0	13.4	**8.8

*In cartel with a regionalist *party*.

**This treats the Flemish Christian Democrats and their allies, N-VA, as separate parliamentary groups.

Other parties with MPs: UDRT (1978–87), Rossem (1991–95), Vivant (1999–2003), Lijst De Decker (2007–).

terms, the current Belgian situation clearly represents a case of extreme multipartism.[33] As far as the direction of competition between the two regions is concerned, it does not follow the polarized type in respect of the religious and socioeconomic founding cleavages, but it certainly does so for the widening linguistic cleavage. On this cleavage, practically all the Flemish parties are situated at the pole of defense of Flemish interests, while the Francophone parties are situated at the pole of the defense of Francophone or Walloon interests. Only the Flemish and Francophone Green parties have remained relatively close to the center, as they have kept a unitary parliamentary group in the federal parliament and have generally aimed at developing a common program on linguistic and regional problems.

Towards a New Accommodation

The demand for distinct types of self-government voiced by regionalist parties and the now autonomous branches of the three former state-wide parties were accommodated by the gradual introduction of a complex type of federal state, through a series of constitutional reforms starting in 1970. The complexity of the institutional system is a direct consequence of the compromise made between two separate but complementary concepts. Flemish nationalists defended the idea of a federal structure with two components—Flemish and Walloon—based on the existence of two distinct cultures, or presumably even nations. The Walloon movement in favor of autonomy supported the idea of delegating economic policy to three regions (Flanders, Wallonia, and Brussels) that would then control their own economic development.[34]

These two trajectories towards two types of self-government led to several major constitutional revisions (in 1971, 1980, 1988, 1993, and 2001). The first three reforms had the effect of deepening the level of regional and communal autonomy. The 1971 reform created three community assemblies in charge of cultural affairs, composed of federal representatives and senators of different language groups. It envisaged the creation of three regional assemblies (created provisionally in 1974) in charge of urban planning, regional economic expansion, housing, family policy and public health, energy and industrial policies, and local government. Within the federal government, each region and community had its minister(s) in charge of these competences.

The 1980 reform further clarified the distribution of competences and the manner in which they were financed, and installed separate executives for the regions and communities. The 1988 reforms dramatically expanded the competences and financing of the substate level (from about 10% to 30% of public expenditures), including the huge sector of education and the remaining parts of economic policy. It should be noted that Belgian federalism is generally based on the principle of dual federalism (a particular competence is attributed to one level only), but that within policy sectors, specific competences are allotted to different levels. For instance, while financing of health care remains mainly federal, preventive health care is a community competence.

In a change of considerable significance, the 1993 constitutional revision institutionally consolidated the transformation of Belgium into a federal country based on three partially overlapping linguistic communities (Flemish, French, and German, the last a tiny minority) and three socioeconomic regions (Flanders, Brussels, and Wallonia), with directly elected assemblies. However, in spite of its "double" form (three regions and three communities), the asymmetry of Belgian federalism was increased by the merger, from the start, of the Flemish community and region (see Figure 1). More recently the Walloon region and the Francophone community have pooled some competences (often with a single minister in charge of regional as well as community affairs), while there has also been a gradual transfer of appropriate Walloon regional competences to the German-speaking community.

Federalization created an entirely new political system in the regions and communities, each of which has its own directly elected legislature, an executive headed by a minister-president and a civil service. This level of government controls more than one-third of overall public spending. After the 1993 reforms, regional competences included urban planning, environment, local government, housing, as well as parts of the following sectors: agriculture, economy, energy, employment, public works, transportation, science and research, and even international relations. The communities' competences include nearly all educational matters, culture, parts of health policy and assistance to families, the disabled, elderly, youth, and other groups. In the most recent reform, in 2001, agriculture, developmental aid and subregional government were added.

Hence, with the creation of this *sui generis* form of federalism, the self-government movements in the three regions managed to transform a basic zero-sum game into a win-win solution, a fine example of consociational arrangements previously applied with success to other major divisions in Belgian society, including the question of the king in 1945–50, the school pact of 1958, and the culture pact of 1974.[35]

It should be noted that these changes were accompanied by another consociational rule: government by mutual consent. The 1970 constitutional revision neutralized the Flemish parliamentary majority by giving veto powers to the Francophone minority (in respect of representation in the Council of Ministers, parliamentary procedures, and special provisions for particular kinds of legislation). First, the cabinet (excluding the prime minister and junior ministers) has to include as many Francophones as Dutch-speaking members. Second, linguistic groups have power to delay or block legislation threatening their interests through the use of an "alarm-bell" procedure (this requires support from at least three quarters of the members of that group).[36] Third, in order to protect the rights of regional and

3 Regions

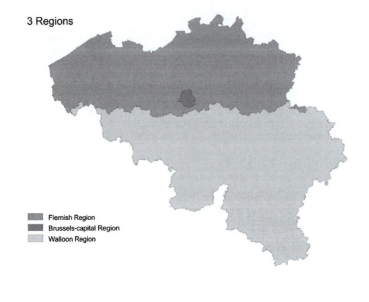

Flemish Region
Brussels-capital Region
Walloon Region

3 Communities

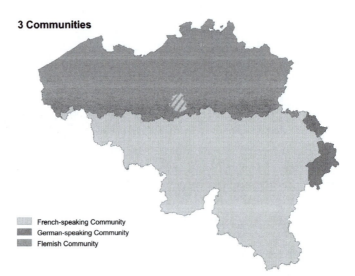

French-speaking Community
German-speaking Community
Flemish Community

FIGURE 1 Belgium: Federal State Organization. *Source*: IGEAT-ULB.

linguistic minorities, some bills have to be approved by qualified majorities: overall support by a two-thirds majority of the valid votes, and a majority of valid votes within each linguistic group in each chamber. Since 1831, constitutional amendments have also required approval by a two-thirds majority of valid votes in each chamber.

Since 1970, no Flemish demand for further autonomy can be granted unless the Francophones agree. But other "minorities" have also been given special protection: the Flemish in the Brussels region (at the regional level, and in each of the 19 Brussels communes), the Francophones in Flemish *"facilités"* communes in the Brussels periphery (see below), and the German-speaking minority in Belgium. Each of these veto-power arrangements has been contested in the postfederalism phase.

BEYOND FEDERALISM, 1995–PRESENT

Redefining the Conflict

In spite of this successful exercise in the "politics of accommodation"—the transformation of a unitary state into a full-fledged federal state in less than three decades—community conflicts did not disappear from the political agenda, though the main ethnoregionalist parties have declined since the late 1980s.[37]

There are several reasons for this absence of political peace. First, federalization did not solve all issues that fed into the community conflict, and once the main issues of federal institutional reform were solved, these relatively minor issues gained in importance. Amongst these "unfinished businesses," linguistic issues regarding the Brussels region and its periphery are prominent. But from the mid-1990s, socioeconomic issues have dominated the agenda. While nobody doubts that Belgium is by now a fully fledged federal state, there is no full elite or public consensus about the most appropriate balance in the division of labor between the federal, regional, and, indeed, European levels, as in most other federal or regionalized states.[38]

The remaining linguistic problems are essentially due to a "mismatch" between the language regimes installed in certain communes and the actual language use of the local population.[39] The most important linguistic problem from a demographic perspective concerns the Francophones living in the Brussels periphery—on "Flemish soil." Large numbers of Francophone (as well as Flemish) Bruxellois have left the capital to live in the greener Flemish countryside around Brussels. This suburbanization process started long before the linguistic arrangements of 1963, which acknowledged this situation by granting the Francophones special minority rights ("facilités" [facilities]) in six Flemish communes in the Brussels periphery (numbers 1 to 6 in Figure 2). There Francophone citizens may communicate with the communal administration in French, an exception to the rule that in Flanders the official administrative language is Dutch only.

By now (2009), in all six communes, the Francophones constitute a majority of inhabitants (ranging from 50% to 80%). Hence, Francophone politicians run the local council and executive. Formally they are obliged to conduct business in Dutch, and certainly they would prefer their commune to be given bilingual status (as in the Brussels communes). However, all Flemish parties, ethnoregionalist movements, and wider Flemish public opinion are unanimously and vehemently opposed to this threat to the "unity and monolingual character of the Flemish territory." The experience of the "loss" of

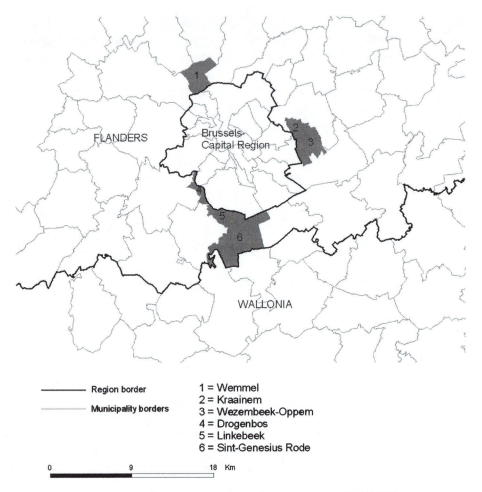

FIGURE 2 Belgium: Greater Brussels area. *Source*: IGEAT-ULB.

Brussels to the Francophones, a city that still in the nineteenth century was predominantly Flemish, pushes all Flemish parties to call an unconditional halt to further linguistic assimilation in the Brussels periphery. In fact, most Flemish parties try proactively to hold back this process, by interpreting the use of "facilities" restrictively as well as by positively discriminating in favor of the Flemish, for instance in terms of access to housing and to infrastructure for organizing French cultural events. The quasi-unanimous Flemish position is that Francophones who move to Flemish territory should adapt to the monolingual language regime.

Assimilation to French is also substantial in many other Flemish communes in the Brussels periphery, where French speakers do not enjoy any linguistic facilities. Estimates are that by now well over 100,000 Francophones live in the Flemish periphery around the capital. Most Francophone local civil society organizations and parties call for changing the official monolingual status of these communes to a regime that would recognize the bilingual sociological reality, for instance by granting language facilities in these communes, or more radically by extending the regional territory of Brussels and the bilingual language regime.[40] Belgian members of the Council of Europe have called several times (1998, 2001, 2005, and 2009) for a report on potential discrimination against linguistic minorities in Belgium and the violation of the charter of local autonomy; the resulting reports that generally tend to support the Francophone theses regarding the unfair treatment of the Francophone "minority" in the Brussels periphery.[41]

Linked to these linguistic problems in the periphery is the highly symbolic but technically complex issue of "BHV"—the proposed division of the electoral constituency of Brussels-Halle-Vilvoorde. While federalization established three regions, an anomaly remained regarding the redrawing of electoral constituencies. For general elections, the Brussels region continued to constitute a single constituency together with the 35 Flemish communes of the Halle and Vilvoorde electoral *arrondissements* that surround the capital region. The Flemish want an unconditional partition of the BHV constituency—the largest in the country with 1.6 million inhabitants—as they claim that the current system allows Francophone parties to take easy advantage of the votes of the numerous Francophones living in the Flemish periphery. This long-standing claim (voiced already in 1961) has gotten some sense of urgency, due to the 2001 enlargement of the electoral constituencies, which now coincide with provincial borders, except for the BHV case. A 2003 ruling of the Constitutional Court declared the current situation unconstitutional, and this may even invalidate any further general elections. But splitting the constituency is not the only way to restore constitutionality, and Francophone parties argue for a return to the previous subprovincial electoral constituencies. It appears that the issue is more important symbolically than in substance: it is by no means clear that concession of the Flemish demand for partition of BHV would in practice result in any significant change in representation.

Finally, the definition of the status of Brussels as a third region during the different waves of federalization has produced a complex system—one that has functioned relatively well until now—for the protection of the linguistic and cultural interests of the Flemish minority, at least at the level of the regional executive institutions. The Flemish enjoy a constitutionally fixed representation of 17 out of the 89 members of the Brussels parliament, and two ministers (plus a secretary of state) in the regional executive. Yet, because of the continuing decline of the Flemish demographic presence in Brussels, their representation at the communal level has become insignificant.[42] As the 19 Brussels communes are responsible for many welfare functions, including the public hospitals, social aid, and pensioners' care, the Flemish would like to transfer these competences to the Brussels regional level where they are better represented.[43] Finally, the Flemish argue that the principle of bilingualism of local and regional public services (compatible with substantial unilingualism among individual public servants, provided there are enough speakers of each language to satisfy local needs) should be replaced by the principle of bilingualism of public *servants*. This measure would boost Flemish employment in the Brussels public sector.[44] The Francophones threaten to reduce Flemish protection in Brussels, especially the obligation of bilingual public services, if Flanders does not compromise on issues concerning the status of Francophone minorities, like the "BHV" issue and the "facilities" that French speakers enjoy in the Flemish periphery.

While these linguistic issues remain salient and difficult to resolve due to their zero-sum nature, socioeconomic issues have increasingly become predominant. The growing economic north-south differences have triggered huge financial transfers from Flanders to Brussels and Wallonia (estimated at 2 billion euro per year by the Belgian Federation of Employers, but at up to 11 billion by the Flemish nationalist party *Nieuw-Vlaamse Alliantie* [N-VA]) through the redistributive mechanism of the social security system (still a federal competence), of federal grants to regions and communities (which take population, economic performance, and size of the territory into consideration), and general federal policies.[45] While these solidarity transfers are based on objective differences (for instance, the higher degree of unemployment and professional health hazards), many Flemish parties and media would like to reduce them. They are not considered to be a normal consequence of interpersonal solidarity but are attributed to abuses of the social security system. Populist interpretations of "lazy Walloons living on the rents of hardworking Flemish," and of an inefficient, clientelistic, and even corrupt Walloon public management, are widely voiced by Flemish parties and media.[46]

Hence, the Flemish increasingly call for more fiscal and financial autonomy, a Flemish social security system, and devolution of full policy competences in the labor market, transport and telecommunications, science and technology, foreign trade, development aid, and occasionally also police and justice. Francophones call for better financing of current competences, especially in the education sector, and the Bruxellois for more resources in general (in view of the paradox of being the region with the highest gross regional product while at the same time having the highest unemployment and poverty rates, a big unskilled labor force, and a pressing need for affordable housing). Francophones fear that Flemish calls for more competences are just another step in the region's march towards full independence. Hence, since the last constitutional reform of 2001 (see above), Francophones have called for a halt to the further disempowerment of the federal state. The conflict between the institutional status quo defended by the Francophones and the call of the Flemish for a "huge" state reform created the stalemate that blocked the formation of the federal government after the June 2007 elections for seven months.

Repositioning the Actors

Compared to the first phase, the main actors in the Belgian community conflict have gradually changed. First, the capacity of the Flemish movement to mobilize hundreds of thousands of demonstrators to endorse its demands has vanished (the last mass mobilization was in 1978). Traditional regular mass gatherings, such as the annual Yser pilgrimage (a Flemish nationalist commemoration of deaths in the First World War) and the Flemish National Song Festival, by now draw only a few thousand participants. The regionalist parties have also lost appeal since the mid-1980s. The *Rassemblement Wallon* had lost its last MPs by 1985 (many of its members and MPs joined the Liberals or the Socialists), while the FDF managed to keep a few seats by forming a federation with the Francophone Liberals after 1993.

Although the VU lost about two-thirds of its 1981 voters over the next 20 years, this decline led—contrary to the shrinking of the Francophone party system—to extreme fragmentation. First there was the breakthrough of the separatist *Vlaams Blok*, a splinter from the VU dating from 1978. This has boomed since the early 1990s, mainly through anti-immigrant and anti-establishment stands. The VU's struggle for survival in the 1990s (including the search for collaboration with a large Flemish party) radicalized the traditional Flemish parties, whose electoral scores tended to converge in the 20%–25% range. With the VU's 10% of the votes potentially "up for grabs" and given a general trend of growing volatility, whichever party would manage to get the biggest slice of the VU electorate could claim political leadership in the Flemish political system and thus also at the federal level.[47] Thus political competition focused on seducing the drifting VU voters, by offering a credible Flemish nationalist program (and even party name).[48]

This new focus of the traditional parties on competition with the Volksunie occurred also at the level of political personnel. Already in the 1990s, several leading VU MPs had joined other parties, mainly the Liberals. But in 2001, the VU split into the "post-nationalist" left-liberal *SPIRIT* (which formed an electorally beneficial cartel with the Flemish Socialists in 2003), while the traditional supporters of independence formed the *Nieuw-Vlaamse Alliantie* (N-VA), which eventually formed an electoral cartel with the Flemish Christian Democrats in 2004. Both cartels were triggered by the implementation of a provincial threshold of 5% in 2001 for regional and federal elections. Hence, by 2004, the regional branches of the mainstream Flemish parties had become the main protagonists in the postfederalization phase, each party counting a considerable number of former VU Flemish nationalists in its ranks, and these further radicalized the respective parties' positions on the community question.

Ethnic entrepreneurship has shifted towards regional institutional actors. The creation of directly elected regional parliaments (since 1995) and democratically legitimized regional governments created a new class of Flemish political entrepreneurs, who exploited their institutional position as members of the Flemish executive or parliament to push the "Flemish agenda" further. In 1999 the Flemish parliament voted for five radical resolutions almost unanimously (with only the Socialists and the Greens failing to endorse all), and these have remained up until now the yardstick of Flemish demands, although some have been implemented by the 2001 constitutional reform. The most contentious resolutions call for the current "3 + 3" federal state structure (Flanders, Wallonia, and Brussels as regions; Dutch, French, and German speakers as linguistic communities) to be transformed into a "2 + 2" formula, with two strong *deelstaten* or substate entities (Flanders and Wallonia) responsible for the management of the "second order" regions, Brussels and the German-speaking community, respectively. Second, it calls for fiscal and financial autonomy, the exclusive attribution of residual competences to the regions, and the right of the Flemish community to draft its own constitution. In terms of competences, it calls for full transfer away from the center of health and family policy, science and technology, rail infrastructure, communication, agriculture and fisheries, foreign trade, developmental aid, and parts of labor market policy. While the resolutions were mainly legitimated by reference to the principles of subsidiarity, good governance, fiscal accountability, and efficiency (with demands for more coherent policy packages tailored to diverging regional needs), the Francophones perceived them as a road map to full Flemish independence.

The main calls for larger Flemish autonomy are voiced by the Flemish executive, and especially by the various Flemish Christian Democratic minister-presidents. Most of these demands are made in the name of the Flemish "general interest," on the grounds that they are good for the Flemish people; but for the Francophones this resonates alarmingly with the more primitive calls of the racist *Vlaams Blok* (VB), a party that does not hide its clear separatist goals, *Eigen volk eerst* ("Our own people first"). Hence, the VB's growing success (until 2006) serves as a democratic legitimation (and a kind of alibi) for Francophone resistance to what they describe as "VB-driven" Flemish demands—though the Flemish consider these as democratically fully legitimate.

Finally, these institutionally based calls for more autonomy have been reinforced recently by the decoupling of federal and regional elections and the occurrence of asymmetrical majorities. Before 2003, the seat distributions within the national and regional parliaments within each region tended to coincide. Up to 1995, the regional and community parliaments were composed of national MPs, while the first two direct elections of the regional parliaments were organized on the same day as the federal elections (1995 and 1999). Hence, until 2004, symmetrical coalitions were formed at the federal and regional level (with the exception of the Brussels region). However, the 2004 regional elections, which for the first time did not coincide with federal elections, were won in Flanders by the Christian Democrats, a party in opposition at the federal level since 1999. The Christian Democrat minister-president used this legitimate power base to vehemently attack the federal Liberal-Socialist government, reproaching its neglect of Flemish interests and lack of good governance.[49] The federal prime minister, preoccupied with keeping his "unnatural" coalition of Flemish and Francophone Liberals and Socialists together, tried as much as possible to downplay community conflicts. Hence, asymmetrical coalitions between the federal and regional level tend to enhance competition between government levels and between parties, especially on community issues.

Thus, the completion of a federal state in 1993 did not lead to peace at the elite level, rather the contrary. At the level of the citizens, however, we do find significant indications of diminishing salience of community issues. First, all longitudinal surveys indicate that, since the early 1990s, community issues are very low in salience vis-à-vis mainstream issues such as unemployment, security, and migration.[50] Neither do Flemish citizens seem to follow the radicalization pattern found amongst elites. While in the late 1970s Flemish citizens identified more with the Flemish community than with Belgium, from the late 1980s this situation was reversed, and by now about twice as many Flemish identify with Belgium as with Flanders.[51] The so-called "Moreno question" shows a "normal" and stable distribution around the center position "I feel as much Flemish as Belgian," with systematically less than 10% opting for the position "I feel Flemish only." As regards constitutional options, a majority still opts for more power to the Belgian level rather than for more power to the regions. Finally, when asked to choose between the regional, national, and European levels as the most appropriate decision-making level to solve problems of unemployment, migration, health, environment, and criminality, the regional level is always overshadowed by the Belgian (or European) level.[52] However, Flemish MPs clearly prefer the region over Belgium in all policy sectors (apart from issues of crime control).

Hence, at the Flemish level there seems to be a serious gap between elite and mass opinion, while on the Francophone side there is a strong mass identification with Belgium, shared by the elites. Thus, the "divorce des Belges" is mainly situated at the elite level, rather than at the mass level, in spite of the existence of two distinct "public spheres." In fact, Belgium has two media landscapes segregated by language, with very little interaction between them.[53] Since the media only cater for the information needs of their own community, they have no interest in paying much attention to presenting an objective picture of what happens in the other community.[54] In addition, the Flemish media always consider themselves as watchdogs of the "Flemish cause" and tend to focus on news that confirms the large north-south differences, whether in cultural, economic or political matters, societal values, or lifestyle issues. The European Values Studies and European Social Surveys, however, systematically indicate that while value differences between Flemish and Walloons do exist, they tend to be smaller than those between Flemish and Dutch, or between Walloons and French.[55]

A Path towards Settlement?

Since the completion of a federal state in 1993, the institutional structure of Belgium has changed little, apart from a minor expansion of regional competences during the last state reform of 2001. This relative institutional inertia creates a huge potential for a major (and perhaps lethal) community conflict between Flemish demands for fundamental state reform, and Francophone preferences for the institutional status quo.

Traditional consociational strategies have lost a good part of their traditional bridge-building potential, for a variety of reasons. First, intercommunal peace in Belgium was often achieved by turning conflicts into a win-win situation that usually included granting large subsidies to the conflicting camps. However, since the budgetary crisis of the 1990s (with a record public debt of 139% in 1993), there have been few financial resources left to distribute. The current economic and financial crisis further diminishes the possibility of buying off conflicting communities.

Second, there is a breakdown of communication between political elites from different sides of the conflict, especially between Flemish and Francophone Christian Democrats, the backbone of most postwar federal governments. However, socioeconomic elites tend to remain on better speaking terms (the trade unions and mutual health associations, the backbones of the Socialist and Christian Democratic pillars, are still organized in a national, though federalized, structure).[56]

Third, due to the contest for political leadership in Flanders between the three traditional parties, there is considerable irresponsible outbidding in respect of Flemish demands, which can never be realized through normal interparty bargaining with the Francophones, who defend the status quo. Given the latter's strong institutional veto power, most radical Flemish sectors plead for a blackmail strategy, reducing Flemish transfers to the south or even threatening the pursuit of full Flemish independence.[57]

CONCLUSION

In the eyes of many observers, Belgium has moved into a final stage of disintegration. The original community conflict on language issues has become predominantly one over socioeconomic policy and autonomy, essentially opposing on the one hand the Francophones in Wallonia and Brussels, unanimously defending the institutional status quo of the current federal state, and on the other hand most Flemish political elites, calling for radical autonomy, and some even for independence.

It is quite hazardous to make predictions about the evolution of the community conflict in the near future. The status quo is the most unlikely outcome, as it could lead to a federal decision-making deadlock. Fear of further radicalization and support for independence in Flanders is gradually pushing Francophones to accept further devolution in some policy sectors (such as the labor market), in exchange for monetary compensation and some measures that would improve the functioning of the federal state also (such as resynchronization of regional and federal elections, and the introduction of a single federal constituency that would counterbalance the centrifugal tendencies of the two party systems).

But will this "lighter but fitter Belgium" outcome satisfy Flemish elites? Is this win-win option financially still affordable, given the structural budgetary problems enhanced by the current financial crisis? If the answer is "no," the breakup option will gain further momentum in Flanders. In any case, in both camps various think tanks prepare road maps in case such a breakdown becomes unavoidable.

However, there are several factors that make such a drastic solution unrealistic. First, there is the issue of Brussels, representing the economic and diplomatic crown jewels of the Kingdom of Belgium.[58] An independent Flanders would certainly have to surrender Brussels, given the large majority of Francophones living in that region. Most recently, some minority factions of the Flemish Movement (at the latest Yser Pilgrimage) have indeed accepted this as a price to pay for Flemish independence. Second, there is the problem of the division of the enormous public debt. Third, many large European Union (EU) countries that themselves face independence movements are unlikely to support Flemish independence. Neither would the EU be enthusiastic about the breakup of a state in the heart of Europe along ethnic lines.[59] Fourth, the Flemish economy, which is highly export oriented, may suffer from the loss of the label "Made in Belgium," as Flanders still lacks a strong brand name in international markets. Finally, the high transaction costs incurred from transforming the existing state into a new Flemish state and the remaining "Wallo-Brux" parts of the Belgian federation would be enormous and would create a lose-lose situation for all.

NOTES

1. As it has been put, "Belgium can legitimately claim to be the most thorough example of consociational democracy, the type of democracy that is most suitable for deeply divided societies"; see Arend Lijphart (ed.), *Conflict and Coexistence in Belgium: The Dynamics of a Culturally Divided Society* (Berkeley: Institute of International Studies, University of Berkeley, 1981), p. 1. Lijphart also heralds Belgium, with Switzerland, as the best real-world approximation of the ideal type of a consensus democracy; see *Patterns of Democracy* (New Haven, CT: Yale University Press, 1999).

2. Liesbet Hooghe, Gary Marks, and Arjan Schakel, "Patterns of Regional Authority," *Regional and Federal Studies*, Vol. 18, Nos. 2–3 (2008), pp. 167–81.

3. Frans Schrijver, *Regionalism after Regionalisation: Spain, France and the United Kingdom* (Amsterdam: Amsterdam University Press, 2006).

4. Stein Rokkan and Derek Urwin (eds.), *The Politics of Territorial Identity: Studies in European Regionalism* (London: Sage, 1982); André-Paul Frognier, "Application du modèle de Lipset et Rokkan à la Belgique," *Revue Internationale de Politique Comparée*, Vol. 14, No. 2 (2007), pp. 303–24; Vincent De Coorebyter, "Clivages et partis en Belgique," *Courrier Hebdomadaire du CRISP*, No. 2000 (2008), pp. 7–95.

5. Liesbet Hooghe, "Nationalist Movements and Social Factors: A Theoretical Perspective," in John Coakley (ed.), *The Social Origins of Nationalist Movements* (London: Sage, 1992).

6. Lieven De Winter, "Conclusion: A Comparative Analysis of the Electoral Office and Policy Success of Ethnoregionalist Parties," in Lieven De Winter and H. Türsan (eds.), *Regionalist Parties in Western Europe* (London: Routledge, 1998), pp. 204–47.

7. Certainly, one can apply a different periodization. Many authors writing entire volumes about the community conflict use more phases. Yet all consider the linguistic laws of 1962–63 and the federal constitution of 1993 as milestones in the Belgian community conflict; see Kas Deprez and Louis Vos (eds.), *Nationalism in Belgium: Shifting Identities, 1780–1995* (Basingstoke, UK: Palgrave, 2001); Els Witte, Jan Craeybeckx, and Alain Meynen, *Political History of Belgium from 1830 onwards* (Brussels: VUB University Press, 2000); Xavier Mabille, *Histoire politique de la Belgique, facteurs et acteurs de changement* (Bruxelles: CRISP, 2001); Lode Wils, *Histoire des nations belges: Belgique, Flandre, Wallonie: quinze siècles de passé commun* (Bruxelles: Éditions Labor, 2005); Jos Bouveroux and Luc Huyse, *Het onvoltooide Land* (Leuven, Belgium: Van Halewyck, 2009).

8. The various dialects spoken in Flanders were standardized under the label *Nederlands* in 1844 by adopting the standard of the Dutch language used in the Netherlands. After the First World War, a small territory with a German-speaking population was added. This community now counts about 70,000 German speakers, less than 1% of the Belgian population.

9. The distribution of the Dutch- and French-speaking populations has always been a contested issue. Linguistic censuses have been held since 1842, but their methodology was questionable. After the First World War these censuses were used to determine the language regime of the communes along the linguistic border, especially in and around Brussels; Reginald de Schryver, Bruno de Wever, Gaston Durnez, Lieve Gevers, Pieter van Hees, and Machteld de Metsenaere (eds.), *Nieuwe Encyclopedie van de Vlaamse Beweging* (Tielt, Belgium: Lannoo, 1998). Given the politicization of "language counting," no more census data on the language use of Belgians have been published since 1954, when the final results of the 1947 census appeared.

10. It had already played the role of administrative center in the past when Belgian provinces were part of different empires.

11. In addition, there were religious differences between Flanders and Wallonia, with a very Catholic Flanders, and a Wallonia and Brussels more disposed towards anticlericalism.

12. This peripheral position of Flanders fits Rokkan and Urwin's definition (*Politics of Territorial Identity*, 1982, p. 5) of the center and the periphery well. They define the center as the "privileged location within a territory where key military/administrative, economic and cultural resource-holders most frequently meet; with established arenas for deliberations, negotiations and decision-making; where people convene for ritual ceremonies of affirmation of identity; with monuments that symbolize this identity; with the largest proportion of the economically active population engaged in the processing and communication of information and instructions over long distances. Centers, then, are both locations providing services and nodes in a communication network." On the other side, a periphery is defined as "dependent, controlling at best only its own resources and more exposed to fluctuations in long-distance markets; [it] is isolated from all other regions except the central one; and contributes little to the total flow of communication within the territory, with a marginal culture that is fragmented and parochial, yet not fully dominant across the politically defined territory" (ibid). Also, in Rokkan's terms, the initial territorial structure is clearly monocephalic, with political power and economic and cultural resources all highly concentrated in a well-defined and clearly prevailing geographical area. Initially, the Flemish periphery did not possess any political, economic, and cultural resources. Hence, Flanders in the nineteenth century was more peripheral than the industrial regions of, for instance, Catalonia, the Basque Country, Scotland, or Wales.

13. Lode Wils, *Van de Belgische naar de Vlaamse natie. Een geschiedenis van de Vlaamse beweging* (Leuven, Belgium: Acco, 2009).

14. The name of the party referred to the war front where many Flemish soldiers had given their lives for their country while serving under officers who did not speak or understand their language. On the other hand, some Flemish nationalists had collaborated with the German occupiers, trying to achieve nationalist objectives that had been refused before the war, such as the conversion of the State University of Ghent into a Dutch-speaking one.

15. Consequently, the VNV captured most political and administrative positions in the occupied state. It also recruited Flemish volunteers to fight bolshevism with the German army and fully adopted national socialist ideology.

16. Luc Huyse and Steven Dhondt, *Onverwerkt Verleden. Collaboratie en Repressie in België 1942–1952* (Leuven, Belgium: Kritak, 1991).

17. A new Flemish nationalist party, the Christelijke Vlaamse Volksunie (Christian Flemish Peoples Union), was founded in 1954, but before 1965 it managed to capture only one or two seats.

18. Even though Dutch was recognized as an official language by the end of the century, it was not used in higher education in Flanders until 1930.

19. The "linguistic laws" of 1963 constituted the final step in this process. The process of assimilation to French was even reversed as the elites in Flanders gradually became Dutch speaking.

20. Wilfried Dewachter, *Van oppositie tot elite. Over macht, visie en leiding* (Leuven, Belgium: Acco, 2003).

21. Between 1945 and 1965, no reapportionment of seats according to voting population had occurred.

22. Michel Quévit, *Les causes du déclin Wallon* (Brussels: Vie Ouvrière, 1998).

23. Paul Delforge, Philipe Destatte, and Micheline Libon (eds.), *Encyclopédie du Mouvement wallon* (Charleroi, Belgium: Institut Destrée, 2000).

24. In 1999, the effective number of parties reached its peak at 9.1; Lieven De Winter and Patrick Dumont, "Belgium: Party System(s) on the Eve of Disintegration?", in David Broughton and Marc Donovan (eds.), *Changing Party Systems in Western Europe* (London and New York: Pinter, 1999), pp. 183–206.

25. De Winter and Dumont, "Belgium," pp. 183–206.

26. Lieven De Winter, "In Memoriam the Volksunie 1954–2001: Death by Overdose of Success," in Lieven De Winter, Marga Gómez-Reino Cachafeiro, and Peter Lynch (eds.), *Autonomist Parties in Europe: Identity Politics and the Revival of the Territorial Cleavage,* vol. 2 (Barcelona: Institut de Ciènces Polítiques i Socials, 2006), pp. 11–45.

27. Ruth Van Dyck and Jo Buelens, "Regionalist Parties in French-Speaking Belgium: The Rassemblement Wallon and the Front Démocratique des Francophones," in Lieven De Winter and Huri Türsan, *Regionalist Parties in Western Europe* (London: Routledge, 1998), pp. 51–69.

28. Chantal Kesteloot, *Au nom de la Wallonie et de Bruxelles français. Les origines du FDF* (Bruxelles: Complexe/CEGES, 2004).

29. Note that the Liberals initially split into three parties, including a Brussels Francophone wing that merged with the Walloon wing in 1979. For the specific circumstances of these splits and the evolution of the successor parties of these three party families, see Lieven De Winter, "Socialist Parties in Belgium," in José Maravall (ed.), *Socialist Parties in Europe* (Barcelona: Institut de Sciencies Politiques i Socials, 1991), pp. 123–56; Lieven De Winter, "Christian Democratic Parties in Belgium," in Mario Caciagli, Lieven De Winter, Alf Mintzel, Joan Culla, and Alain De Brouwer, *Christian Democracy in Europe* (Barcelona: Institut de Ciènces Polítiques i Socials, 1992), pp. 29–54; Lieven De Winter, "Liberal Parties in Belgium: From Freemasons to Free Citizens," in Lieven De Winter (ed.), *Liberalism and Liberal Parties in the European Union* (Barcelona: Institut de Ciènces Polítiques i Socials, 2000), pp. 141–82.

30. Lieven De Winter, Marga Gomez-Reino, and Jo Buelens, "The Extreme-Right Flemish-Nationalist Vlaams Blok," in Lieven De Winter-Marga Gomez, and Peter Lynch (eds.), *Autonomist Parties,* Vol. II (2006), pp. 47–78.

31. Benoit Rihoux, "Belgium: Greens in a Divided Society," in Dick Richardson and Christopher Rootes (eds.), *The Green Challenge: The Development of Green Parties in Europe* (London: Routledge, 1995), pp. 91–108.

32. Lieven De Winter, Marc Swyngedouw, and Patrick Dumont, "Party System(s) and Electoral Behaviour in Belgium: From Stability to Balkanisation," in Marleen Brans, Lieven De Winter, and Wilfried Swenden (eds.), *The Politics of Belgium* (London: Routledge, 2009), pp. 71–94.

33. Giovanni Sartori, *Parties and Party Systems* (Cambridge: Cambridge University Press, 1976); see Lieven De Winter, "Multi-Level Party Competition and Coordination in Belgium," in Charley Jeffery

42 L. De Winter and P. Baudewyns

and Dan Hough (eds.), *Devolution and Electoral Politics* (Manchester, UK: Manchester University Press, 2006), pp. 76–95.

34. Chantal Kesteloot, "The Growth of the Walloon Movement," in Kas Deprez and Louis Vos (eds.), *Nationalism in Belgium: Shifting Identities, 1780–1995* (Houndmills, UK: Macmillan, 1998), pp. 139–52; Delforge, Destatte, and Libon, *Encyclopédie*.

35. The *royal question* arose from the attitude of Leopold III (1934–50) towards the Nazis during the Second World War, when he ordered the country's surrender in 1940 and remained captive throughout the war while a government in exile was formed in London. The question of his return after the war created a major division that brought the country to the brink of civil war. In a 1950 referendum on the issue, the North and the South voted differently, with a majority of Flemings (72%) in favor of the King, but only 42% of Walloons accepting this position. Leopold ultimately abdicated in favor of his son Baudouin. The *school pact* between the Catholics, Socialists, and Liberals was concluded in 1958 and brought to an end a conflict that had been simmering for 130 years, by providing for a package on the financing of Catholic schools. The *culture pact* was concluded between the same three traditional parties in 1974 and made large sums of money available to organizations of different pillars, imposing "pluralist" management on all publicly financed or subsidized entities, such as public radio and television, theatres and libraries, universities, school boards, sports organizations, tourism bodies, and museums. For the operation of the consociational model in respect of the Belgian community conflict, see Kris Deschouwer, "And the Peace Goes On? Consociational Democracy and Belgian Politics in the Twenty-First Century," in Brans, De Winter, and Swenden, *Politics of Belgium* (2009), pp. 33–49; Jos Bouveroux and Luc Huyse, *Het onvoltooide Land* (Leuven, Belgium: Van Halewyck, 2009).

36. If at least three quarters of the members of a linguistic group introduce a motion to that effect on a specific bill, parliamentary procedure is suspended, and the Council of Ministers makes a judgement on the "alarm-bell" motion within 30 days, inviting the relevant chamber to reconsider in the light of this. In practice, this procedure has been used effectively only once, but it has been used more often as a threat, given the fact that once a conflict has reached this stage, it rings the funeral bells for the federal government too. There is also a procedure to govern cases of "conflict of interest" between federal or substate chambers.

37. Arend Lijphart, *The Politics of Accommodation: Pluralism and Democracy in the Netherlands* (Berkeley: University of California Press, 1968).

38. Lieven De Winter and Marc Swyngedouw, "The Scope of EU Government," in Hermann Schmitt and Jacques Thomassen (eds.), *Political Representation and Legitimacy in the European Union* (Oxford, UK: Oxford University Press, 1999), pp. 47–73; Lieven De Winter, Marc Swyngedouw, and Bart Goeminne "The Level of Decision Making: The Preferences of the Citizens after Enlargement," in Jacques Thomassen (ed.), *The Legitimacy of the European Union after Enlargement* (Oxford, UK: Oxford University Press, 2009), pp. 117–40.

39. During the 1970s and 1980s, the focus of conflict regarding the linguistic border was the commune of Voeren (Fourons in French), allocated to the Flemish Community in 1963 (Limburg province), but populated by a narrow majority of French speakers (57% in 1947, only 19% in 1930). In fact, the Walloon Socialists were happy to exchange rural, Catholic Voeren for the industrial communes of Comines and Mouscron. The Fourons French speakers regularly violated the monolingual Dutch status of this commune (while enjoying facilities) and wanted to protect their linguistic rights by reattaching their commune to the French-speaking province of Liège. The Voeren question regularly cropped up on the national political agenda, and a few governments fell over the issue. Since the 1990s, the issue has lost momentum. Dutch immigrants—having received local suffrage since the Maastricht Treaty (1992)—toppled the political majority in the local council in favor of the Flemish, thus eliminating the town hall as a legitimate institutional power base for Francophone resistance.

40. Other models include a "federal district" status for Brussels, a merger between the Walloon and Brussels regions, or even a "District of Europe"; see Nicolas Lagasse, "Gouverner Bruxelles. Règles en vigueur et débat," *Courrier Hebdomadaire du CRISP*, No. 1628–1629 (1999).

41. Belgium has not yet ratified the cadre convention on the protection of national minorities of the Council of Europe. The Flemish still refuse to recognize the Francophones in the Brussels periphery as a national minority.

42. This fear of further assimilation in and around Brussels is reinforced by the extension of local suffrage to EU citizens since 2000, under the Maastricht Treaty, and to non-EU legally established migrants (law of 2004). Since these groups are much more likely to use French than Dutch, this is likely to further reinforce the predominance of the Francophone parties. In several communes, the local

council no longer includes any Flemish councillor (and thus neither a Flemish alderman nor a representative in the management of the administratively important *Commission Publique d'Assistance Sociale*, (CPAS)).

43. One of the recurrent complaints of the Flemish minority is that the doctors and nurses of the public (and particularly private) hospitals and pensioners' homes are not (or not sufficiently) bilingual; Jean-Paul Nassaux, "Les relations communautaires à l'Assemblée réunie de la Commission communautaire commune," *Courrier Hebdomadaire du CRISP*, No. 1633– 634 (1999).

44. In fact, the requirement of bilingualism for all Brussels civil servants is quite beneficial for the Flemish population, which tends to be more fluent in both national languages. Hence, many "Brussels" jobs are occupied by Flemish workers, who commute daily to Brussels from all over Flanders.

45. Note that redistribution occurs not only between north and south, but in other directions as well. Capron's detailed analyses based on the difference between gross and net income per capita, which constitutes a rough indicator of interregional transfers, showed that (in 2003) the difference for the inhabitants of the Flemish region was 108.1 versus 105.5, for Wallonia 86.2 versus 90.6, and for Brussels 97.5 versus 98.1 (Belgium = 100). However, in pure terms of regional economic performance, that is, in terms of gross regional product, Brussels is far ahead of the other two regions with 200.5, by contrast to 99.0 for Flanders and 71.8 for Wallonia, due to the fact that many Flemish and Walloons gain their income in the Brussels region. Hence, Brussels politicians call for a tax regime that is based less on the current system of income tax (collected at the level of the commune of residence), and more on the commune of employment (where this income is earned). In addition, Capron demonstrates that several Flemish *arrondissements* (administrative and statistical units) are net receivers, while some Walloon arrondissements are net contributors; see H. Capron, "Croissance et développement spatial inégal des regions," in B. Bayent, H. Capron, and P. Liégeois (eds.), *L'espace Wallonie-Bruxelles. Voyage au bout de la Belgique* (Bruxelles: De Boeck, 2007), pp. 199–225.

46. Alain Destexhe, Alain Eraly, and Eric Gillet, *Démocratie ou particratie? 120 propositions pour refonder le système belge* (Bruxelles: Editions Labor, la Noria, 2003).

47. At the 2003 general elections, four Flemish parties could hope to claim leadership: the Liberals with 25 MPs, the Socialists with 23, the Christian Democrats with 21, and the Vlaams Blok with 18. The last of these, however, remained "uncoalitionable"—excluded by other parties on ideological grounds as a potential coalition partner.

48. The Liberals changed from *Partij voor Vrijheid en Vooruitgang* (Party for Liberty and Progress) into the *Vlaamse Liberalen en Democraten* (Flemish Liberals and Democrats) in 1992; the *Christelijke Volkspartij* (Christian Peoples Party) became *Christen Democratisch en Vlaams* (Christian Democratic and Flemish) in 2001.

49. In addition, the Flemish minister-president Yves Leterme made several insulting comments about Walloon profiteerism and Francophones' intellectual incapacity to learn Dutch. Hence, while he gradually became the most popular politician in Flanders (as shown when he won 800,000 personal votes at the 2007 federal elections), his popularity among Francophones was nil, a serious handicap when he was in the process of forming a federal government.

50. The Instituut voor Sociaal en Politiek Opinieonderzoek (ISPO) at the Katholieke Universiteit Leuven and Pôle Interuniversitaire Opinion publique et Politique (PIOP) at the Université Catholique de Louvain have been conducting postelectoral and longitudinal surveys since 1991 (for methods, data, and publications, see www.ispo.be and www.piop.be); see Pierre Baudewyns, Daniel Bol, Virginie Van Ingelgom, and Caroline Van Wynsberghe, *Questions de société et comportement electoral*, PIOP Working paper 2008/3; available www.uclouvain.be/261359.html; Marc Swyndegouw, *Politieke kwesties en stemgedrag, Instituut voor Sociaal en Politiek Opinieonderzoek* (ISPO), Onderzoeksverslag, CeSO/ISPO/2008-9 (2008); available soc.kuleuven.be/ceso/onderzoek/9/pdf/Politieke kwesties en stemgedrag_Swyngedouw.pdf [accessed 16 Nov. 2009].

51. Lieven De Winter, "La recherche sur les identités ethno-territoriales en Belgique," *Revue Internationale de Politique Comparée*, Vol. 14, No. 4 (2007), pp. 575–96; Lieven De Winter, "Les identités territoriales: 25 ans d'évolution," in André-Paul Frognier, Lieven De Winter, and Pierre Baudewyns (eds.), *Elections: le reflux? Comportements et attitudes lors des élections en Belgique* (Bruxelles: De Boeck, 2007), pp. 141–56; Marc Swyngedouw and Nathalie Rink, *Hoe Vlaams-Belgischgezind zijn de Vlamingen?*, Instituut voor Sociaal en Politiek Opinieonderzoek (ISPO), Onderzoeksverslag CeSO/ISPO/2008-6 (2008); available soc.kuleuven.be/ceso/onderzoek/9/pdf/ISPO07vlaanderenbelgie.pdf [accessed 16 Nov. 2009]; André-Paul Frognier, Lieven De Winter and Pierre Baudewyns, *Les Wallons et la réforme de l'Etat. Une analyse sur la base de l'enquête post-électorale de 2007*, Document de travail du PIOP, 2008; available www.uclouvain.be/209208.html/ [accessed 16 Nov. 2009].

52. André-Paul Frognier and Lieven De Winter, "Les Belges et le Fédéralisme. Les leçons des enquêtes de 1970 à 2007," in Régis Dandoy, Geoffroy Matagne, and Caroline Van Wynsberghe, *Le fédéralisme belge* (Bruxelles: Academia Bruylant, forthcoming)

53. For instance, during the campaign for federal elections, no debates are organized between Flemish and Francophone politicians; see Marc Lits, "Media in Belgium: Two Separate Public Opinions," E-book Rethinking Belgium, 2009; available www.rethinkingbelgium.eu/rebel-initiative-files/ebooks/ebook-3/Lits.pdf [accessed 16 Nov. 2009]. French newspapers are hardly read in the Flemish side of the country and vice versa. The same applies to radio and television news. Topics differ in saliency; see Dave Sinardet, Knut de Swert, and Régis Dandoy, "Les sujets des journaux télévisés Francophones et flamands: une comparaison longitudinale," *Courrier hebdomadaire du CRISP*, No. 1864 (2005). Even interview styles differ; see Martina Temmerman and Dave Sinardet, "Political Journalism across the Language Border: Communicative Behaviour in Political Interviews by Dutch- and French-Speaking Journalists with Dutch- and French-Speaking Politicians in Federal Belgium," in Jeroen Darquennes (ed.), *Multilingualism and Applied Comparative Linguistics: Vol. 2: Cross-Cultural Communication, Translation Studies and Multilingual Terminology* (Cambridge, UK: Cambridge Scholars Publishing, 2008), pp. 110–38.

54. Lits, *Media in Belgium*, pp. 43–7.

55. Bernadette Bawin-Legros, Liliane Voyé, Karel Dobbelaere, and Mark Elchardus (eds.), *Belge toujours. Fidélité, stabilité, tolérance. Les valeurs des Belges en l'an 2000* (Bruxelles: De Boeck Université, 2001); Jaak Billiet, Bart Maddens, and André-Paul Frognier, "Does Belgium (still) Exist? Differences in Political Culture between Flemings and Walloons," in Marleen Brans, Lieven De Winter, and Wilfried Swenden, *Politics of Belgium* (2009), pp. 50–70; Nicole Voss and Pierre Lebrun, *Divergences et Convergences Régionales en Belgique. Les Wallons et les Flamands à l'épreuve des 275 questions de l'European Social Survey* (Bruxelles: Academie Royale des Sciences et des Lettres de Belgique, 2006).

56. The employers are more divided, given the fact that a minority of Flemish entrepreneurs have embraced the idea of Flemish independence and support separatist think tanks and even separtist political parties. These entrepreneurs hope that an independent Flanders would be more entrepreneur friendly, with lower taxes and wages, weaker trade unions, and more efficient public services.

57. At the June regional elections of 2009, the parties that defended the independence option (N-VA, *Vlaams Belang*, and *Lijst De Decker*) totalled about 35% of Flemish voters (although many of them are not motivated by community issues).

58. This is one of the reasons that the Flemish leadership decided to make Brussels the capital of the Flemish region and community, rather than selecting a provincial capital within Flemish territory.

59. On the other hand, as in many other countries, European integration has also boosted the independence option of Flemish ethnoregionalist parties; Lieven De Winter and Marga Gomez-Reino Cachafeiro, "European Integration and Ethnoregionalist Parties," *Party Politics*, Vol. 8, No. 4 (2002), pp. 483–503.

3

Spain: Identity Boundaries and Political Reconstruction

FRANCISCO JOSÉ LLERA
University of the Basque Country

The aim of this article is to look at the political implications of identity patterns in one case that is of exceptional interest, that of Spain. It begins by looking at the nature of identity, and the challenges it poses in the contemporary world. This is followed by a section examining the issue of collective identity in the Spanish context, exploring variation in forms of regional identity and relating this to new political structures in the regions. The two last sections look respectively at the manner in which the regional party systems reflect diverse patterns of identity and the challenges posed by these patterns for the system of government.

INTRODUCTION

The question of identity, whether of the individual or the group, is as old as civilization itself. Collective identity, as a component of the culture of a human group, defines its sense of *us,* distinguishing it from *them*, articulates its mechanisms of social and community cohesion and organizes group activities that bring about feelings of belonging, loyalty, and social control. Reflections on this topic are not new to modern sociology, since Tönnies, Weber, and Pareto each underscored the role of subjectivity as a source of social action. Yet, identity has gained a renewed academic interest in the last couple of decades and has been the subject of special focus, not only among sociologists but also anthropologists, historians, philosophers, economists, and political scientists.[1]

The aim of this article is to look at the political implications of identity patterns in one case that is of exceptional interest—that of Spain. For more than three decades, the structure of the Spanish state has been subjected to a dramatic form of territorial reconstruction. While some of the momentum behind this derived from the new energy and enthusiasm for state building that followed the end of the dictatorship, it was in particular a response to a fascinating interplay between the social psychological domain (that of identity) and the political world (that of institutional organization). The article therefore begins by looking at the nature of identity and the challenges it poses in the contemporary world. This is followed by a section examining the issue of collective identity in the Spanish context, exploring variation in forms of regional identity and relating this to new political structures in the regions. The two last sections look respectively at the manner in which the regional party systems reflect diverse patterns of identity and the challenges posed by these patterns for the system of government.

IDENTITY AND IDENTITIES

One of the reasons for the renewed interest in the identity question in our contemporary societies lies in the very fragmentation associated with its growing complexity and the societal fatigue that has been accumulated by pressure from nations and markets to be homogeneous. In a very basic way, individuals and groups have a problem adapting to the social changes and superimposed models of mechanisms of control and social cohesion that define group and community structures within complex societies.[2] The impact of globalization on this phenomenon must also be taken into account—generally speaking, this includes the processes of internationalization and supra-state integration. Inevitably, the result is the manifestation of a plurality of loyalties that are in varying degrees concentric or eccentric, hierarchical or at odds, and intertwined or fragmented. This process also includes a weakening of some of the group's connections with respect to certain of its other attachments, thereby altering the structure of its hierarchy. Therefore, it is no mere coincidence, when faced with overall uncertainty and chaos, that renewal of the concept of "glocal" may take on the strength of an identity, in the same way that self-affirmation has gained strength in territorialized communities or in ethnic groups faced with the inefficiencies of nation-state homogenization. In this manner, social cohesion along with the language of solidarity and community are converted into a political topic.

   It is the politicization of the identity question that interests us most here. The progressive contemplation of the nation-state paradigm of state building was created precisely in order to highlight the advantages of reinforcing state power in European societies.[3] The state-centered view, according to the early Weberian approach, conceives of the state as a geographically sovereign political entity with a permanent population, a defined territory, a government, the ability to relate to other states in accordance with international law, and a series of social institutions that confer a monopoly in the legitimate use of force over such a territory. State and nation are two sides of the same coin, although both may take on distinct shapes and models, not only in their structure but in their composition and also in their way of relating to each other. If the ability of the state refers to the strength and performance of its institutions, the nation brings us back to the population itself, unified and connected by identity links of history, culture, or language. States have been more or less efficient instruments in modernizing societies, bringing about economic development and social cohesion, and creating and stabilizing democratic institutions within stable borders. However, this has not always been designed to homogenize the population culturally, or otherwise convert it into a "national community." In other words, state building needs and is complemented by nation building—the state needs its population to share, in its own way, what Benedict Anderson called the "imagined community," an expression of the mutual dependence of state and nation.[4]

The process of constructing modern states, to the extent that they originate from or operate within sociodemographic and territorial realities or complex cultures and have played the lead role in histories that are more or less broken and laden with state-nation centralization, has generated a central-peripheral dynamic that is the source of conflicts that are often very difficult to resolve.[5] Although this dynamic does not always have a practical translation that is spatial or geographical, as occurs in the Spanish case with its regional peripheries, we may associate it with the existence of a national political identity that is hegemonic or central, that integrates, competes with or opposes local identities that are more or less strong, and that is either preexisting or not. In the case of some nation-states, ethnocultural diversity, sociodemographic displacements, and the complexity of the territorial and productive model have to be considered in assessing the territorial tensions that drive political processes of decentralization or adjustment.[6]

Going back to Benedict Anderson, our national communities are, at the very least, *invented* social and cultural organizations, or constructed mentally, based on cultural materials derived from sharing histories, languages, land, traditions, and mythologies. That is how we build our community identities, whether they are inclusive or exclusive of one another, and with ethnocultural boundaries that are more or less clear or diffuse. In any case, we are now faced with one of the dimensions of identity construction: the cognitive dimension (necessary for imagining and understanding the community) that encodes, stores, processes and recycles information from the community heritage. However, one may easily verify the possible existence of two other dimensions that complement this and that make a lived reality out of that which was imagined: the emotional dimension (the interpretation of perceptions, information, and collective knowledge), and the motivational or voluntary dimension (the connection between knowledge, emotions, and behavior). Nevertheless, the imagined identities can, in the end, be converted into lived realities, closing the circle of community identity.[7]

It is out of the materials of the ethnocultural domain that human groups begin to construct their collective identity, their sense of community cohesion, and eventually their national consciousness and their sovereignty, equipped with a state entity.[8] The complexity and dynamics of the setting in which ethnic groups, nations, and states find their realities rooted is quite apparent if we bear in mind a few details.[9] First, the number of states has multiplied considerably in the last century, particularly if we recall that the 44 states that were integrated into the United Nations in 1945 are about 200 states today, leaving aside states that had merged or unified. Second, more than 15,000 ethnic groups and 7,000 languages can be identified and recorded worldwide, although half of the world's population can be identified with the 10 most widely spoken languages.[10] Third, globalization, while it produces supra-state integration, strengthens the migratory mobility of populations and the ethnic complexity of states. Fourth, many states feel obliged to decentralize or to adjust their way of exerting or organizing sovereignty, responding to ethnoterritorial or other types of demands.

Emilio Lamo de Espinosa, beginning with the bidirectional relationship or identification of "state = nation = language" as the heart of the question, reaches several important conclusions.[11] First, he argues, ethnic dispersion through political structures is apparent; second, the majority of states are characterized by ethnic plurality; and third, the romantic ideal of the nation-state as having a monoethnic character is an exception (no more than 5% of all ethnicities have achieved such an ideal). For that reason, it appears that languages, nations, and states can adjust easily, notwithstanding the romantic ideal of nationalism.[12] According to Manuel Castells, "the real question is how you build a form of social and cultural organization that calls itself a nation . . . any objective observation shows that, in the modern age, there are nations, there are states and different forms of relating among one another: nations with a state, nation-states, multinational states, and imperial nation-states that integrate various nations by force."[13] Emilio Lamo de Espinosa himself, questioning the state-nation model, concludes that "if the state-nation model is not useful for us, then the nation-state model is even less useful for us," referring to the national secularization of the current state itself that rejects the cultural homogenization of its people, who have a plurality of sentiments and loyalties.[14]

SPAIN: A COMPLEX STATE AND A PLURAL NATION

Many of these dilemmas of identity are illustrated strikingly in the Spanish case. The Spanish political system that emerged from the Constitution of 1978 and the consociational politics of the democratic transition played a key part in one of the major innovations in the political processes of the advanced democracies.[15] It was described by Juan P. Fusi as "the greatest change that we have made here since 1700."[16] The intense and quick decentralization that the structures of the state underwent, right in the middle of a democratic consolidation, and its unusual form of territorial organization, have defined what we might call "Spanish exceptionalism."[17] This exceptionalism also articulates itself in the role that the territorial and identity dimensions play. There is no other advanced democracy in which between five and nine regional parties almost always obtain representation in the national parliament, and in which these parties, with no more than a total of 11% of the votes, are the key players in the national government. In addition, in 14 of the 17 regional parliaments, these parties typically obtain a level of representation that is more or less constant; they have been or currently are key players in regional governments, leading coalition governments (in five regions), forming part of them (in another five), lending external parliamentary support (in two), and maintaining a steady parliamentary presence (in another two).

The complexity and uniqueness of the Spanish political process are determined by the country's swift and profound path towards territorial and regional decentralization, leading to the so-called *Estado de las Autonomías* (State of the Autonomies).[18] This refers to a process by which four Spanish regions ("autonomous communities") were initially (1979–81) granted autonomy (the Basque Country, Catalonia, Galicia, and Andalusia). Autonomy was later (1983) extended on a symmetrical basis to the remaining 13 regions.[19]

In fact, this unique Spanish process of decentralization, since it began with the Basque elections of 1980, has brought about a second-level platform of competition of increasing importance. In reality, this platform has been diversifying along with the very dynamic of the electoral processes in the 17 Spanish autonomous communities, with their different subsystems of parties and their own guidelines regarding government—a process covered only superficially in the academic literature.[20] In the rest of this section we consider three aspects of this process: the implications of identity for the new territorial structures, the character of Spanish regional identity as revealed by survey data, and public opinion on Spain's territorial restructuring.

Nationalism and Political Change

The data bank at the Centro de Investigaciones Sociológicas (CIS), Spain's most important public opinion research center, has accumulated a substantial number of sample and national quantitative studies since the beginning of the democratic transition. The earlier studies focused on the territorial, identity, and linguistic questions facing the Spanish.[21] These were followed by studies of the structure of the Spanish autonomous communities.[22] In addition, there are more than one hundred specific studies pertaining to each of the different autonomous communities, whether having to do with their

electoral processes, statutes, or individual or shared problems, particularly in
the 1980s. More recently, opinion polls and studies of the political culture in
each region have been carried out as a result of various academic initiatives,
not to mention the official surveys conducted by some of the Spanish regional
governments.[23]

The Spanish constitution, as we have seen, is based on the integration of
diverse nationalities and regions organized into autonomous communities.[24]
To be precise, it reaffirms the coexistence of various national events within
the same state framework, facilitating an array of shared loyalties and dual
or plural identities. The citizenship of the political nation expresses and
establishes its diversity in the plurality of cultural nationalities, which are, in
turn, unavoidably plural in their loyalties and sentiments. Some of them are
defined individually and by an exclusive nationalism of one type or another.
The significance of this complexity was summed up on the bicentenary of
the popular insurrection against the Napoleonic invasion on 2 May 1808 (the
so-called "Independence War") by Arturo Pérez-Reverte, who tells us that it is
"key in order to understand the certainty of this nation, questionable perhaps
in its modern arrangement, but unquestionable in its collective substance,
in its culture and in its historic dimension."[25] In fact, it is possible that a
distinctive Spanish nationalist project has failed in its attempt to create a
culturally homogeneous nation; the vigor of peripheral forms of nationalism
illustrates this failure to homogenize the respective communities.[26]

Today, the political nation exhibits itself in the plurality of cultural and
linguistic identities, with feelings of belonging and loyalties that are also
plural. The reforms of the statutes (the basic laws that define structures of
government in the autonomous communities) that are underway illustrate
this plural reality, as may be seen in the first new reformed statutes of six of
these:

• The statute of Catalonia speaks of a definition of a "majority of Catalonia
  as a nation . . . and that the European Union recognizes the national reality
  of Catalonia as a nationality" without any mention of the Spanish nation;
• The statute of the Valencian Community speaks of its "identity as differing
  from the historic nationality," but in reference to the "unity of the Spanish
  nation";
• The statute of Andalusia refers to the description of Andalusia as a "national
  reality" in the Andalusian Manifesto of 1919, but in reference to the constitutional recognition of Andalusia "as a nationality within the framework
  of the inseparable unity of the Spanish nation";
• The statute of the Balearic Islands speaks of "historic nationality" as a form
  of expressing the collective will of the islands and in the framework of the
  constitution;
• The statute of Aragón also speaks of "historic nationality" in reference to
  the constitution; and

- The statute of Castilla and León defines the national reality as "a historic and cultural community ... that has contributed decisively to the shaping of Spain as a nation."

These six examples reflect the process of identity and organizational self-affirmation that emerged as a result of the constitutional decentralization following nearly three decades of institutionalization.

Nation, Region, and Public Opinion

For the purposes of this analysis, we conducted a recent survey about these matters, in which we asked a Spanish sample their opinions about the autonomous communities defining themselves as a "nation" within the framework of the reform of their statutes. The results showed that almost two-thirds of the Spanish population over the age of 18 (64%) are against the idea, a little more than one out of four view it positively (29%), 5% of those surveyed were indifferent, and 2% did not offer an opinion.[27] An earlier series of similar questions dating back to 1990, asking citizens whether they prefer the label "national" or "regional" for their respective autonomous communities, revealed that almost eight out of every ten Spanish people (77%) preferred the term "region," whereas a little more than one out of every ten (13%) chose the term "nation."[28] Significantly, the Basques leaned towards the first term (44%) rather than the second (38%), while the Catalans were almost equally divided between the two (40% and 45%, respectively). This suggests a certain lack of internal homogeneity in each of these communities; and opinion is also volatile, if we take a look at the way this indicator has evolved over the period of time since we have been conducting such surveys.

In probing the matter further, in 2005 the CIS asked citizens about their feelings of pride in being Spanish, as well as Andalusian, Galician, Extremaduran, and so on. The results show 85% saying that they were very proud or quite proud to be both Spanish and regional in their identity (that is, also Basque, Catalan, Galician, Andalusian, Asturian, or other); a mere 13% said that they were not proud to be Spanish.

We also asked the Spanish sample to describe their idea of Spain.[29] The results are reported in Figure 1. This shows that for almost two out of three Spanish people (63%), the preferred option is "my nation or my country"; the idea of citizenship ("the state of which I am a citizen") is supported by 16%; the notion of the multinational state by another 18%; and just 2% stated that they identified with "another state" or felt a sense of national alienation. Only in the cases of Catalonia and the Basque Country is there a different distribution.[30] The Basques and the Catalans lean towards the multinational state idea (42% and 45%, respectively), followed by the idea of a Spanish

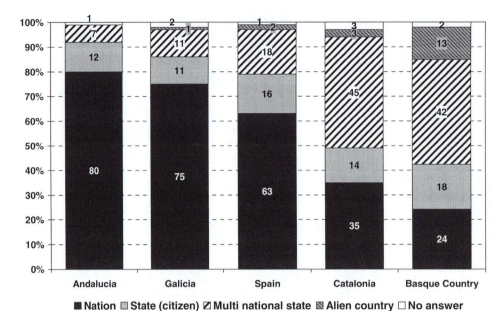

FIGURE 1 Spain: Perceptions of the Idea of Spain, 2007.
Note. The question asked "What does Spain mean to you?" "Nation" refers to "My country, my nation"; "State (citizen)" to "The country which I belong to as a citizen. *Source*: Eusko-barometro SEJ 2006-15076. Survey on Political Culture and Representation in Spain, 2007. Data from Andalucia, Galicia, and Pais Vasco come to their respective regional observatories from November 2006, Cataluña from 2005 (OPA 5, 2006).

nation (24% and 35%), that of citizenship (18% and 14%), and, to a lesser extent, they identify with a sense of national alienation (13% and 3%).

Finally, in our survey, we repeated a question that we have been asking for a long time, especially in the Basque Country; we specifically asked whether respondents feel or do not feel that they are "Spanish nationalists" and whether they feel or do not feel that they are Basque, Catalan, Galician, Asturian nationalists, and so on, as a way of exploring contradictory national sentiments.[31] The results were extremely surprising: more than two-thirds of the Spanish sample stated that they do not feel like Spanish nationalists (68%), nor nationalists of any other place (69%), compared with almost one-third who state that they feel that they are Spanish nationalists (29%) or nationalists of their respective regional groups (30%). In the Basque case, the percentage of those who feel that they are nationalists versus those who feel that they are non-nationalists is practically the same, with a small slant towards being non-nationalist (51%). In the Basque case, furthermore, we asked about level of agreement with an emphatic declaration by a nationalist leader in 2002 ("The Basques are not Spanish, and we do not believe in the Spanish nation"), revealing a majority who disagree with the statement

(50%, or 78% among non-nationalists), versus a minority (28% or 59% among nationalists) who subscribe to that idea.

This handful of sample indicators shows that there is not only a national plurality in Spain but also a plurality of its most vital nationalistic components. At the same time, there is a strong regionalist tension in respect of what defines the Spanish nation, and a slight nationalist tint within the Spanish nation. Finally, Spanish national consciousness shows itself as being more inclusive of local sentiments and identities than the more exclusive pattern of certain peripheral nationalist movements, self-defined against the Spanish nation. Without a doubt, the leaders of the nineteenth-century liberal state, while they failed to modernize and democratize the country, were also misguided in their strategy of homogenizing and centralizing it; and this was especially true of their successors' attempt to impose a nationalistic and unified vision of the Francoist dictatorship after the civil war. There is very little doubt about the counterproductive effect of such strategies, and especially that of the dictatorship, but it is also clear that a national consciousness exists, even though it is without nationalists.[32] These failures and political errors, which led to the so-called "two Spains" that clashed in the civil war (1936–39), offered a reactive opportunity to the regional cultures to reaffirm their differing consciousness, and, in some cases, the consolidation of forms of nationalism that have been nurtured exclusively of one another, especially feeding on an anti-Spanish victimization that is initially linked to an agonizing view of having lost the regional languages.[33]

A good indicator of the dual reality of Spanish and regional identities is to be seen in Figure 2. This reports responses to a question widely used by the CIS and showing great consistency over time, one we usually call subjective national identity.[34] The dual identity of those who associate themselves with feeling just as Spanish as they do about the region they are from clearly prevails (56%), to which must also be added those who share a feeling of being Spanish with a national accent (9%) or a regional accent (12%), thus bringing the compatibility of identities up to more than three-fourths of the Spanish people. Compared with those figures, only 16% say they feel Spanish only, and another 4% say that they identify with their respective autonomous community only, with a significant increase in the first group over the years 2005–07. If we look at how Basques and Catalans responded to the same question, we find that the compatibility of identities is somewhat reduced in both cases but still continues to have majority support (76% in Catalonia and 61% in the Basque Country), with a very clear regional accent in both cases (23% and 22%, respectively). In the case of Catalonia, the percentage of those who are opposed to the Spanish (8%) and the Catalan identities (14%) are almost symmetrical, whereas in the Basque Country there is a clearly exclusive nationalistic slant (24%) and an extremely small percentage of those who identify with Spanish nationalism (6%).

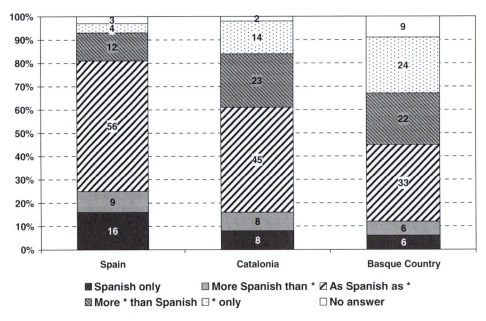

FIGURE 2 Spain: Patterns of Dual Identification, 2007.
Note. See text for question wording. "*" refers to a regional identity, for example, Catalan, Basque. *Source*: Euskobarometro SEJ 2006-15076; Survey on Political Culture and Representation in Spain, 2007; evolution from CIS study 2610 (Dec. 2005); data from Cataluña and Pais Vasco come to their respective regional observatories from October and November 2006 (OPA 6, 2007).

Without a doubt, the case that is the most far-removed from the common pattern is the Basque one. Precisely for that reason, and in view of the intensity of nationalist motivated violence, we have tried to delve into its primordial or voluntaristic elements, according to the definition already mentioned by Juan J. Linz.[35] In Table 1, we show the relationship between subjective national identity and a sense of being nationalist in the Basque Country. As may be observed, there is a clear pro-Basque bias in the adult Basque population and in the core of the more radical nationalists (interpreted as nationalists who identify with being Basque only). "Basque only"

TABLE 1 Basque Country: Nationalist Feeling and Identity, 2006

Identity	Spanish only	More Spanish than Basque	As Basque as Spanish	More Basque than Spanish	Basque only	No answer	N
Basque nationalists	—	—	6	36	57	1	514
Basque non-nationalists	11	7	57	14	6	4	604
No answer	—	—	29	35	19	17	82
N	70	53	400	300	344	33	1, 200

Note. Percentages total 100 horizontally.
Source: Euskobarómetro 2006/2.

Basque nationalists represent a little less than one-quarter of the sample; though they make up the vast majority of the electorate supporting militant nationalism, and less than half of the electorate of the moderate Basque nationalist parties. This is the hard core of the ethnic community of Basque nationalism and uses the identity clash as an element of cohesion. This is not replicated at the other end of the spectrum, where the pro-Spanish group lacks a similarly cohesive force.

The Basque case also stands out due to the confusion of perceptions of identity, probably caused by the impact of terrorist violence in the construction of the so-called "Basque problem." In an effort to delve into the roots and characteristics of these attitudes, we asked the adult Basque population what they understand as "being Basque," obtaining a series of results that are reported in Table 2. This shows a certain movement away from the "ethnic" conception of Basque identity (with declining minorities endorsing the importance of speaking Euskera or being of Basque descent), in favor of a more "civic" concept, with the subjective criterion of sharing "the will to be a Basque" enjoying consistently strong support, and a striking increase in 2005 in the proportion viewing living and working in the Basque Country as important. When we ask respondents to choose the most important of these criteria, half of the Basques support the last of these (residence; this breaks down into six out of every ten non-nationalists and one-third of nationalists).

Spanish history records the emergence of a plural nation, culturally rich, socially and politically complex, and difficult but viable. It has graduated into becoming one of the oldest European state-nations despite its repeated

TABLE 2 Basque Country: Conditions for Becoming Basque, 1979–2005

Condition	1979* Yes	1989 Yes	1989 No	1996 Yes	1996 No	1999 Yes	1999 No	2002 Yes	2002 No	2005 Yes	2005 No
1. Living and working in the Basque Country	69	54	31	46	50	55	36	63	35	85	14
2. Speaking Euskera	30	30	53	34	61	31	60	24	74	20	76
3. Descending from a Basque lineage	61	36	49	30	65	40	51	23	70	28	68
4. To be born in the Basque Country	62	41	44	49	45	53	39	52	46	57	40
5. Defending the Basque nation	—	57	23	—	—	—	—	—	—	—	—
6. The will to be a Basque	—	79	8	86	8	82	8	85	11	73	23
7. Having nationalist feelings	—	—	—	42	49	36	52	32	65	23	71

*Only positive percentages are included for 1979.
Sources: For 1979, Linz, 1986: 31 et seq; for 1989, CIS, Study no. 1795; and for 1996–2005, Euskobarómetro.

failure to modernize and its delayed and dramatic democratization.[36] An essential trait of the new political culture is the dual identity of Spanish territories and the model of a plural nation. It is true that in the Spanish regions there are nationalist parties, and voters who place their confidence in them, and even governments that are predominantly nationalist, but there is no pattern of regional identity that extends to a predominantly nationalist sentiment of exclusion. This does not even occur in the most problematic and conflict-ridden part of the country, the Basque Country. We may conclude that after 30 years of implementing and developing a decentralized democratic system, Spain has clearly moved on to a new political and constitutional culture, with only the Basque case remaining atypical.

The Territorial Reshuffling of Identity

How has this plural nation been constructed? To what degree is it successful? We find the answers in the views of citizens themselves. These allow us to really see the reshuffling of this plural nation from each of the different corners of its heterogeneous territory, and the progressive materialization of a new political culture. The citizens of many autonomous communities may find their territorial identity in the very evolution of the "state of the autonomies," as the Spanish state is sometimes described. In other cases, they find their identity by contrast or competition, and some citizens feel that their expectations have been frustrated because their leaders fail to resolve the grievances they have expressed.

In the autonomous communities in which political leaders have maintained an institutional stability or have consolidated a stable political leadership (for example, in Extremadura or Castilla-La Mancha), despite their inferior level of development and the traditional weakness of their identity, they have managed to generate a level of satisfaction with the current system that exceeds that of other communities that might surpass them in the other respects mentioned (for example, Asturias, Aragón, Cantabria, and Murcia). Almost three-fourths of the Spanish population expresses a satisfaction with the "state of the autonomies." This figure is on the rise especially in Catalonia (77%) and in the Basque Country (74%), leaving the remainder of those who feel dissatisfied for various reasons as a minority that does not exceed 20%.[37] However, most importantly, according to the CIS, none of the communities express a dissatisfaction level that exceeds the maximum of 11% recorded in Catalonia.[38] Notwithstanding tensions emerging as a result of the new reforms of the statutes of the autonomous communities, the Spanish people appear to be mostly optimistic (53%) when evaluating how well the organization of the state functions right now, and only a small minority is pessimistic (8%).[39]

How do citizens rate the decentralizing dynamic? The vast majority (73%), a proportion on the rise in almost all of the autonomous communities, believe that the autonomous communities have contributed to bringing the administration of public affairs closer to the actual citizens. On the matter of delivery of material benefits, views are more divided: 48% agree and 45% disagree with the view that the autonomous communities have contributed to an increase in spending without improving public services. There are also many doubts about whether the new territorial model has actually served to improve coexistence between the provinces, despite the fact that there are more who believe that they have helped than who say that they have not been helpful (48% versus 44%). This may be due in part to the fact that close to a majority (47%) thinks that the model has contributed to the growth of separatist groups. On the other hand, this may arise from an evaluation of the dynamic differences in regional development and wealth. A third factor that may have an influence on this popular perception of such a centrifugal dynamic may be related to comparative grievances at the perceived preferential treatment of the various autonomous communities by the central government.

In fact, after an evolution that has not been at all positive in the last few years, more than two-thirds (69%) of Spanish respondents continue to think that the central government does not treat the communities equally, but that it gives preferential treatment to some over others.[40] This may be attributed to the political leanings of the respective governments or to the ability of local leaders to put pressure on citizens, especially if they are nationalists who play a role in governing the state.[41] In identifying regions that are perceived beneficiaries of such unequal treatment, the finger points at Catalonia (so regarded by 69% in 1992 and by 87% in 1996) and the Basque Country (38% and 57%, respectively), but with Madrid (27% and 18%) and Andalusia (48% and 12%) also appearing.

As may be observed in Figure 3, the current territorial model (represented by the top line, showing support for the current system of autonomy) has been gaining strength and legitimizing itself over the years (from 31% in 1984 to 57% in 2007), especially due to a weakening of the skepticism and resistance of the more centralist and homogenizing provincial models (from 29% to 12% during these same years). Nevertheless, it has not succeeded in winning over those who continue to be in favor of a greater degree of decentralization in the federal core (between 20% and 22%, almost consistently and with little fluctuation) and, to an even lesser extent, the supporters of regional independence, who continue to fight for the right of secession (represented by the bottom "confederal" line, always less than 10%). Even in Catalonia (73%) and in the Basque Country (63%), the integrationist options (either autonomous or federal) are predominant, with more of a slant towards autonomy-supporting groups in the case of the former than in the Basque Country. However, the Basque Country stands out due to the greater

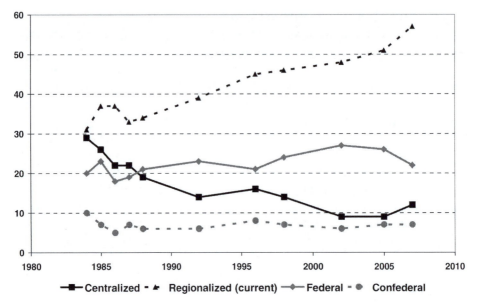

FIGURE 3 Spain: Type of State Preferred, 1984–2007.
Note. The respective positions refer to (1) a state with one central government and no autonomous governments; (2) a state with regions and nationalities as at present; (3) a state with regions and nationalities with more autonomy than at present; and (4) a state acknowledging the right of nationalities to independent statehood. *Source*: CIS and Euskobarómetro SEJ 2006-15076. *Encuesta de Cultura y Representación Política en España*, 2007.

influence of secessionism (around 30%). Thus, the constitutional model of self-government, whether in its static version or favoring evolution towards a higher level of self-government, obtains overwhelming and growing support from all corners of the country. Neither those with centralist aspirations nor those (like the Basques and Catalans) with proindependence tendencies have much capacity to challenge the model.[42]

This complex process of decentralization has been carried out asymmetrically and at a different pace from one autonomous community to another, and this has inevitably been the cause of political tensions, comparative grievances, financial dysfunctions or deficiencies in public services, and, especially, problems in achieving cooperation and social and regional cohesion.[43] The Spanish system of decentralization still needs to learn how to forge interregional cooperation and cohesion. If we exclude the Basque case and the tensions of the new autonomous public financial system (the so called *Concierto económico*), it is true that the initial tendency towards conflict has been reduced. In addition, the statutes of autonomy of the 13 autonomous communities of the common system were reformed by expanding their levels of self-government without increasing tensions (except in the case of Aragón), and by agreement between the dominant political forces, in cooperation with the independent plans of Ibarretxe, the president of the

Basque government (1998–2008). However, the recent reform of the statute of Catalonia has also intensified tensions.[44] In any case, the mechanisms of multilateral cooperation have yet to be institutionalized, and that is necessary for the system to progress efficiently and in a balanced manner. To be specific, as of today, two-thirds of the Spanish people (67%) advocate that the state reassign the authorities of the autonomous communities, and 60% believe that the central government should give top priority to the multilateral agreements with all of the autonomous communities (versus 35% of the population that advocates a bilateral model).[45]

THE POLITICIZATION OF REGIONAL IDENTITIES AND DEMANDS

For more than two decades, Western political science literature has focused increasingly on territorial, nationalist, and regionalist parties.[46] Despite their asymmetrical foundation, trajectory, political impact, and ideological configuration, these are a reality in many Western democracies. Italy, France, Belgium, Canada, and the United Kingdom, among others, share this partisan mixture with Spain. These territorial parties have been changing the almost exclusively pro-state image of European party systems and are no longer viewed as something exceptional or as simple vestiges of the past.[47] The very decentralization in the regional core of states, and most especially the complex dynamics of the new democracies of Central and Eastern Europe, have introduced a new cleavage in the definition of political identities and aggregation of interests, challenging the older, omnipresent ideological dimension with its classical and functional roots.[48]

The Spanish party system, which was moderately pluralist at the beginning of the democratic transition, has been gradually moving towards an imperfect bipartisan model in the national arena, tempered only by the territorial axis.[49] This may be seen in Table 3, which shows its evolution since 1977. Only the Popular Party (PP, with its de facto predecessor, the Union of the Democratic Centre, UCD) on the right and the Socialist Party (PSOE) on the left have a strong presence throughout the country, and only they are in a position to alternate with each other in the national government, as well as in the majority of the autonomous communities. They form the core of the government in the other communities. Election after election, these two major parties have gradually extended their vote share. Only the former communists of the United Left (IU) fall outside this bipartisan model, with a minimal presence at the national level and a lack of representation in many of the provinces, but a limited political influence in the government of some of the autonomous communities or larger city councils. In addition to this national partisan model, a small number of voters, an average of approximately 10%, support territorial, nationalist or regionalist parties—some

TABLE 3 Spain: Votes and Seats in National Elections, 1977–2008

Year	PSOE/PSP	AP/PP	UCD/CDS	PCE/IU	Nationalists	Others	Turnout
1977	33.8	8.2	34.4	9.3	7.0	6.9	78.8
	(124)	(16)	(166)	(19)	(24)	(1)	
1979	30.4	6.1	34.8	10.8	9.1	8.5	68.0
	(121)	(10)	(168)	(23)	(27)	(1)	
1982	48.1	26.4	9.7	4.0	8.4	3.1	80.0
	(202)	(107)	(13)	(4)	(24)	(0)	
1986	44.1	26.0	9.2	4.6	10.5	4.9	70.5
	(184)	(105)	(19)	(7)	(35)	(0)	
1989	39.6	25.8	7.9	9.1	11.5	5.4	69.7
	(175)	(107)	(14)	(17)	(37)	(0)	
1993	38.8	34.8	1.8	9.6	11.2	3.0	76.4
	(159)	(141)	(0)	(18)	(32)	(0)	
1996	37.6	38.8	—	10.5	10.5	1.7	77.4
	(141)	(156)	—	(21)	(32)	(0)	
2000	34.2	44.5	—	5.4	10.6	3.5	68.7
	(125)	(183)	—	(9)	(33)	(0)	
2004	42.6	37.7	—	5.1	10.1	2.1	75.7
	(164)	(148)	—	(5)	(33)	(0)	
2008	43.6	40.1	—	3.8	7.7	3.4	75.3
	(169)	(154)	—	(2)	(24)	(1)	

Note. For each year, the first row indicates percentage of total votes cast (for turnout, votes as a percentage of electorate); the figures in parentheses refer to numbers of seats; the total number of seats was 350 in each year. "Nationalists" include Catalans (CiU, ERC), Basques (PNV, HB, EE, EA, NaBai), Galicians (BNG, CG), Aragonese (PAR, CHA), Canarians (UPC, AIC/CC), Andalusians (PA), and Valencians (UV); "Others" include CIC, UN, and UPD; see appendix for explanation of party abbreviations.
Source: Calculations by the author from data of the Ministry of Interior.

of which become key players in the central government of Spain when the winning party does not obtain an absolute majority.

As regards its party system, then, Spain is exceptional, though this phenomenon has attracted relatively little academic attention.[50] We make a distinction here between *nationalist* and *regionalist* parties, though it is not always accepted by the partisan actors themselves; we may use the broader label *territorial parties* to refer to the heterogeneous reality of almost 50 parties of this type. These compete or have a public presence that is more or less relevant in 14 of the 17 autonomous communities (the exceptions are Murcia, Madrid, and Castilla-La Mancha). In this they are assisted by the greater accessibility of the electoral systems at the regional level to local political forces.[51] They collaborate with the major national parties while playing a hinge role linking government and society.

We may summarize the political influence and the parliamentary presence of these parties as follows. First, there are two autonomous communities where nationalist or regionalist parties together have a majority in the regional assembly. Catalan nationalism is led by *Convergència i Unió* (CiU) and *Esquerra Republicana de Catalunya* (ERC), to which we might add, although it plays a much less relevant role, *Estat Català*, the latter also having a presence in the Valencian Community and in the Balearic Islands. In the Basque Country, the pro-statute or Alava regionalist party, Aleves Unity (UA), is added to the four surviving nationalist parties, the Basque Nationalist Party (PNV), *Eusko Alkartasuna (EA)*, Aralar, and the illegal Batasuna party.[52] Second, there are other autonomous communities where regionalist or nationalist parties are significant. This will be clear from the appendix, which lists such parties, though it should be acknowledged that their presence is slight in certain communities, and some of the parties listed here are very small indeed. Third, there are three autonomous communities where parties of this kind are entirely absent. This pattern will also be clear from Table 4, which shows the balance between national-level parties and their regional and nationalist competitors in the regional assemblies and governments.

TABLE 4 Spain: Structure of Party Systems in Parliaments and Governments of Autonomous Communities, 2006–09

Autonomous Community	Composition of Assembly					Composition of government
	PP	PSOE	IU	Nationalist/Regionalist parties	Total	
Andalucía, 2008	47	56	6	0	109	PSOE
Aragón	23	30	1	13 (PAR-9, CHA-4)	67	PSOE-PAR
Asturias	20	21	4	0	45	PSOE-IU/BA
Baleares	28	20	0	11 (PSM-EN-5, UM-3, ExC-2, AIPF-1)	59	PSOE-UM-Bloc
Canarias	15	26	0	19 (CC-17, AHI-2)	60	CC-PP
Cantabria	17	10	0	12 (PRC-12)	39	PRC-PSOE
Castilla y León	48	33	0	2 (UPL-2)	83	PP
Castilla-La Mancha	21	26	0	0	47	PSOE
Cataluña, 2007	14	37	0	84 (CiU-48, ERC-21, ICV-12, Ciut.-3)	135	PSC-ERC-ICV
C. Valenciana	54	38	5	2 (Bloc-2)	99	PP
Extremadura	27	38	0	0	65	PSOE
Galicia, 2009	38	25	0	12 (BNG-12)	75	PP
Madrid	67	42	11	0	120	PP
Murcia	29	15	1	0	45	PP
Navarra	0	12	2	36 (UPN-22, NaBai-12, CDN-2)	50	UPN-CDN
País Vasco, 2009	13	25	1	36 (PNV-30, Aralar-4, EA-1, UPD-1)	75	PSE/EE
La Rioja	17	14	0	2 (PR-2)	33	PP

Note. The most recent elections for the "common statute" autonomous communities took place in 2007, with the four "special" communities following a separate cycle: Cataluña (2006), Andalucia (2008), and Galicia and País Vasco (2009). IU was in coalition with the regional group of the "Bloque por Asturias" (Asturias), with the PSM (Baleares), and with ICV (Cataluña). In Navarra, UPN has replaced PP in autonomous elections since 1991. The new national party (UPD) has one seat in the Basque Parliament. *Source*: Calculations by the author from data of the regional parliaments.

These regionalist and nationalist parties have also used elections to the European Parliament as mechanisms for organizing themselves into broader groups, thus maximizing their electoral interests. A number of such coalitions were obvious in the 2009 European election: the Coalition for Europe, formed mainly by three important center-right parties from Catalonia, the Basque Country, and the Canaries (CiU, PNV, and CC; see appendix for a list of abbreviations); a coalition of two small centrist parties of the Balearic Islands (UM and UMe) with two leftist parties, the Andalusian PA and the Valencian Bloc; and a progressive, republican tendency, the European Peoples (EdP), formed by the Basque EA and Aralar, the Catalan ERC, the Galician BNG, and the CHA from Aragón, as well as two small parties, ExM from the Balearic Islands and PB (Party of El Bierzo) from a region inside Castilla. Other nationalist and regionalist parties participated on their own, with the banned Basque party Batasuna supporting the "Internationalist Initiative" list.

GOVERNING COMPLEXITY AND INTEGRATING DIVERSITY

Paradoxically, the exchange of national and territorial support among the large national parties and the more important nationalist and regionalist parties described above has served to lend stability to the government of Spain, but at the expense of a lack of stability at the level of autonomous governments. It has also produced a dynamic of adversary politics among the large national parties and a disposition on the part of some nationalist parties to take advantage of this. The need to compete and to pursue government office at any price, especially by the regionalist or nationalist parties of the right, has been a stumbling block for the major national parties that seek unity and consensus about the idea of Spain. The question that arises is an obvious one. How is it possible that the two major national parties have not been capable of preserving a consensus where it is most needed—in respect of the territorial dilemma and its parallel terrorist violence?

It is true that efforts have been made to harmonize the system of autonomy in the communities where it was instituted at an early stage, and, more recently, there have been similar reforms in the statutes of the communities of a common regime. But during a period of over two decades there has been more discord than agreement between the PSOE and the PP.[53] This assists the negotiating position of the regionalist and nationalist parties, giving them an incentive to maximize territorial conflicts to bolster their own role. It also causes public unease: in 2007, 81% of Spaniards thought that the fact that PSOE and PP maintained confrontational positions on almost everything was negative for democracy. This idea was shared between socialist voters (84%) and conservative voters (77%). Moreover, this confrontation between the two main parties' political elites affects the daily lives of citizens. In this same survey, 58% of Spaniards took the view that the current divisions between political parties generate more tensions and arguments in their social environment, as acknowledged by two out of three PSOE and PP supporters.[54]

Yet, some degree of consensus between the large national parties is increasingly necessary, as the nationalist parties favor participation in coalition governments at the level of the central state. Catalan and Basque nationalism are clear cases: they are prepared to support incumbent governments, thus playing the role of territorial hinges in the national party system. However, the large national parties have not been able to develop a culture of coalition with the nationalists, which would mean allowing them to have more involvement, not only in the central government but in the national reconstruction of Spain. This arises from an absence of strategic consensus on matters of national or state policy, and a failure to overcome the adversary politics that has been imposed as a behavioral model for Spain's national partisan leaders. In 2007, 63% of the Spanish people indicated that they would prefer a coalition government to another minority government (29%), if, after the next national elections, neither of the two major parties should obtain an absolute majority.

Those who designed the democratic transition and their successors who planned its consolidation were agreed on the guidelines for democratic representation.[55] Their objective was to procure a mechanism for obtaining a system of party government that would be stable and efficient, avoiding partisan fragmentation while ensuring sufficient representation of minority demands. They did so knowing about the interwoven ideological and territorial tensions that could threaten the future of the democratic system with a weak partisan structure and a fragile democratic political culture following decades of the dictatorship. The result has been a country with a high level of government stability, unique in the continental European Union in combining proportional representation with stable majority or even minority government. This has been possible both because of Spain's particular form of proportional representation (with low district magnitude favoring large parties) and elite priorities (the willingness of political leaders to form a coalition or to tolerate minority governments).

After a process of political and administrative decentralization carried out in record time, as we have seen, there are now 17 regional parliaments in Spain, with their respective governments, autonomous administrations, superior courts, and networks of institutional organizations and public businesses that require a regional political leadership of more than 3,000 authorities for a country of 40 million inhabitants.[56] To this we may add about 1,100,000 public employees who are dependent on such regional administrations—more or less half of all of the personnel in Spain's public administration system (completed by about 600,000 in the central administration and another 500,000 in local administration).[57] Regional and cultural diversity is reflected in the fact that at least eight regional languages are recognized (six of them with the status of coofficial language), along with Spanish, and in seven autonomous communities there is an official bilingualism that applies to almost half of the Spanish population, although the bilingual inhabitants amount to no more than one-fourth of the Spanish people. This new political-administrative reality has led to 17 health care systems, 17 educational systems, 3 autonomous police departments (in the Basque Country, Catalonia, and Navarre), various systems and methods of public communication (radio and television), and autonomous public infrastructures (highways and railways). Policies pertaining to agriculture, fishing, food, and tourism, and to industrial, commercial, urban, environmental, labor, and housing development, as well as territorial organization and social protection, are exclusively dependent on the new regional administrations. They account for about 33% of total public spending for all public administration in Spain (with the central administration accounting for 53% and the local administration for 14%).

Governance in Spain consists of making sure that this complexity operates efficiently, cooperates institutionally, maintains national cohesion and generates an output, both in democratic terms and in services for citizens. It is true that, generally speaking, we do not usually find the same governmental stability at the territorial level as we see in the national arena, although the political gains are unequal. The difference, however, is that the ability to form a coalition is more developed in the autonomous communities in which there is a greater variety of party subsystems (in Table 4, we saw the actual format of the regional party systems; Table 5 shows how these have been translated into governing coalitions).[58]

Thus, we do not encounter the national two-party system in a more or less pure state, but some autonomous communities come close to this model: Castilla, Madrid, Extremadura, Murcia, La Rioja, now the Valencian Community, and, with a little more variation, Andalusia and Asturias. Moderate pluralism is to be found in Catalonia, the Canary Islands, Aragón, the Balearic Islands, and Galicia, though with a strong bipartisan tendency. Finally, extreme pluralism occurs, though in very different forms, in the Basque Country and Navarra.[59] Local actors tend to play a limited role in territorial parliaments and politics. The cases of Catalan, Canarian, and Basque nationalism are exceptions: their main actors (CiU, CC, and PNV), in addition to being in charge of government responsibilities in their respective communities, have been occupying a hinge role in the national arena, usually sharing reciprocal parliamentary support or coalition governments on a territorial level, and parliamentary agreements in the national arena. Once again, the exception to this dynamic of progressive moderation, stability, and adjustment is the Basque Country with its deeply divisive politics.

TABLE 5 Spain: Coalition Governments in Autonomous Communities, 1983–2009

	Only Left	Mixed	Only Centre-Right
Only Territorial Parties		Cataluña: CIU-ERC (1984–87) Pais Vasco: PNV-EA-EE (1990–91) Pais Vasco: PNV-EA (1998–2001)	Canarias: CC-AHI (1993–95) Navarra: UPN-CDN (2003–)
Territorial and state-wide parties	Andalucía: PSOE-PA (1996–2004) Asturias. PSOE-IU-BA (2003–07/2008–) Baleares: PSOE-PSM-EN-IU-EV (1999–2003) Cataluña: PSC-ERC-ICV (2003–) Galicia: PSOE-BNG (2005–09)	Aragón: PSOE-PAR (1999–) Baleares: PSOE-UM-Bloc* (2007–) Cantabria: PSOE-PP-PRC-CDS (1990–91) Cantabria: PRC-PSOE (2003–) Canarias: PSOE-AIC (1991–93) Galicia: PSOE-CG-PNG (1987–89) Pais Vasco: PNV-PSE (1987–90) Pais Vasco: PNV-PSE-EE (1991–94) Pais Vasco: PNV-PSE/EE-EA (1994–98) Pais Vasco: PNV-EA-IU (2001–09) La Rioja: PSOE-PR (91–95) Navarra: PSOE-CDN-EA (1995–96)	Aragón: PAR-PP (1989–93) Aragón: PP-PAR (1995–99) Baleares: AP/PP-UM (1987–95) C. Valenciana: PP-UV (1995–99) Canarias: CDS-AIC-AP-AHI (1987–91) Canarias: CC-PP (1996–) Cantabria: UPCA-PP (1991–95) Cantabria: PP-PRC (1995–2003) Galicia: PP-CdeG (1989–93)
Only State-wide Parties			Galicia: AP-GPI/UCD (1983–85) Castilla y León: PP-CDS (1990–91)

*Coalition formed by PSM-EN, EU, EV, and ERC.

CONCLUSION

The dynamic of competition and partisan alignment in Spain has a double dimension. On the one hand we have the traditional left-right cleavage, which is the most important one, above all in national elections.[60] On the other hand, we find the center-periphery dimension, which is secondary at the national level but gains more relevance in regional elections and is even more important than the left-right one in certain communities such as the Basque Country.[61] This dynamic of complex governance has had some influence on party culture; according to our 2007 survey, more than one out of three Spaniards (36%) reject the view that the decisions of the central headquarters of the big national parties prevail over their territorial organizations (while almost half of them, just under 50%, agree with this).[62] This internalizes the competitive impact and the blackmail potential of the territorial parties, on the one hand, and the relevance of the territorial powers in the distribution of the national political power, on the other.

The current model of territorial organization in Spain has enjoyed some success, but it also has a few deficiencies that require correction or modification. Areas of particular challenge include the following:

• the dynamics of state consensus for matters related to the definition and coordination of national cohesion;
• the institutionalization and effective implementation of multilateral intergovernmental cooperation, as well as interterritorial solidarity;
• the reciprocal constitutional loyalty in the plural definition of the nation and in the application of the principles of equality, distinctiveness, and solidarity that integrate the model of self-government;
• the motivation of shared nationalist responsibility and the ability of the state government to form a coalition;
• the institutional expression of regional participation in shaping the Spanish position in the context of the institutions of the European Union;
• the top-down decentralization, which implies that the local entities and, above all, the cities must play a larger and more central role in creating a network that will offset the centrifugal tensions from the center and periphery; and
• the implementation of a reform mechanism that anticipates the dysfunctional features of the model and implements the necessary corrections, such as the overhaul and reform of the Senate.

We may conclude by returning to our central questions. Cohesion, centripetal dynamics, and competition are the dominant patterns in the political culture and behavior of Spanish political leaders and parties, even taking account of the fact that there are powerful centrifugal tensions, center-periphery conflicts, partisan fragmentation, and patterns of adversary politics, features with the capacity to threaten the stability of the decentralized model in the future. A critical issue is the point at which the impact of separatist dynamics, encouraged by certain leaders of peripheral nationalism, establishes itself within the structure of social pluralism in the political culture, with big implications for territorial cohesion and for the coherence of the national ideological families and their social supports.

After 30 years of the new decentralized democratic system, Spaniards have clearly moved on to a new political and constitutional culture, which, for the most part, whatever the region, allows them to share the plural identity of the Spanish common nation alongside strong local sentiments and identities (with the Basques as the major exception). The process of reconstruction of the Spanish plural nation and governance of the complexity of this renewed old state-nation has achieved positive political results. Yet, nowadays, the ability to govern affects not just the central government but also the territorial governments, defining a national arena than is both complex and plural.

ACKNOWLEDGMENT

This contribution is a result of the research projects SEJ2006-15076-C03-01 and IT-323-07, funded by the Spanish and Basque Governments.

NOTES

1. For an update of the old problem of identity, see Jonathan Friedman, *Cultural Identity and Global Process* (London: Sage, 1994), and Stuart Hall and Paul du Gay (eds.), *Questions of Cultural Identity* (London: Sage, 1996).

2. See Ulrich Beck, Anthony Giddens, and Scott Lash, *Reflexive Modernization: Politics, Tradition and Aesthetics in the Modern Social Order* (Stanford, CA: Stanford University Press, 1969).

3. For an updated view of the vast scientific production on the state-building paradigm, see Aidan Hehir and Neil Robinson (eds.), *State Building: Theory and Practice* (London: Routledge, 2007); see also Charles Tilly, *The Formation of National States in Western Europe* (Princeton, NJ: Princeton University Press, 1975).

4. Benedict Anderson, *Imagined Communities: Reflections on the Origin and Spread of Nationalism* (London: Verso, 1983), defines the nation as an "imagined political community," such that it is idealized as inherently limited, sovereign, and distinct from a specific community based on the daily interaction of its members, because what they really share is the mental image of their identity affinity and of their fellowship. See also Joel S. Migdal, *State in Society: Studying how States and Societies Transform and Constitute One Another* (Cambridge, UK: Cambridge University Press, 2001).

5. See Seymour M. Lipset and Stein Rokkan (eds.), *Party Systems and Voter Alignments* (New York: Free Press, 1967), and Stein Rokkan and Derek W. Urwin, *Economy, Territory, Identity* (London: Sage, 1983). See also Anthony D. Smith, *The Ethnic Origins of Nations* (London: Basil Blackwell, 1986); Jennifer Todd, N. Rougier, and L. Canas Bottos (eds.), *Political Transformation and National Identity Change: Comparative Perspectives* (London: Routledge, 2008); Christian Deschouwer, Michael Keating, and John Loughlin, *Culture, Institutions and Developments: A Study of Eight European Regions* (London: E. Elgar, 2002), among others.

6. See Ernest Gellner, *Nations and Nationalism* (Oxford, UK: Basil Blackwell, 1983); John Coakley (ed.), *The Social Origins of Nationalist Movements* (London: Sage, 1992); Brendan O'Leary and John McGarry (eds.), *The Politics of Ethnic Conflict Regulation: Case Studies of Protracted Ethnic Conflict* (London: Routledge, 1993); Andrés de Blas, *Nacionalismo y naciones en Europa* (Madrid: Alianza, 1994); On comparing the management of such tensions and the role of the partisan leaders, see Kurt Richard Luther and Christian Deschouwer (eds.), *Party Elites in Divided Societies: Political Parties in Consociational Democracies* (London: Routledge, 1999); John Coakley (ed.), *The Territorial Management of Ethnic Conflict*, 2nd ed. (London: Frank Cass, 2003).

7. The distinction between "fundamentalism" and "nationalism" made by Juan Linz is very appropriate in describing the national sentiments in Spain; see Juan Linz, "From Primordialism to Nationalism," in Edward A. Tiryakian and Ronald Rogowski (eds.), *New Nationalisms of the Developed West* (Boston: Allen and Unwin, 1985), pp. 203–53.

8. We may recall the definition in Fredrick Barth (ed.), *Ethnic Groups and Boundaries: The Social Organization of Cultural Difference* (London: Allen and Unwin, 1969), of ethnic groups as organizational types that are based on associating oneself with a certain category, or being associated with such a category, based on the perception of others, which allows the ethnic groups to define collective identities and to establish limits to interaction.

9. See Gunnar P. Nielsson, "States and Nation-Groups: A Global Taxonomy," in Tiryakian and Rogowski, *New Nationalisms* (1985), pp. 57–86, who analyzed the distribution of the 575 ethnicities that were recorded in 1985, and more recently Wsevolod W. Isajiw, *Understanding Diversity: Ethnicity and Race in the Canadian Context* (Toronto: Thompson Educational Publishing, 1999).

10. Raymond G. Gordon (ed.), *Ethnologue: Languages of the World*, 15th ed. (Dallas, TX: SIL International, 2005); also available at www.ethnologue.com.

11. Emilio Lamo de Espinosa, "¿Importa ser nación? Lenguas, naciones y Estados," *Revista de Occidente*, No. 301 (2006), pp. 118–39.

12. Elie Kedourie in *Nationalism* (London: Hutchinson, 1960) identified the three supposed ideals of this type of nationalism as the only source of legitimacy: the natural division of humanity into nations; the simple and empirical identification of the nations; and the right of these nations to have their own state.

13. In "Inventar naciones," *La Vanguardia*, 26 Jan. 2008.

14. Ibid., p. 137.

15. Arend Lijphart, *Democracies: Patterns of Majoritarian and Consensus Government in Twenty-One Countries* (New Haven, CT: Yale University Press, 1984), p. 21.

16. Interview published in *El País*, 28 May 2006.

17. This borrows the concept of American exceptionalism coined by S. M. Lipset in *American Exceptionalism: A Double-Edged Sword* (New York: W. W. Norton & Co, 1996) to highlight the most unique aspects of Spanish democratic dynamics. The historical roots and peculiarities of the "Spanish case" were first discussed in international comparative studies by Juan J. Linz, "Early State-Building and Late Peripheral Nationalisms Against the State: The Case of Spain," in S. N. Eisenstadt and Stein Rokkan (eds.), *Building States and Nations: Models, Analyses, and Data across Three Worlds* (Beverly Hills, CA: Sage, 1973), vol. 2, pp. 32–112; "Politics in a Multi-Lingual Society with a Dominant World Language: The Case of Spain," in Jean-Guy Savard and Richard Vigneault (eds.), *Les Etats multilingues: Problèmes et solutions* (Quebec, Canada: Presses de l'Université Laval, 1975), pp. 367–444; "La política en sociedades multilingües y multinacionales," in Fundes, *Como articular las autonomías españolas* (Madrid: Fundes, 1980), pp. 83–107; "The Basques in Spain: Nationalism and Political Conflict in a New Democracy," in Phillips Davison and Leon Gordenker (eds.), *Resolving Nationality Conflicts: The Role of Public Opinion Research* (New York: Praeger, 1980), pp. 11–52; "Peripheries Within the Periphery?" in Per Torsvik (ed.), *Mobilization, Center-Periphery Periphery Structure and Nation Building: A Volume in Commemoration of Stein Rokkan* (Bergen: Universitetsforlaget, 1982), pp. 335–89.

18. See Juan J. Linz, "La crisis de un Estado unitario, nacionalismos periféricos y regionalismo," in Ramon Acosta (ed.), *La España de las autonomías (pasado, presente y futuro)* (Madrid: Espasa Calpe, 1981), Vol. II, pp. 651–751; Eduardo García de Enterría, "El futuro de las autonomías territoriales," in E. García de Enterría (ed.), *España: un presente para el futuro* (Madrid: Instituto de Estudios Económicos, 1984), vol II; *Estudios sobre autonomías territoriales* (Madrid: Civitas, 1985); *La revisión del sistema de autonomías* (Madrid: Civitas, 1988); Andrés de Blas, "Instituciones, procesos de decisión y políticas en el Estado Autonómico: hacia un nuevo modelo de Estado de las Autonomías," *Revista del Centro de Estudios Constitucionales*, No. 4 (1989), pp. 255–67. See also Robert Agranoff and Rafael Bañón (eds.), *Publius*, Vol. 27, No. 4 (1997), pp. 99–120.

19. The Spanish Constitution refers in Art. 2 to the Spanish Nation as composed of "nationalities" and "regions," and Title VIII distinguishes two pathways for autonomy: the four historical communities that established this status during the Second Republic (1936–39) with special status, and the remaining regions.

20. Exceptions include Pilar Del Castillo (ed.), *Comportamiento político y electoral* (Madrid: CIS, 1994), and Manuel Alcántara and Antonia Martínez (eds.), *Las elecciones autonómicas en España, 1980–1997* (Madrid: CIS, 1998), which refer to the electoral processes, and Francisco J. Llera, "La opinion pública: la diversidad de una nación plural," in Joan Subirats and Raquel Gallego (eds.), *Veinte años de autonomías en España. Leyes, políticas públicas, instituciones y opinión pública* (Madrid: CIS, 2002), pp. 321–76; "Las arenas autonómicas de 2003," in Juan Montabes (coord.), *Instituciones y procesos políticos. Libro homenaje a José Cazorla Pérez* (Madrid: CIS, 2005), pp. 273–308; "La dimension territorial e identitaria en la competición y la gobernabilidad españolas," in F. Murrillo, J. L. García de la Serrana et al. (eds.), *Transformaciones políticas y sociales en la España democrática* (Valencia: Tirant lo Blanc, 2006), pp. 239–317; and José R. Montero, Francisco J. Llera, and Mariano Torcal, "Sistemas electorales en España: una recapitulación," *Revista Española de Investigaciones Sociológicas*, Vol. 58 (1992), pp. 7–56, which evaluates the electoral systems in the Spanish autonomous communities. See also Equipo ERA, In ERA: "*15 años de experiencia autonómica. Un balance*" in CECS, *Informe España 1996* (Madrid: Fundación Encuentro, 1997), pp. 371–576.

21. See also studies no. 1109 (in 1976, with 6,340 interviews), 1174 (in 1978, with 10,971 interviews), and 1190 (in 1979 with 8,800 interviews). These are analyzed in Salustiano Del Campo, Manuel Navarro, and José F. Tezanos, *La cuestión regional española* (Madrid: Edicusa, 1977); Jiménez Blanco, García Ferrando, López-Aranguren, and Miguel Beltrán, *La conciencia regional en España* (Madrid: CIS, 1977); and Manuel Garcia Ferrando, *Regionalismo y autonomía en España, 1976–1979* (Madrid: CIS, 1982).

22. See also studies no. 2025 to 2041 (in 1992, with 27,357 representative interviews and samples conducted on a provincial level), 2123 (in 1994, with 2,993 interviews), 2228 (in 1996, with 4,932 interviews), and 2286 (in 1998, with 9,991 interviews), referring only to those included in such publications. These are analyzed in Eduardo Lopez-Aranguren, *La conciencia regional en el proceso autonómico español* (Madrid: CIS, 1983); José R. Montero, Francisco J. Llera, and Françesc Pallares, *Autonomías y Comunidades Autónomas: actitudes, opiniones y cultura política* (Madrid: CIS, unpublished report, 1992); Manuel García Ferrando, Eduardo López-Aranguren, and Miguel Beltrán, *La conciencia nacional y regional en la España de las autonomías* (Madrid: CIS, 1994); José L.Sangrador, *Identidades, actitudes y estereotipos en la España de las Autonomías* (Madrid: CIS, 1996); Francisco Moral, *Identidad regional y nacionalismo en el estado de las Autonomías* (Madrid: CIS, 1998).

23. Among the pioneers are those of the Political and Social Sciences Institute (ICPS) of the Autonomous University of Barcelona for Catalonia; the Basque barometer of the Political Science research team of the University of the Basque Country (www.ehu.es/euskobarometro); the surveys of the Institute for Advanced Social Studies (IESA) of Cordoba for Andalusia; the Political Science research team of the Department of Political Science and Sociology at the University of Granada; in Galicia, the barometer of the Political Science research team of the University of Santiago de Compostela; and most recently, the barometer of the region of Murcia, carried out by the Political Science research team of the University of Murcia. The first four have just finished creating the Observatory of Autonomous Politics (OPA), www.opa151.com, which tries to synchronize and offer combined products about the respective regional opinions.

24. "Nación y nacionalidad," *El País*, 2 Dec. 2004; Andrés de Blas defends the sense of belonging and the profound meaning of such a distinction.

25. "Cólera de un pueblo, certeza de una nación," *El País*, 24 Jan. 2008.

26. See José Alvarez Junco, *Mater Dolorosa. La idea de España en el s. XIX* (Madrid: Taurus, 2001); Clare Mar-Molinero and Angel Smith (eds.), *Nationalism and the Nation in the Iberian Peninsula* (Oxford, UK: Berg, 1996); Juan Pablo Fusi, *Identidades proscritas. El no nacionalismo en las sociedades nacionalistas* (Barcelona: Seix Barral, 2006).

27. Carried out by our Basque barometer team of the University of the Basque Country, based on a random sample of 1,035 interviews conducted in Nov. and Dec. 2007 for the project SEJ 2006-15076 (See www.ehu.es/euskobarometro [accessed 1 January 2008]).

28. Study no. 2610, 2005 (See www.cis.es [accessed 1 January 2008]).

29. As the CIS has also been doing for many years in reference to the question: "What does 'Spain' mean to you?"

30. We took the data from our Observatory of Autonomous Politics, referring to the year 2005 (for Catalonia) and 2006 (for Andalucia, Galicia, and the Basque Country); see www.opa151.com [accessed 1 January 2008].

31. For the Basque Country, we usually ask, "Would you say that you identify with being a Basque nationalist, or not?" and the results can be consulted in the survey series of the Basque barometer (www.ehu.es/euskobarometro [accessed 1 January 2008]).

32. As Emilio Lamo de Espinosa ("Importa ser nación?", p. 130) eloquently states, "Spain is one of the countries that has the strongest and most pronounced regional identities in the world, yet a smaller Spanish nationalism."

33. The postwar generation of Basque nationalists comprises the children of a century and a half of civil wars and symbolic violence; this was manifested first in the Carlist Wars (1833-76), leading to a rise in nationalist discourse and the emergence of an ethnonationalist movement headed by Sabino Arana (the founder of the Basque Nationalist Party) a century ago; and second, in the violent resistance of the younger generations beginning in the 1960s in response to the political consequences of the civil war of 1936–39 and Francoist dictatorship. For Basque nationalism, see Stanley Payne, *Basque Nationalism* (Reno, NV: University of Nevada Press, 1975); Antonio Elorza, *Ideologías del nacionalismo vasco* (Madrid: Guadarrama, 1978); Javier Corcuera, *Orígenes, ideología y organización del nacionalismo vasco, 1876–1904* (Madrid: Siglo XXI, 1979); Jon Juaristi, *El linaje de Aitor. La invención de la tradición vasca* (Madrid: Taurus, 1987); Jon Juaristi, *El bucle melancólico. Historias de nacionalistas vascos* (Madrid: Espasa, 1997); Jon Juaristi, *Cambio de destino* (Barcelona: Seix Barral, 2006); Mikel Azurmendi, *La herida patriótica* (Madrid: Taurus, 1998); J. De Pablo, J. L. De la Granja, and L. Mess, *Documentos para la historia del nacionalismo vasco* (Barcelona: Ariel, 1998); Alfonso Perez-Agote, *La reproducción del nacionalismo vasco* (Madrid: CIS, 1984); Alfonso Perez-Agote, *El nacionalismo vasco a la salida del Franquismo* (Madrid: CIS, 1987); Ander Gurutxaga, *El código nacionalista vasco durante el Franquismo* (Barcelona: Anthropos, 1985).

34. The question is: "Of the phrases below, which one best expresses your own feelings? (1) I only feel Spanish; (2) I feel more Spanish than ... ; (3) I feel as Spanish as ... ; (4) I feel more ... than Spanish; (5) I only feel ... " (where the blanks refer to the corresponding regional group).

35. We are referring to ETA's radical nationalism, terrorism, and its social and political backing. Unfortunately, violence continues to be one of the sad characteristics of the Basque polity. See José M. Garmendia, *Historia de ETA* (San Sebastián, Spain: Haranburu, 1979); Gurutz Jauregui, *Ideología y estrategia política de ETA. Análisis y evolución entre 1959 y 1968* (Madrid: S. XXI, 1981); Joseba Zulaika, *Basque Violence: Metaphor and Sacrament* (Reno, NV: University of Nevada Press, 1988); John Sullivan, *ETA and Basque Nationalism* (London: Routledge and Kegan Paul, 1988); Robert P. Clark, *The Basque Insurgents: ETA, 1952–1980* (Madison, WI: University of Wisconsin Press, 1984); Robert P. Clark, *Negotiating with ETA: Obstacles to Peace in the Basque Country, 1975–1988* (Reno, NV: University Of Nevada Press, 1990); José M. Mata, *El nacionalismo vasco radical. Discurso, organización y expresiones* (Bilbao, Spain: Universidad del País Vasco, 1993); Francisco Llera, José M. Mata, and Cynthia L. Irvin, "ETA: From Secret Army to Social Movement: The Post-Franco Schism of the Basque Nationalist Movement," *Terrorism and Political Violence,* Vol. 5, No. 3 (1993), pp. 106–34; Goldie Shabad and Francisco Llera, "Political Violence in a Democratic State: Basque Terrorism in Spain," in Martha Crenshaw (ed.), *Terrorism in Context* (Philadelphia: University of Pennsylvania Press, 1995), pp. 410–69; Florencio Dominguez, *De la negociación a la tregua. ¿El final de ETA?* (Madrid: Taurus, 1998), among others. Juan J. Linz and his team spoke very poignantly about the Basque case during the early stages of the democratic transition; see Juan J. Linz, Manuel Gomez Reino, Francisco A. Orizo, and D. Vila, *Conflicto en Euskadi, Estudio sociológico sobre el cambio político en el País Vasco 1975–1980* (Madrid: Espasa Calpe, 1984), continued by Francisco J. Llera, "*Conflicto en Euskadi* revisited," in Richard Gunther (ed.), *Politics, Society and Democracy. Vol. I The Spanish Case* (Boulder, CO: Westview Press, 1993), pp. 169–95; and Francisco J. Llera, "Basque Polarization: Between Autonomy and Independence," in William Safran and Ramón Maiz (eds.), *Identity and Territorial Autonomy in Plural Societies* (Boulder, CO: Frank Cass, 2000), pp. 101–20.

36. Linz, "Early State Building" (1973) gave a very correct and early diagnosis of the difficulties and the role of nationalism in the national construction of identity.

37. Study no. SEJ 2006-15076, Dec. 2007; see www.ehu.es/euskobarometro [accessed 1 January 2008].

38. Study no. 2610 of the CIS (2005); see www.cis.es [accessed 1 January 2008].

39. Study no. SEJ 2006-15076, Dec. 2007; see www.ehu.es/euskobarometro [accessed 1 January 2008].

40. Study no. SEJ 2006-15076, Dec. 2007; see www.ehu.es/euskobarometro [accessed 1 January 2008].

41. Study no. 2228 of the CIS (1996); see www.cis.es [accessed 1 January 2008].

42. On the regulatory or contextual question of the succession, based on a comparative perspective, see Bruno Coppieters and Richard Sakwa (eds.), *Contextualizing Secession: Normative Studies in Comparative Perspective* (Oxford, UK: Oxford University Press, 2003); Michel Huysseune, *Modernity and Secession: The Social Sciences and the Political Discourse of the Lega Nord in Italy* (Oxford, UK: Berghahn, 2006).

43. On the asymmetry and institutional diversity acquired in the process of constructing the territorial model, see the excellent contributions found in the essays of Eliseo Aja, *El Estado Autonómico. Federalismo y hechos diferenciales* (Madrid: Alianza, 1999).

44. The critical view of this moment is offered by Francisco and Igor Sosa, *El Estado fragmentado: modelo austrohungaro y brote de naciones en España* (Madrid: Trotta, 2007).

45. Study no. SEJ 2006-15076, Dec. 2007; see www.ehu.es/euskobarometro.

46. See Daniel-Louis Seiler, *Les Parties autonomistes* (Paris: PUF, 1982); Daniel-Louis Seiler, *Sur les parties autonomists dans la CEE* (Barcelona: ICPS, 1990); Rokkan and Urwin, *Economy, Territory, Identity* (1983); Ferdinand Müller-Rommel and Geoffrey Pridham (eds.), *Small Parties in Western Europe* (London: Sage, 1991); Lieven De Winter (ed.), *Non-State Wide Parties in Europe* (Barcelona: ICPS, 1994); Michael Keating, *The New Regionalism in Western Europe: Territorial Restructuring and Political Change* (Cheltenham: Edward Elgar, 1998); Lieven De Winter and Hüri Türsan (eds.), *Regionalist Parties in Western Europe* (London: Routledge, 1998); Joseph Ruane, Jennifer Todd, and Anne Mandeville (eds.), *Europe's Old State in the New World Order: The Politics of Transition in Britain, France and Spain* (Dublin: University College Dublin Press, 2003).

47. Hans Daalder and Peter Mair (eds.), *Western European Party Systems: Continuity and Change* (London: Sage, 1983); Rokkan and Urwin, *Economy, Territory, Identity* (1983).

48. Lipset and Rokkan, *Party Systems* (1967).

49. Richard Gunther, Giacomo Sani, and Goldie Shabad, *Spain after Franco: The Making of a Competitive Party System* (Berkeley, CA: University of California Press, 1986); Llera, "Dimension Territorial" (2006).

50. Exceptions include the pioneering essay written by Isidre Molas, "Los partidos de ámbito no estatal y los sistemas de partidos," in Pedro de Vega (ed.), *Teoría y práctica de los partidos políticos* (Madrid: EDICUSA, 1977), or the more recent studies by Juan Montabes, "Non-State Wide Parties within the Framework of the Spanish Party System," in De Winter, *Non-State Wide Parties*, pp. 117–61; and Françesc Pallarés, José R. Montero, and Francisco Llera, "Non State-Wide Parties in Spain: An Attitudinal Study of Nationalism and Regionalism," *Publius: The Journal of Federalism*, Vol. 27, No. 4 (1997), pp. 135–69.

51. Francisco J. Llera, "The Performance of the Autonomous Communities' Electoral Systems: The Predominance of the Imperfect Two-Party System," *Revista Española de Investigaciones Sociológicas* (1999), pp. 93–123.

52. *Batasuna* ("Unity") was one of the different forms (HB, EH, EHAK, ANV) of representation and competition from 1979 of the so-called *patriotic left*; Batasuna, EHAK, and ANV were made illegal by the Spanish Supreme Court because of their support for and dependence on the ETA terrorist organization.

53. José Tornos, *Informe sobre las autonomías* (Madrid: Civitas, 1988).

54. Study no. SEJ 2006-15076, Dec. 2007; see www.ehu.es/euskobarometro [accessed 1 January 2008].

55. Juan Montabes (ed.), *El sistema electoral a debate* (Madrid: CIS, 1998).

56. A good study of the statutes of autonomy, and of their legal system, contents, and chronology can be found in Ignacio Torres, *Los Estatutos de Autonomía* (Madrid: CEPCO, 1999).

57. Registro Central de Personal, *Boletín Estadístico,* Jan. 2009.

58. Jordi Matas (ed.), *Coaliciones políticas y gobernabilidad* (Barcelona: ICPS, 2000).

59. Francisco J. Llera, *The Construction of the Basque Polarised Pluralism* (Barcelona: Institut de Ciences Politiques i Socials, 1993).

60. Isidre Molas and Oriol Bartomeus, *Estructura de la competencia política en España (1986–2000)* (Barcelona: ICPS, 2001).

61. Llera, "Basque Polarisation", pp. 101–10.

62. Study no. SEJ 2006-15076, Dec. 2007; see www.ehu.es/euskobarometro [accessed 1 January 2008].

APPENDIX
LIST OF SPANISH POLITICAL PARTIES

National Parties

AP	Alianza Popular/People's Alliance
CD	Coalición Democrática/Democratic Coalition
CDS	Centro Democrático y Social/Democratic and Social Center

IU	Izquierda Unida/United Left
PCE	Partido Comunista de España/Spanish Communist Party
PP	Partido Popular/People's Party
PSOE	Partido Socialista Obrero Español/Spanish Workers Socialist Party
UCD	Unión de Centro Democrático/Unity of Democratic Center
UN	Unión Nacional/National Unity
UPyD	Unión, Progreso y Democracia/Unity, Progress and Democracy

Territorial Parties

Andalucía

| PA | Partido Andalucista/Andalusist Party |
| PSA | Partido Socialista de Andalucía/Socialist Party of Andalusia (left) |

Aragon

| CHA | Chunta Aragonesista/Aragonesist Council (nationalist; left) |
| PAR | Partido Aragonés Regionalista/Regionalist Aragonese Party (regionalist; right) |

Asturias

AA	Andecha Astur/Asturian Coalition (nationalist; left)
BA	Bloque por Asturias/Bloc for Asturias (nationalist; left)
PAS	Partíu Asturianista/Asturianist Party (regionalist; left)
URAS	Unión Renovadora Asturiana/Asturias Renewal Union (regionalist; right)

Baleares

AIPF	Agrupació Independent Popular de Formentera/Popular Independent Association of Formentera (right)
Bloc	Bloc/Nationalist Balearic Left Bloc
EN	Entesa Nacionalista/Nationalist Coalition (left)
EC	Estat Catalá/Catalan State (nationalist; left)
ExC	Eivissa pel Canvi/Ibiza for Change (left)
PSM-EN	Partit Socialista de Maiorca-Entesa Nacionalista/Mallorcan Socialist Party-Nationalist Coalition (left; nationalist)
UM	Unió Mallorquina/Majorcan Unity (regionalist; right)

País Vasco

| Aralar | Aralar (nationalist; left) |
| EA | Eusko Alkartasuna/Basque Solidarity (nationalist; left) |

EE	Euskadiko Ezkerra/Basque Left (nationalist; left)
EH	Euskal Herritarrok/We the Basques (nationalist; left)
HB	Herri Batasuna/People's Unity (nationalist; left)
PCTV/EHAK	Partido Comunista de las Tierras Vascas/Euskal Herrialdeetako Alderdi Komunista/Comunist Party of Basque Lands (nationalist; left)
PNV	Partido Nacionalista Vasco/Basque Nationalist Party (nationalist; right)
UA	Unidad Alavesa/Alavese Unity (regionalist; right)

Canarias

AC	Asamblea Canaria/Canarian Assembly (left)
AHI	Agrupación Herreña Independiente/Independent Association of El Hierro (right)
AIC	Agrupaciones Independientes de Canarias/Canarian Independent Associations (right; regionalist)
CC	Coalición Canaria/Canarian Coalition (right; regionalist)
CNC	Congreso Nacional de Canarias/National Congress of Canarias (right)
FNC	Federación Nacionalista Canaria/Canarian Nationalist Federation (right)
INC	Izquierda Nacionalista Canaria/Canarian Nationalist Left (left)
PCN	Plataforma Canaria Nacionalista/Nationalist Canarian Platform (right)
PNC	Partido Nacionalista de Canarias/Canarian Nationalist Party (nationalist)
UPC	Unión del Pueblo Canario/Union of Canarian People (left)

Cantabria

CNC	Consejo Nacionalista de Cantabria/Cantabrian Nationalist Council (nationalist)
PRC	Partido Regionalista de Cantabria/Cantabrian Regionalist Party (regionalist; right)
UPCA	Unión para el Progreso de Cantabria/Unity for Cantabria's Progress (right)

Cataluña

CiU	Convergència i Unió/Convergence and Unity (nationalist; right)
ERC	Esquerra Republicana de Catalunya/Republican Left of Catalonia (nationalist; left)
ICV	Iniciativa per Catalunya Verds/Initiative for Catalonia— Greens (left)

| PSA | Partido Socialista de Andalucía/Socialist Party of Andalusia (left) |
| EC | Estat Catalá/Catalan State (nationalist; left) |

Castilla y Leon

PRPL	Partido Regionalista del País Leonés/Regionalist Party of the Leonese Country (regionalist)
SI	Solución Independiente/Independent Solution (left)
TC-PNC	Tierra Comunera/Commoner Land (nationalist; left)
UPL	Unión del Pueblo Leonés/Leonese People's Unity (regionalist; left)

Extremadura

| EU | Extremadura Unida/United Extremadura (regionalist; right) |

Galicia

BNG	Bloque Nacionalista Galego/Galician Nationalist Bloc (left)
CG	Coalición Galega/Galician Coalition (right)
EG	Esquerda Galega/Galician Left (left)
UPG	Nos-Unidade Popular/We—Popular Unity (nationalist, left)
PNG	Partido Nacionalista Galego/Galician Nationalist Party (right)
PSG	Partido Socialista Galego/Galician Socialist Party (left)

Navarra

AEM	Agrupación de Electores de Merindad/Navarrese Association of Electors (left)
Aralar	Aralar (nationalist; left)
CDN	Convergencia de Demócratas de Navarra/Convergence of Navarrese Democrats (regionalist; right)
EA	Eusko Alkartasuna/Basque Solidarity (nationalist; left)
EE	Euskadiko Ezkerra/Basque Left (nationalist; left)
HB	Herri Batasuna/People's Unity (nationalist; left)
IFN	Independientes Forales Navarros/Navarrese Foral Independents (left)
NaBai	Nafarroa Bai/Navarra Si/Navarre Yes (nationalist; left)
PNV	Partido Nacionalista Vasco/Basque Nationalist Party (nationalist; right)
UDF	Unión Demócrata Foral/Navarrese Democratic Unity (right)
UNAI	Unión Navarra de Izquierdas/Left Navarrese Unity (left)
UPN	Unión del Pueblo Navarro/Navarrese People's Unity (regionalist; right)

La Rioja

PR   Partido Riojano/Riojan Party (regionalist; right)
PRP   Partido Riojano Progresista/Progressive Riojan Party
            (regionalist; right)

Valencia

Bloc   Valencian Nationalist Bloc (nationalist; left)
EC   Estat Catalá/Catalan State (nationalist; left)
UV   Unió Valenciana/Valencian Unity (regionalist; right)

4

Northern Ireland: From Multiphased Conflict to Multilevelled Settlement

JENNIFER TODD

University College Dublin

The origins of the Northern Ireland conflict fall into three temporally distinct phases, each of which creates a particular sociostructural context that defines a set of protagonists with conflicting interests, more or less defined aims, and a given temporality of conflict. Each is superimposed on the previous phases, further defining and intensifying conflict. This multilevelled structure explains the difficulties of negotiating and of implementing an agreed settlement and allows assessment of the successes and failures of the 1998 settlement.

INTRODUCTION

Few, if any, contemporary settlement processes designed to resolve long-running ethnic or communal conflicts can be understood without reference to their deep historical roots, and the Northern Ireland case is no exception. This essay has as its starting point the argument that the origins of the Northern Ireland conflict fall into three temporally distinct phases. The first phase begins with the English state's reassertion of control over Ireland in the late sixteenth century and the early seventeenth-century plantation of Ulster, with their profound implications for power relations on the island of Ireland. The second phase starts with late nineteenth- and early twentieth-century nationalist mobilization, partition of the island, and the formation of two states. The third phase dates from the civil rights mobilization in 1968 and the subsequent drift towards violent conflict. In each phase a particular form of conflict is generated and embedded: if the seventeenth century locks in a communal conflict, the creation of Northern Ireland superimposes upon it a national and nation-state form of conflict, and the crisis of the 1969–72 sets in place an intensely violent struggle in the name of conflicting nationalisms.[1]

This framework is used here to sketch an explanation of the difficulties of negotiating and of implementing an agreed settlement and an assessment of the successes and failures of the 1998 settlement.

This historical perspective is not shared by all parties to the conflict. Indeed the political parties defined in the latest phase—unionists (the Ulster Unionist Party and the Democratic Unionist Party), nationalists (the Social Democratic and Labour Party), republicans (Sinn Féin), and their constituencies—disagree profoundly on the interrelation of the different phases.[2] One major issue in contention in the settlement process was whether the violent phase of conflict could be stopped without a reconfiguration of the form of national conflict set in place in 1921, and without tackling the conditions of communal opposition set in place 300 years earlier. Contemporary political and scholarly debates on the character of the present political configuration rest on different judgments of the changes in each of these levels of conflict.

The first section of this essay traces the multiphased origins of conflict; the second shows how this contributed to the formation of communities constituted in a complex way, with multiple aims; and the third section outlines the settlement reached in 1998 and assesses how far it meets the demands of the parties and addresses the key problems at each level of conflict.

THE GENESIS OF THE CONFLICT

Three temporally distinct origins of the conflict in Northern Ireland may be identified: seventeenth-century plantation, early twentieth-century partition, and late twentieth-century mobilization and countermobilization over reform. At each stage, initiating events created a particular sociostructural configuration that "locked in" a propensity for conflict in a path-dependent way, defining a set of protagonists with conflicting interests and more or less defined aims, and leading to a period-specific form of conflict. While it was possible that the later phases could have radically changed, or indeed undone, the form of conflict set in place with the plantation, the tendency at each new phase was instead to further specify, define and intensify the earlier patterns of conflict. Each phase sets a structural level of conflict: the earlier communal struggle does not go away but remains the base and everyday level of a conflict that may be fought in the name of nationalism and intensified by violence and threat of violence, but that is motivated by a much wider and deeper range of interests and values. Dispute over identity and over the aims and the very nature of the conflict becomes endemic to the actors in the conflict: the very range of interests, identities, and repertoires of conflict provides a rationale for almost all the population to take sides.[3]

Seventeenth-Century Plantation and its Legacy

Ireland, conquered in the twelfth century by the Anglo-Normans, had a sociopolitical structure that was resistant to the state-building and modernizing efforts of the early modern English monarchs. Ulster, the most Northern and most Gaelic province, was particularly difficult to bring under the new English order.[4] Plantation (colonization of confiscated land by loyal settlers) had been tried, relatively unsuccessfully, in other parts of Ireland in the sixteenth century. It was imposed on a larger scale on Ulster in the early seventeenth century: vast tracts of land were distributed to English companies, and to English and Scottish settlers brought in to work it.[5] The conflict in what is now Northern Ireland lies in a direct line of descent from this English reconquest and colonization (plantation) of Ulster.

Colonization was never separable from religious differences. Counter-reformation, via Irish priests trained on the continent, came to Ireland before the English reformation had taken hold, so that by the early seventeenth century, when the bulk of plantation took place, religious conflict was already under way.[6] Colonization required settlers who were not just ethnically distinct (English and Scots) but also distinct in respect of religion (Protestants). Subsequent power relations were tied around the religious distinction, legally in the "penal laws" directed against Catholics, informally in Protestant resistance to reform. The result was a multilevel conflict, where power relations (expressed in military force, economic resources, class position, legal status, and political representation) were partially organized by formal and informal religious institutions and networks, and where symbolic boundaries were multiple, with religious beliefs, moral-political norms and civilizational values, as well as historical narratives of plantation and ethno-national identities, overlapping if never quite coinciding.[7]

This created a strong tendency towards a triangular form of conflict typical of the colonial period where the English or British state was a key player in securing the dominance of the "settlers" even if, by the eighteenth century, the latter had developed their own distinctive political agenda.[8] To put the point crudely, Protestants had a vital interest in retaining their possessions and security against resentful majoritarian Catholics and relied on alliance with the state to do so; Catholics had an interest in undoing the power imbalance and multiple oppressions they suffered and were indifferent as to whether this meant that just the British state or also the Protestant people had to go.[9] The British state soon became relatively indifferent to the religio-cultural character of its supporters in Ireland (by the eighteenth century it had an interest in conciliating the Irish majority, not least because it needed recruits to the navy). However, its overriding interest was in stability, and this could best be guaranteed by alliance with the dominant, Protestant, partner.

The result was a multilevel communal conflict, where the precise role of religion, ethnicity, or political loyalty varied over time and between subgroups. Religious difference did not map perfectly onto ethnic distinction. Catholics were of both "Old English" (Anglo-Norman) and Gaelic Irish provenance, and the class position and interests of each group in the early seventeenth century were quite distinct. Meanwhile, many of the seventeenth-century incomers had only the vaguest concept of religion or religious distinction.[10] By the eighteenth century, religious distinctions between Presbyterians and Anglicans were more important among Protestants than was ethnic provenance. In the late eighteenth century, the rebellion of the United Irishmen, a denominationally mixed revolutionary movement under mainly Protestant leadership, showed the extent to which political loyalty and religious affiliation cut across each other. Even if, for the most part, the varying dimensions of difference ultimately converged in creating loyal Protestant and disaffected Catholic populations, the reasons for this loyalty and disaffection differed quite dramatically within each population, as also did the extent to which some might be (or might have been) won over to a different political position. There were opportunities to win groups of Catholics to the state cause, not just in the seventeenth century but also immediately after the Union of 1800, when Ireland became a more fully integrated part of the new United Kingdom, with the merger of the Irish and British parliaments.[11] If Catholic emancipation had been conceded at this time, it might have forestalled the kind of mobilization that was led by the Catholic and nationalist activist Daniel O'Connell in the early nineteenth century. Conversely, in the late nineteenth and early twentieth centuries, if the state had stood up decisively to Ulster Protestants while brokering a better deal for them under a scheme of devolution or "home rule" for Ireland, a different outcome might have been possible.[12]

To summarize, the seventeenth century created a colonial-style conflict between native and settler, set in place and reproduced by a state that cemented power relations and inequality and provided the cultural and economic resources that the settlers used to augment their power, status, and self-respect. This was not typical colonialism. It differed in its early genesis—in the sixteenth and seventeenth centuries—and, largely because of this early stage in English state and empire building, in a certain fluidity as to where kingdom ended and colony began.[13] In addition, there was the key role played by religion in communal differentiation, and this superimposed a reformation dynamic on a quasi-colonial mode of state-building and massively increased the cultural differentiation of the populations. One legacy of this phase of conflict lies in the multiplicity of dimensions of distinction, so that the actors have multiple repertoires of self-categorization and motivation. Another is the position of the British state as guarantor of deep-set communal inequality.

Nineteenth-Century Nationalist Mobilization and Twentieth-Century State-Building

The Union of 1800 created a new political regime in Ireland, now subject directly to the Westminster parliament. It left communal relations and communal antagonisms intact. Slowly, but increasing in momentum with democratization, the relative economic and political position of Catholics in Ireland improved through the nineteenth century. At the same time, nationalist mobilization increased in scope and effectiveness. For much of the period nationalism, although with a largely Catholic social base, was driven more by a sense of peripheral grievances against Britain than by the communal inequality and antagonism set in place centuries earlier. Much nineteenth-century nationalist literature, like the reformist or "constructive" unionist critique of nationalism, focused on the benefits and disbenefits to Ireland of the Union, and the best ways to increase Irish prosperity and to reduce sectarian division.[14]

By the beginning of the twentieth century, however, nationalist ideology and grievance became superimposed upon the deeper communal oppositions.[15] The questions of how this happened, and whether it could have been avoided, lie beyond the scope of this paper. That it happened is clear. There were periods in the nineteenth century when Protestants—including Ulster Protestants—played a role in the nationalist movement, and in the latter quarter of the century the Irish Protestant Home Rule Association had a significant Ulster membership.[16] Through the century, and even after nationalist politicization, many Catholics remained loyal to the empire, if not to the state. To be sure, this coexisted with continuing local communal division in Ulster, as Frank Wright has documented.[17] But it was only from 1885 (just before the first "home rule" bill proposed devolved government for Ireland) that this communal division was politicized and came to be expressed in clear nationalist terms.[18] As a result of this, and of similar tensions over the second home rule bill (1893), which also failed to reach the statute book, Protestant dissent was silenced and, according to Northern nationalist leader, Tom Campbell, voting behavior became entirely predictable by confessional allegiance.[19] As mobilization for and against the third home rule bill (1912) proceeded in the early twentieth century, ethnic, religious, and political distinctions were forged into a coincidence.[20]

Although the third home rule bill (1912) was eventually passed in 1914, it was never implemented. Instead, the partition of Ireland was legislated for in the Government of Ireland Act of 1920, with devolved government introduced in the six counties of Northern Ireland in 1921, and the 26 counties of what would eventually become independent Ireland forming a "Free State" the following year. Partition changed the political locus of conflict, condensing the most extreme division in Northern Ireland, with Ulster Protestant unionists opposed to Irish Catholic nationalists (and their perceived fifth column inside the Northern state), and only the scattered southern Irish Protestant minority excluded or excluding themselves from each group. Partition also provided a state for each group, and each state was used to dig division still deeper, in nation-building enterprises, in institutionalizing confessionalism, and—in the North—in using state resources in a clientelist way to secure Protestant unity.[21] Each state was used by the dominant political parties to create a world—a set of institutions manned by the dominant group and given meaning by their stories, norms, and rituals—in which one group felt secure and the other was marginalized.

Partition had another effect. It massively increased the importance of sovereignty in Northern Ireland. With another state in the archipelago, British sovereignty became much more important than before, and its importance was more deeply felt in Northern Ireland, where it was challenged, than elsewhere in the United Kingdom. Unionists needed the British state to protect them against a Catholic-dominated society in the South, and they identified with the British state for a whole range of reasons—economic, religious, and moral—that are not reducible simply to ethnic origin or national solidarity.[22]

In summary, both Irish nationalists and Ulster unionists were formed in a process of mobilization and countermobilization in the late nineteenth century—a period when nationalism was strong throughout Europe. Irish nationalism is a paradigmatic case of peripheral nationalism successfully asserting itself against an old imperial center. Ulster unionism unites ethnic, religious, and political loyalties in a way that is sometimes defined as a form of ethno-national loyalty to "Britain." However, the ways in which the ethnic, religious, political, and national categories were interrelated, and the motives that went into British loyalty, were considerably more diverse than those described in a classic nationalist model, or seen in the Irish nationalist paradigm.

Partition created the conditions for lasting conflict in Northern Ireland, institutionalizing unionist majority power such that only unionists could be relied upon for loyalty to the state. In effect it created a structural bind, in which nationalist equality came to threaten unionist security.[23] It became extremely difficult for unionist leaders—even liberal ones—to conceive of what was necessary to secure nationalist acquiescence, and those few who did were marginalized or defeated.[24]

The Late Twentieth Century: A Dynamic of Violence

The third period saw the end of the devolved government put in place in 1921, as mobilization within Northern Ireland for civil rights met unionist opposition and produced nationalist (and later armed republican) responses.

As the British state again took control, a quarter-century of intense violence ensued, costing over 3,000 deaths, with the Irish Republican Army (IRA) effectively carrying on a guerrilla campaign against the state, and indirectly against its Protestant supporters, while Protestant paramilitaries targeted Catholics.[25] The intense violence became self-perpetuating. The IRA gained a foothold in local communities, whose populations were targeted by loyalists, and many of whose members were harassed, intimidated and killed by the British army, but whose support for republicanism remained strong through the period.[26] The period also saw the creation of a British state apparatus of repression and administration in Northern Ireland, heavily reliant on Protestants in the security industry, which provided another experiential focus of British identification.

Meanwhile, another struggle was going on, largely independent of what the IRA, and later the British and Irish states, called the "war." This was a struggle between nationalists and unionists to try to create an acceptable form of society and state, waged by the political parties who were constantly called to account by politicized populations. This struggle was not centrally about state sovereignty: actual negotiations, policies, and failed initiatives were about attempts to secure equality, respect, participation, and recognition within Northern Ireland; the manner in which state institutions and practices impacted on this; and the role that the British and Irish states could and should play to ensure these aims. State sovereignty was highlighted when reform appeared (to nationalists) to be impossible, or when it appeared (to unionists) to weaken the Union. That this political struggle was so difficult to resolve, however, is a product of the longer term processes and aims set in place with plantation and partition: a division of communities, a set of overlapping, deep cultural divisions, and deep-set inequalities justified in terms of values and beliefs embedded in cultural traditions of empire- and state-building and fought out in terms of the rights of natives as well as of nationalists. Political struggle was also entwined with the violence. The IRA campaign ensured that the grievances of Catholics could not simply be ignored as they were before 1968 and might well have been again had the IRA been defeated.[27] Protestant mobilization and the threat of a loyalist paramilitary backlash ensured that Protestants could not be coerced. The British state—as holder of massive power resources in the region—kept some control over the escalation of violence, and slowly implemented reforms, while guaranteeing a social structure that systematically reproduced conflict.

In summary, the period of British direct rule between 1972 and 1998 saw an intense and violent power struggle in the name of nationalism that had three separate aspects. There was a war waged by republicans and loyalist paramilitaries, dependent on a level of popular acquiescence and local community support. There was a party political struggle and usually a party political stalemate between nationalist and unionist parties over the proper form of political institutions for the region. There was an intermittent mobilization and assertion of aims, identities, and oppositions by the wider populations, together with a slow renegotiation and rethinking of these aims and oppositions. This underpinned the political stalemate, bringing down political leaders who compromised too far. The political stalemate was broken, a change in popular aims was confirmed, and an alternative to violence was provided only by a repositioning of the British government in Northern Ireland. The first step was the Anglo-Irish Agreement of 1985, which gave the Irish government a role "more than consultative but less than executive" in the governance of Northern Ireland.

THE PARTIES TO THE CONFLICT

Plantation in the seventeenth century left "two communities" in the northeast of Ireland, defined as Protestant and Catholic, locally and regionally opposed, and looking to the English or British state as a tool or power resource. This continued into the twentieth century, when the British state, rather than constituting an arena of democracy, continued to be seen as a power resource for the communities in Northern Ireland. Equally, despite the formal democracy of the devolved system of government in Stormont, politics in Northern Ireland turned into a communal power play. Individuals—for good historical reasons—constructed their sense of themselves by a subtle intersection of political aims, religious belonging, and ethnic provenance, and this part-merging of religious values, ethnic solidarity, and political loyalties at once made for deeper and more hard-fought opposition. What was at stake was power, but power for the sake of the very highest of values. What did the communities want? They had a whole range of varied aims, from the everyday to the religious to the geopolitical, and on all of them they were opposed.[28] The "constitutional question" symbolized and crystallized all of these aspects, and that is why the issue of state sovereignty was so powerful a motivating force and so difficult to bypass.

Partition defined the two communities in opposing national and state-centric terms. As is well documented, the partition of Ireland and the formation of the Northern Ireland devolved institutions in 1921 was a product of unionist mobilization; the extent of the devolved territory was explicitly designed to produce a large unionist majority (approximately two-thirds Protestant and one-third Catholic).[29] The dominant party was the Ulster Unionist Party and it united the Protestant population through judicious use of state resources and opportunities.[30] It was opposed by a Catholic and nationalist population whose organizations and cultural reference points were lost with partition, and who only slowly reorganized politically under a Nationalist Party that was closely integrated in a church-dominated society.[31] The Nationalist Party was unable to achieve any of its political goals, either when it participated as a minority within a parliament dominated by the unionist majority, or when it abstained from participation. There was also a small Labour party (and several republican-labor groupings), recruiting from both the Protestant and Catholic working class, and continually outmaneuvered as a competitor for the Protestant vote by a Unionist Party with state resources under its control. The party system was bipolar, with all elections focused on the overarching unionist-nationalist opposition. Within this overarching division, each population was internally divided and politically fractious.[32]

The overarching division was defined in political—indeed constitutional —terms but fuelled by religious ethos, economic conditions, and perceived injustice. More precisely, these motivations reinforced a national division that—for many—was of decreasing salience in the period after the Second World War. By the 1960s, for example, many Catholics and "nationalists" were willing to settle, in the middle term, for a reformed Northern Ireland.[33] Many Protestants and unionists were willing to contemplate closer relations with the Irish state and reform within Northern Ireland.[34] Divisions were increasingly visible within the Protestant population, while Catholics were increasingly impatient with the old nationalist-Catholic consensus.[35] As the civil rights movement began, the motivations of different segments of the population were varied, and there seemed to be potential space for compromise.[36] However, conflict focused on the form and stability of the unionist-devolved state. Even unionist liberals were slow to endanger their state by giving up on the unionist alliance, nor were nationalist moderates willing to help bolster the state and trust unionists to change in their own time.

The civil rights movement of the late 1960s, initially opposed by loyalist militants (who were supported by sections of the security forces), secured some reform in Northern Ireland but at the expense of exposing the Protestant nature of the state and of the security forces. The resulting street violence, increasing steadily in intensity, showed the inability of the unionist devolved government to control its own supporters, let alone the population as a whole. It required first British army and later (in 1972) British state intervention to take government from the hands of the unionists before a measure of order was secured. By this stage, the IRA campaign of violence was not only underway but had secured public support in key neighborhoods.[37]

From 1971, the issues of equality within Northern Ireland and of links with the South took a low place on a political agenda dominated by increasing violence and repression. A new party system was developing, with a fragmentation of the unionist parties, divided as to the best strategy to maintain the union (integration within the United Kingdom, direct rule from London, devolution, and, if devolution, in what form). The Rev. Ian Paisley's Protestant Unionist Party was renamed the Democratic Unionist Party (DUP) in 1971 and was soon to become the main contender for the Protestant vote against mainstream unionism, in the Ulster (or Official) Unionist Party (UUP), which won about two thirds of the Protestant vote over the next 25 years.

The Social Democratic and Labour Party (SDLP) was formed by the notables who led the civil rights movement and replaced the old Nationalist Party by a younger, more socially concerned leadership. The SDLP had aspirations for a united Ireland, but these were long term, conditional on the consent of a majority in Northern Ireland; its leadership was open to a variety of constitutional and institutional compromises.[38] Meanwhile the Provisional IRA—whose political wing, Sinn Féin, did not contest elections until the early 1980s—created a secure home base in marginalized and underprivileged urban and rural neighborhoods.[39] A cross-community party, the Alliance Party of Northern Ireland (APNI) peaked in support at 16% of the popular vote in 1981, thereafter gaining no more than 10% of the poll. Under direct rule it had considerable influence on British policy, but it never seriously challenged the support of the main parties.

What did the parties want? Their strategies varied with the different policies and practices of the British state. In 1973–74 unionists were divided between those who wanted a return to devolution with majority rule and those who would accept a level of power sharing; by the late 1970s and into the 1980s the division was between devolutionists and integrationists (the latter supporting complete absorption of Northern Ireland within the United Kingdom). As both integration and majority rule devolution were ruled out by the British, new divisions emerged between those who wanted no change in the status quo (direct British rule) and those who would contemplate change to ward off nationalist advance (and in particular to reverse the Irish government's role in Northern Ireland granted in the 1985 Anglo-Irish Agreement).[40] All, however, saw republican violence as criminal terrorism and wanted it defeated independently of and prior to any political settlement that included republicans.[41] For them, there was no rationale to armed struggle, and any attempt to lessen support for the IRA by reforming the state in Northern Ireland (as nationalists in the SDLP and the Irish state advocated) was at once unprincipled appeasement and practically useless. Politically, they were willing to allow reform within the union; how much reform, and how much equality and what equality would mean, slowly changed over time and under pressure of increasing reform from 1985.[42]

Nationalists in the SDLP wanted equality in Northern Ireland and an open agenda on Irish unity, with an institutionalized and at least symbolic link with the Republic of Ireland. How this Irish dimension was to be institutionalized, and what exactly would count as equality, were matters on which views changed over time and with events. In the New Ireland Forum of 1983–84, an all-Ireland nationalist consensus emerged not on the form of the Irish dimension (different options were given) but on the necessity of it.[43] Republicans, in turn, wanted the "Brits"—that is the British state—out, as a prerequisite for further change. They wanted a settlement that would resolve the historic causes of conflict, which, in the republican analysis, went right back to plantation and required a strong "equality agenda" as well as a path to Irish unity. When they were convinced that Irish unity could not come in one step, but that other political opportunities were being held open, they slowly opened negotiations that would lead to not just to the end of war but also to the end of the political stalemate.[44]

PATHS TOWARDS A SETTLEMENT, 1997–2007

The Anglo-Irish Agreement of 1985 was followed by an accelerating reform program and the outlining of a complex multileveled and multilocated form of governance. Negotiations between the unionists, the SDLP, the Alliance Party, and the governments, and between IRA representatives and the SDLP (and the British and Irish governments), were intermittent through the 1990s. At first an IRA ceasefire was called in 1994, followed by loyalist paramilitary ceasefires, but violence recommenced after a delay in commencing talks. A second ceasefire was called in 1997, and in September of that year Sinn Féin was admitted for the first time to all-party talks, which the DUP and the small UK Unionist Party immediately left. A settlement was finally, unexpectedly, reached in April 1998, between the UUP, SDLP, Sinn Féin, and smaller parties, with only the DUP and the UK Unionist Party outside the consensus. The DUP was eventually brought in, once it had electorally destroyed the more moderate UUP, but that took almost another decade.

The settlement was a complex package put together by the two governments and approved after amendments by the parties.[45] It had three strands—internal to Northern Ireland, North-South, and East-West—and a number of important constitutional components and provisions for institutional reform. Constitutional change was made dependent on the vote of a majority in both parts of the island of Ireland, with guarantees by both governments to hold referenda and to implement the agreed changes, and with a change in the Irish constitution to reflect the aim of unity by consent (and only by consent) of a majority in Northern Ireland. New consociational representative institutions were created: an Assembly with 108 members elected by the single transferable vote system of proportional representation, whose members would self-designate as unionist, nationalist, or other; bloc vetoes for unionists and nationalists in the form of weighted majority voting on contentious issues; a First and Deputy First Minister with equivalent powers to be appointed by simultaneous majorities of unionists and nationalists in the Assembly; and a proportionally representative executive appointed by the d'Hondt method.

The existence of the Assembly was codependent on the existence of a North-South council of ministers, created by British and Irish legislation but functioning by consensus between northern and southern ministers. That Council would in turn have a standing secretariat and would set up six all-Ireland "implementation bodies" to promote consultation, cooperation, and action in the areas of trade, European Union (EU) programs, language, inland waterways, fisheries, and food safety, with the prospect of further harmonization at policy and implementation levels left open to agreement.[46] The Irish government retained some say in the governance of Northern Ireland through a British-Irish intergovernmental conference, responsible for policy areas not devolved to the Assembly. In addition, a British-Irish Council was instituted, bringing together representatives of the British and Irish governments, the Scottish, Welsh, and Northern Irish executives, and representatives from the Isle of Man and the Channel (Anglo-Norman) Isles.

Aside from these major institutional innovations, there were far-reaching reform policies involving the mainstreaming of equality in all public decision making, and human rights guarantees (though the latter have yet to be fully codified).[47] There was agreement to institute an independent international commission on the reform of policing, with the remit to create a police service "capable of attracting and sustaining support from the community as a whole."[48] When the Commission reported in 1999, it proposed a radical reorganization of the policing system, to intense unionist protest.[49] In addition, reform of the administration of justice was promised. Qualifying prisoners (from paramilitary organizations on ceasefire) were to be released within two years. Decommissioning and demilitarization were each promised, the latter dependent on the security situation, and the former dependent on the implementation of the agreement, with the parties committing to "use any influence they may have" to achieve decommissioning within two years "in the context of the implementation of the overall settlement."[50] These qualifications lost important unionist support. Successive crises of implementation led to serial unionist withdrawals from government and an eventual parking of the representative institutions between 2002 and 2007.[51]

What was the balance of gains and losses to the parties and to their wider constituencies? Unionists secured British sovereignty, and an end to the Irish constitutional claim to Northern Ireland. Nationalists, meanwhile, ensured that the fact of sovereignty was diluted in its cultural impact and became significantly less important in institutional organization: as unionist Peter Weir commented, the "dimmer switch" was applied to Britishness. A radical equalization of conditions in Northern Ireland was underway politically, economically, and culturally, with every institution, including the judicial system, vetted for its openness to nationalist perspectives and presence. Decommissioning of republican weapons was eventually achieved, five years after the agreed date, and British security installations were finally dismantled in 2007. In the meantime, the moderate UUP and SDLP were overtaken in the polls by the more extreme DUP and Sinn Féin, even while the latter parties considerably moderated their policies and, from 2007, entered government together.[52]

How successful was the agreement at regulating conflict? When we look at elites and activists, the 1998 settlement has proven an undoubted success.

There has been a definitive end to violence, with paramilitary decommissioning and British army demilitarization. A resurgence of dissident republican
violence in spring 2009 appears to have been contained. There has been
a restructuring of institutions to remedy inequality, and this has been effective at the middle and upper levels of employment, although Catholics
remain disproportionately present in the most marginalized sections of the
population.[53] The new institutional configuration, with its multicentered loci
of political decision making, remains in existence a decade later and is
now worked by the "extreme" political parties. If policy-making achieve-
ments have been questioned, it is at least in part because the devolved
assembly has functioned for only a fraction of the decade since 1998. Major
change has, however, occurred in the structure of governance, the institutional setting (including the creation of a range of British-Irish and North-
South institutions), the security system, and the expectations of the political
parties. Indeed the main parties currently in government—the DUP and
Sinn Féin—have moderated their policies very considerably, with the DUP
sitting in government with ex-paramilitaries and Sinn Féin supporting the
police.

At the everyday level, the record is less clear. There are radically opposing views among experts on Northern Ireland as to whether, ten years on,
the settlement has reduced or increased sectarianism, as to whether it has
crystallized or softened opposing views, and as to whether it has solidified
or moderated opposing blocs, or perhaps even begun to transform them.
Survey research shows some moderation of popular views: Protestants now
largely support the devolved institutions and have come to terms with the
reform of the police; Catholics are willing to make the new settlement work,
and the desire for a united Ireland has remained stable over ten years.[54]
However, levels of segregation have risen, and the numbers of "peace walls"
dividing the populations in Belfast have increased. Reports of sectarian violence and intimidation have increased, although, as Jarman notes, this may
be because police reports have only recently included this as a category.[55]
Qualitative research is starkly divided over whether individuals are in the
process of rethinking or of reaffirming older oppositions.[56] In some central
city neighborhoods and among male activists, real dangers of a renewal of
conflict exist. There is, however, more rethinking among the less-politicized
groups (often made up of women), particularly outside the segregated city
neighbourhoods. The trend, however, remains uncertain, and it is crucial to
the success or failure of the settlement itself. Will the institutions continue to
stumble from crisis to crisis until nationalists reach just over 50% of the voting
population, and unionists have to put up with a united Ireland or fight? Or is
there a slow movement towards participation and dialogue that—unevenly,
and for different subgroups—is gradually decoupling the constitutional question from its ethno-religious basis? And, if the latter is occurring, will it be
enough to forestall future crisis?

CONCLUSION

How far has the Good Friday Agreement of 1998 been successful in conflict management and resolution? To answer the question we need to situate the Agreement as an intervention in the three nested patterns of conflict traced above: the intense and violent conflict that has marked the quarter century from 1969; the zero-sum conflict between nationalism and unionism that characterized Northern Ireland since its foundation; and the British state entanglement in communal conflict that has been a feature of modern Irish history for four centuries.

From early in the conflict, Irish government officials and ministers had come to the conclusion that the three patterns were interrelated, that the partition settlement of 1920–21 had precluded any change in the long-term relationships of sectarian opposition, that this had created nationalist anger and alienation that made the IRA campaign possible, and that a new settlement had to address all three levels of conflict.[57] They disagreed on priorities and strategy, and until the Anglo-Irish Agreement of 1985, had little part to play in conflict management. The 1985 agreement marked the beginning of change: in giving the Irish government a small role, it acted as a wedge that allowed diplomats and politicians to argue for a more radical repositioning of the British state that would also change the structure of relations between unionists and nationalists. Nationalists and republicans shared this broad vision, although republicans had a distinctive view of the causality involved and came late to recognize the importance of creating an institutional settlement as a stepping stone to further constitutional change.

British politicians and officials varied greatly in their interest in and understanding of the Northern Ireland conflict. While some "maximalists" were intuitively open to an Irish involvement in Northern Ireland up to and including joint sovereignty and easily forged understanding with their Irish counterparts, they were unable to drive policy until the 1990s.[58] Others adopted a sovereigntist view, either keeping Northern Ireland British or seeing the alternative as an immediate united Ireland. However, key figures at government and official levels had come to accept the interrelation of the three levels of conflict, and by the 1990s they had begun to converge in their views on the way forward with the Irish government.[59] Unionists, as Farrington points out in an important article, denied these interrelations.[60] They did not see the quest for a compromise political settlement as intimately connected with the quest to end IRA violence, nor did they think a fair settlement in Northern Ireland required any wider changes in the role of the state, except perhaps as a concomitant of wider global influences on a postdevolution United Kingdom.

The 1998 Good Friday Agreement itself was open to these diametrically opposed unionist and nationalist interpretations. There was disagreement as to whether the agreement was in essence an historic compromise,

guaranteeing equality for nationalists and constitutional security for unionists. This was the view of the UUP leadership, with the fairness and balance
of the compromise questioned by the UUP rank and file and by the DUP.
Most nationalists accepted that the agreement was a historic compromise, but
they thought it went further, to begin a process of dismantling the longer run
causes of conflict. There was further disagreement as to whether paramilitary
violence was to be read as a symptom of a longer term pattern of relationships, which would be resolved only as these relations were changed (the
view of nationalists, republicans, and loyalists), or as an independent problem to be resolved prior to implementation of the agreement (the view of
both the UUP and the DUP). Unionists and nationalists were, in addition,
internally divided as to whether the agreement actually resolved conflict at
any of these levels. They were also divided on whether change had stabilized the balance of power or, as the DUP and UUP rank and file believed,
and some republicans hoped, had given a power bonus to nationalists who
were likely to use it to advance constitutional change.[61]

By the mid-2000s, all parties had come to accept that the power balance
had been stabilized for the medium term. The IRA had decommissioned. The
2001 census showed only a gradual increase (to 44%) in the percentage of
Catholics in Northern Ireland, thus suggesting that it would be decades before
a nationalist voting majority was likely to emerge. The US, British, and Irish
governments made clear to all parties—and most particularly to Sinn Féin
and the DUP—that if they undermined negotiations to revive the institutions,
the alternative would not benefit them, and indeed that the character of that
alternative would depend on which party brought down the institutions.
Eventually a revised settlement was reached in St. Andrews, Scotland, in
2006, and the DUP and Sinn Féin entered government in May 2007, with the
expectation that this would be the structure of governance for the medium
term, carefully watched by Irish and British governments. Whether this gives
space for more thorough transformations of relations, ideals, and aims—an
unlocking of the deeply entrenched communal division and ethnic basis of
constitutional politics—remains to be seen.

ACKNOWLEDGMENTS

This article borrows freely in arguments and occasionally in text from a
much longer joint work—in its final stages of completion—on the conflict
and settlement processes in Northern Ireland coauthored with Joseph Ruane.
The analysis of the settlement process is informed by as yet unattributable
interviews and witness seminars with politicians and officials, made possible
by project *Breaking Patterns of Conflict*, funded by the Irish Research Council
for the Humanities and Social Sciences, undertaken with John Coakley and
Christopher Farrington.

NOTES

1. Joseph Ruane and Jennifer Todd, "Path Dependence in Settlement Processes: Explaining Settlement in Northern Ireland," *Political Studies,* Vol. 55, No. 2 (2007), pp. 442–58.

2. Conventional practice is followed here in distinguishing "republicans" (a term commonly reserved in Northern Ireland for militant nationalists, typically supporters of the IRA) from "nationalists" *simpliciter* (typically supporters of conventional political methods in the pursuit of their aims). One section of militant unionists, prepared to consider the use of violence to advance their cause and commonly of working-class background, is similarly labelled "loyalist."

3. Joseph Ruane and Jennifer Todd, *The Dynamics of Conflict in Northern Ireland* (Cambridge, UK: Cambridge University Press, 1996), p. 30.

4. Nicholas Canny, *The Elizabethan Conquest of Ireland: A Pattern Established 1565–76* (Hassocks, UK: Harvester, 1976); Nicholas Canny, *From Reformation to Restoration: Ireland 1534–1660* (Dublin: Helicon, 1987).

5. Ciaran Brady and Raymond Gillespie (eds.), *Natives and Newcomers: The Makings of Irish Colonial Society 1534–1641* (Dublin: Irish Academic Press, 1986).

6. On the use of religious justifications for revolt by the Ulster lords, see Hiram Morgan, "Hugh O'Neill and the Nine Years War in Tudor Ireland," *Historical Journal*, Vol. 36, No. 1 (1993), pp. 21–37.

7. Ruane and Todd, *Dynamics*, pp. 2–30.

8. For the complexities of the colonial model, and its only partial adequacy to the Irish situation, see Stephen Howe, *Ireland and Empire: Colonial Legacies in Irish History and Culture* (Oxford, UK: Oxford University Press, 2000).

9. Clearly there are important variations within both Catholic and Protestant populations. This schema summarizes the overall result and proffers an explanation for it in terms of the interests generated by state-guaranteed social structure. It does not deal with the complex maneuvers, redefinitions, and challenges of individuals and subgroups within each population who tried to break the pattern and sometimes nearly did. For example the United Irishmen's rebellion of 1798, incorporating both Protestants and Catholics, might have succeeded—with very radical implications for the future of the island and the archipelago—if the planned French military intervention force had landed on schedule.

10. Finlay Holmes, *Our Irish Presbyterian Heritage* (Belfast: Publications Committee of the Presbyterian Church in Ireland, 1985), pp. 9–11.

11. On the earlier period, see, for example, Jane Ohlmeyer, "Colonization within Britain and Ireland," in Nicholas Canny (ed.), *The Origins of Empire,* Vol. I of the *Oxford History of the British Empire* (Oxford, UK: Oxford University Press, 1998), pp. 124–47, in particular pp. 140–3.

12. Ian Lustick sees the moment that defined subsequent relations as March 1914, when the British government failed to assert its authority over officers in the military camp of the Curragh who refused to march on Ulster; Ian S. Lustick, *Unsettled States, Disputed Lands: Britain and Ireland, France and Algeria, Israel and the West Bank-Gaza* (Ithaca, NY: Cornell University Press, 1993), pp. 206–9.

13. Joseph Ruane, "Colonialism and the Interpretation of Irish Historical Development," in Marilyn Silverman and P. H. Gulliver (eds.), *Approaching the Past: Historical Anthropology through Irish Case Studies* (New York: Columbia University Press, 1992), pp. 293–323.

14. D. George Boyce, *Nationalism in Ireland* (London: Croom Helm, 1982); Richard English, *Irish Freedom: The History of Nationalism in Ireland* (London: Macmillan, 2006); S. Rosenbaum (ed.), *Against Home Rule: The Case for the Union* (London: Frederick Warne and Co., 1912); Andrew Gailey, "The Destructiveness of Constructive Unionism: Theories and Practice, 1890s–1960s," in D. George Boyce and Alan O'Day (eds.), *Defenders of the Union: A Survey of British and Irish Unionism since 1801* (London: Routledge, 2001), pp. 227–50.

15. See Tom Garvin, *The Evolution of Irish Nationalist Politics* (Dublin: Gill and Macmillan, 1981), and *Irish Nationalist Revolutionaries 1858–1928* (Oxford, UK: Clarendon, 1987), for the tension between these aspects of Irish nationalism, a theme also discussed in English, *Irish Freedom*.

16. James Loughlin, "The Irish Protestant Home Rule Association and Nationalist Politics, 1886–1893," *Irish Historical Studies,* Vol. 24, No. 95 (1985), pp. 341–60.

17. Frank Wright, *Two Lands on One Soil: Ulster Politics before Home Rule* (Dublin: Gill and Macmillan, 1996).

18. Brian M. Walker, *Ulster Politics: The Formative Years, 1868–1886* (Belfast: Ulster Historical Foundation, 1989).

19. T. J. Campbell, *Fifty Years of Ulster (1890–1940)* (Belfast: The Irish News, 1941), pp. 35–76.

20. One of the best accounts is still that of Peter Gibbon, *The Origins of Ulster Unionism: The Formation of Popular Protestant Politics and Ideology in Nineteenth Century Ireland* (Manchester, UK: Manchester University Press, 1975), pp. 112–40.

21. Scholars from different perspectives converge in this judgement: Patrick Buckland, *The Factory of Grievances: Devolved Government in Northern Ireland 1921–39* (Dublin: Gill and Macmillan, 1979); Paul Bew, Peter Gibbon, and Henry Patterson, *Northern Ireland 1921–2001: Political Forces and Social Classes* (London: Serif, 2002); Graham Walker, *A History of the Ulster Unionist Party: Protest, Pragmatism, Pessimism* (Manchester, UK: Manchester University Press, 2004), for example, pp. 67, 101. On the two Irish states, see David Fitzpatrick, *The Two Irelands 1912–1939* (Oxford, UK: Oxford University Press, 1998).

22. See the study of Belfast Protestant church-goers and their varied reasons for resisting Irish unity in Frederick W. Boal, Margaret C. Keane, and David N. Livingstone, *Them and Us? Attitudinal Variation among Churchgoers in Belfast* (Belfast: Institute for Irish Studies, Queen's University Belfast, 1997), pp. 89–90.

23. Joseph Ruane and Jennifer Todd, "'Why Can't You Get Along with Each Other?': Structure, Culture and the Northern Ireland Conflict," in Eamonn Hughes (ed.), *Culture and Politics in Northern Ireland* (Milton Keynes, UK: Open University Press, 1991), pp. 27–43.

24. Walker, *History*, records only a few cases of dissent, and the predominant inertia even of those with liberal convictions in the face of sectarian practices (for example, pp. 117, 121).

25. David McKittrick, Seamus Kelters, Brian Feeney, Chris Thornton, and David McVea, *Lost Lives: The Stories of the Men and Women who Died as a Result of the Northern Ireland Troubles* (London: Mainstream, 2004).

26. The IRA continued as a small group of "professional rebels" opposed to Northern Ireland's existence from the 1920s through the 1960s. What was different in the recent phase of conflict, and what made it so polarizing, was the implicit and explicit support from large sections of the Catholic community, and the wider understanding of republican motivation even among nationalists who opposed violence. See Joseph Ruane, "Contemporary Republicanism and the Strategy of Armed Struggle," in Maurice J. Bric and John Coakley (eds.), *From Political Violence to Negotiated Settlement* (Dublin: University College Dublin Press, 2004), pp. 115–32.

27. Of course the formal indicators of Protestant rule were finally eliminated in 1972 with the abolition of Stormont and the institution of direct British rule. But deep structural inequality remained up until the 1990s in the economy, the makeup of the security forces and civil service, the marks of cultural capital, the publicly acceptable political positions, and the public culture; see Ruane and Todd, *Dynamics*, pp. 116–203.

28. For discussion of the multiple differences and oppositions, see Denis P. Barritt and Charles F. Carter, *The Northern Ireland Problem: A Study in Group Relations* (London: Oxford University Press, 1962); John Whyte, *Interpreting Northern Ireland* (Oxford, UK: Clarendon Press, 1991); Rosemary Harris, *Prejudice and Tolerance in Ulster: A Study of Neighbours and "Strangers" in a Border Community* (Manchester, UK: Manchester University Press, 1972).

29. J. H. Whyte, "How Much Discrimination Was There under the Unionist Regime?," in Tom Gallagher and James O'Connell (eds.), *Contemporary Irish Studies* (Manchester, UK: Manchester University Press, 1983), pp. 1–35.

30. Buckland, *The Factory of Grievances*, pp. 16–18; Paul Bew, Peter Gibbon, and Henry Patterson, *The State in Northern Ireland 1921–1994: Political Forces and Social Classes* (London: Serif, 1995), pp. 55–80.

31. Eamon Phoenix, *Northern Nationalism: Nationalist Politics, Partition and the Catholic Minority in Northern Ireland 1890–1940* (Belfast: Ulster Historical Foundation, 1994), pp. 252–362.

32. Whyte, *Interpreting Northern Ireland*, pp. 26–51, 67–93; Ruane and Todd, *Dynamics*, pp. 54–78. On nationalist factionalism, see Michael Farrell, *Northern Ireland: The Orange State* (London: Pluto, 1980).

33. Whyte, *Interpreting Northern Ireland*, pp. 77–9.

34. Whyte, *Interpreting Northern Ireland*, pp. 77–9; Marc Mulholland, *Northern Ireland at the Crossroads: Ulster Unionism in the O'Neill years 1960–9* (Basingstoke, UK: Macmillan, 2000), pp. 1–7.

35. This was true even within the seemingly traditionalist Orange Order, as shown by Eric Kaufmann, *The Orange Order: A Contemporary Northern Irish History* (Oxford, UK: Oxford University Press, 2007), pp. 21–80.

36. Mulholland, *Northern Ireland*, pp. 1–11.

37. Frank Burton, *The Politics of Legitimacy: Struggles in a Belfast Community* (London: Routledge, Kegan Paul, 1978).

38. Peter J. McLoughlin, "'. . .it's a United Ireland or Nothing?' John Hume and the Idea of Irish Unity, 1964–72," *Irish Political Studies*, Vol. 21, No. 2 (2006), pp. 157–80.

39. Burton, pp. 68–128.

40. For discussions of the divisions, see Arthur Aughey, *Under Siege: Ulster Unionism and the Anglo-Irish Agreement* (Belfast: Blackstaff, 1989); Feargal Cochrane, *Unionist Politics and the Politics of Unionism since the Anglo-Irish Agreement* (Cork: Cork University Press, 1997); Henry Patterson and Eric Kaufmann, *Unionism and Orangeism in Northern Ireland since 1945: The Decline of the Loyal Family* (Manchester, UK: Manchester University Press, 2007); Christopher Farrington, *Ulster Unionism and the Peace Process in Northern Ireland* (Houndsmills, UK: Palgrave Macmillan, 2006).

41. Christopher Farrington, "Ulster Unionism and the Northern Irish Peace Process," *British Journal of Politics and International Relations,* Vol. 8, No. 2 (2006), pp. 277–94.

42. For a discussion of the reform process, see Bob Osborne and Ian Shuttleworth (eds.), *Fair Employment in Northern Ireland: A Generation On* (Belfast: Blackstaff, 2004).

43. New Ireland Forum, *Report* (Dublin: Stationery Office, 1984).

44. For discussion as to when exactly this was recognized and by whom, see Richard English, *Armed Struggle: A History of the IRA* (London: Macmillan, 2003), pp. 303–16; Ed Moloney, *A Secret History of the IRA* (London: Allen Lane, The Penguin Press, 2002), pp. 3–33.

45. For detailed discussion of the institutional provisions, see John McGarry and Brendan O'Leary, *The Northern Ireland Conflict: Consociational Engagements* (Oxford, UK: Oxford University Press, 2004), pp. 260–93.

46. John Coakley, "The North-South Relationship: Implementing the Agreement," in John Coakley, Brigid Laffan, and Jennifer Todd (eds.), *Renovation or Revolution: New Territorial Politics in Ireland and the United Kingdom* (Dublin: University College Dublin Press, 2005), pp. 110–31.

47. On the equality measures and their effects, see Osborne and Shuttleworth, *Fair Employment in Northern Ireland*, pp. 1–23.

48. Agreement reached in the Multi-Party Negotiations (1998), *Policing and Justice*, para. 1.

49. Independent Commission on Policing for Northern Ireland, *A New Beginning: Policing in Northern Ireland* (London: HMSO, 1999); Dean Godson, *Himself Alone: David Trimble and the Ordeal of Unionism* (London: Harper Collins, 2004), pp. 472–9; Aogán Mulcahy, *Policing Ireland: Conflict, Legitimacy and Reform* (Devon, UK: Willan, 2006).

50. Agreement reached in the Multi-Party Negotiations (1998), *Decommissioning*, para. 3.

51. Some crises were provoked by IRA slowness to decommission, some by the march of reform (particularly reform of policing), and some by actual and alleged continuing IRA activity.

52. Paul Mitchell, Brendan O'Leary, and Geoffrey Evans, "Northern Ireland: Flanking Extremists Bite the Moderates and Emerge in Their Clothes," *Parliamentary Affairs*, Vol. 54, No. 4 (2001), pp. 725–43; Gladys Ganiel and Paul Dixon, "Religion, Pragmatic Fundamentalism and the Transformation of the Northern Ireland Conflict," *Journal of Peace Research*, Vol. 45, No. 3 (2008), pp. 419–36.

53. Paddy Hillyard, Demi Patsios, and Fiona Semillon, "A Daughter to ELSI—NILSI: A Northern Ireland Standard of Living Index or Problematising Wealth in the Analysis of Inequality and Material Well-being," *Social Policy and Society*, Vol. 6, No. 1 (2007), pp. 81–98.

54. Paul Mitchell, Geoffrey Evans, and Brendan O'Leary, "Extremist Outbidding in Ethnic Party Systems Is not Inevitable: Tribune Parties in Northern Ireland," *Political Studies,* Vol. 57, No. 2 (2009), pp. 397–421; Joanne Hughes, "Attitudes towards Equality in Northern Ireland: Evidence of Progress?," in Osborne and Shuttleworth, *Fair Employment*, pp. 166–83.

55. Neil Jarman, *No Longer a Problem? Sectarian Violence in Northern Ireland* (Belfast: Institute for Conflict Research, 2005).

56. For the former view, see Jennifer Todd, Theresa O'Keefe, Nathalie Rougier, and Lorenzo Cañás Bottos, "Does Being Protestant Matter? Protestants, Minorities and the Remaking of Ethno-Religious Identity in Ireland," *National Identities*, Vol. 11, No. 1 (2009), pp. 87–99; Gladys Ganiel, *Evangelicalism and Conflict in Northern Ireland* (New York: Palgrave, 2008); Claire Mitchell, "Protestant Identification and Political Change in Northern Ireland," *Ethnic and Racial Studies*, Vol. 26, No. 4 (2003), pp. 612–31;

Claire Mitchell and Jennifer Todd, "Between the Devil and the Deep Blue Sea: Nationality, Power and Symbolic Trade-Offs among Evangelical Protestants in Northern Ireland," *Nations and Nationalism*, Vol. 13, No. 4 (2007), pp. 637–55. For the latter view, see Peter Shirlow and Brendan Murtagh, *Belfast: Segregation, Violence and the City* (London: Pluto, 2006).

57. John M. [Jack] Lynch, "The Anglo-Irish Problem," *Foreign Affairs,* Vol. 50, No. 4 (1972), pp. 601–17, pointed out (in an article reportedly written by one Department of Foreign Affairs civil servant and "toughened up" by his superior) that there could be no "internal" solution to Northern Ireland, an argument developed in the New Ireland Forum *Report* (1984).

58. On the divisions among the state elite in the 1980s, see Bew, Gibbon, and Patterson, *The State in Northern Ireland*, pp. 204–14.

59. Some had consistently put the Northern Irish conflict in long-term British-Irish perspective; see, for example, Sir David Goodall, "Hillsborough to Belfast: Is It the Final Lap?," in Marianne Elliott (ed.), *The Long Road to Peace in Northern Ireland* (Liverpool, UK: Liverpool University Press, 2002), pp. 120–28.

60. Farrington, "Ulster Unionism," pp. 277–94.

61. For an argument that these factors explain the successive crises of the Agreement, see Joseph Ruane and Jennifer Todd, "The Politics of Transition: Explaining the Crises in the Implementation of the Belfast Agreement," *Political Studies*, Vol. 49, No. 5 (2001), pp. 923–40.

5

Bosnia: Dayton is Dead! Long Live Dayton!

ROBERTO BELLONI
University of Trento

The process of implementation of the Dayton Peace Agreement in Bosnia has come to a halt. Particularly since 2006, nationalist rhetoric has increased, political, economic, and social reforms have stalled, and some analysts warn that the country might be sliding towards collapse. This article traces the roots of the current crisis in the 2006 failed constitutional reform attempt, which has high-lighted the precarious state of the Bosnian political situation and, more broadly, in the limited impact of the international community's illiberal, top-down strategies employed in the country since almost the beginning of the peace process. It concludes by suggesting the need for a new approach, led by the European Union, and aimed at reviving the domestic political process.

INTRODUCTION

From roughly 2006 onwards, the Republic of Bosnia and Herzegovina (here-after Bosnia) has suffered from a deep political crisis. The constitutional edifice devised at Dayton, Ohio, in November 1995, which ended a bloody three-and-a-half year war, has come increasingly under pressure. Not only have Croats been forcefully complaining about an institutional structure that, in their view, marginalizes them, but both Bosniaks and Serbs have hardened their positions. Prominent Bosniak politicians have loudly denounced the ex-istence of the semi-independent Serb Republic, which they consider to be an illegitimate entity carved out using ethnic cleansing, and asked for its aboli-tion. By contrast, the Serb leadership has reaffirmed the Serb Republic's right to exist, enshrined in the Dayton Peace Agreement, and has threatened to hold a referendum on independence. In this context, "the international com-munity," a hodgepodge of international organizations and bilateral donors led by the Office of the High Representative, has responded weakly to the challenge. After more than a decade of international intervention, and with other trouble areas needing attention, the political will to remain engaged has been slowly waning. The 11 September 2001 attacks on the United States have further contributed to a shift in the international community's attention towards other frontiers of conflict, most notably Iraq and Afghanistan. More recently the West, distracted by a global financial crisis, has been giving even more of an impression of indecisiveness and a lack of strategy.

As a result, many analysts and some diplomats fear that Bosnia is in danger of collapsing in on itself, with the international community possibly unable to deal with the challenge. For Richard Holbrooke, the senior American diplomat who was the main architect of the Dayton Peace Agreement, and Paddy Ashdown, who served as High Representative in Bosnia from 2002 to 2006, "the country is in real danger of collapse."[1] According to Patrice McMahon and Jon Western, "[t]he country now stands on the brink of collapse. For the first time since November 1995 ... Bosnians are once again talking about the potential for war."[2] Similarly, a report published by an international think tank, the Democratization Policy Council, warned that Bosnia is "sliding toward the precipice," arguing that "international listlessness has permitted Bosnian politicians to believe they can pursue wartime objectives without challenge."[3] Many further examples of similarly apocalyptic analysis could be cited, all converging on the point that never since the Dayton Agreement of November 1995 has Bosnia faced such a great challenge to its existence. If armed conflict flares up again, the international capacity to stop it might be insufficient, given the current military presence in the country. The European Force (EUFOR), a weak European Union-led mission that replaced the NATO-led Stabilization Force, currently maintains fewer than 2,000 soldiers, and even this small number might soon be reduced to a 200-person training force.

This article assesses the current political stalemate. It traces the genesis of the Bosnian political problem, placing it within the context of the contested nature of the Bosnian state. Second, it identifies the main groups' preferred long-term institutional arrangement and shows how the 1995 Dayton Peace Agreement represented an acceptable compromise among mutually incompatible goals. The main part of the paper addresses the reasons for the recent escalation in political tensions in the country. Following the 2006 failed attempt at constitutional reform, the main political parties have increased their uncompromising rhetoric. Yet, although the situation has certainly deteriorated, fears of renewed fighting seem overstated—at least for the time being. Overall, the crisis in Bosnian politics is a reflection of the failure of the internationally led liberal peacebuilding project. As in other countries where post-Cold War peace operations have been deployed, Bosnia has been subjected to extensive liberal reforms in the political and economic spheres. However, rather than favoring domestic reconciliation and the development of locally flavored political institutions, international assertiveness in the country has reified domestic divisions and perpetuated the existing political hierarchies at the local and national level. The paper concludes with a brief assessment of the European Union's potential for steering Bosnia towards European integration. The EU has the potential to advance a new, less intrusive phase of international intervention, one in which local actors can assume greater responsibilities in the management of Bosnian affairs.

GENESIS OF THE PROBLEM

Throughout the post-Second World War period, Bosnia was part of the Yugoslav Federation. Yugoslavia was reconstituted in 1945 as a political solution to the problem of providing a home to a multitude of south Slav peoples. The new federation was made up of six republics—Slovenia, Croatia, Bosnia, Montenegro, Macedonia, and Serbia. In each republic, a national group possessed a hegemonic status, with the exception of Bosnia, with its mixed population. According to the 1991 census, no group in Bosnia had a numerical majority, with the Muslims (who adopted the religiously neutral term of "Bosniaks" in 1993) constituting a relative majority of 44%, the Serbs 31%, and the Croats 17%. Self-identified Yugoslavs made up 5.5% of the population, and "others" the remaining 2.5%. Despite occasional tensions, these groups coexisted in relative peace for long periods.[4]

The events that led to the war in Bosnia and subsequent Dayton Peace Agreement can only be mentioned in summary here.[5] The beginning of the process of Yugoslav dissolution posed Bosnia's leaders with a dilemma and strained relationships between its main national groups. The northern republics of Slovenia and Croatia declared independence in June 1991, thus ending the existence of post-Second World War Yugoslavia. Bosnia could choose between either remaining in a rump Yugoslavia dominated by Serbia, or attempting to gain independence, hoping that the international community would both recognize the creation of another new state and intervene militarily to defend it in case of external aggression. The presence of Slobodan Milosević at the helm of what was left of the Yugoslav federation accentuated fears among the Bosnian political elite of subordination to Serbian influence. In the second half of the 1980s, Milosević had begun playing the ethnic card to demobilize his internal political opponents and to propose himself as champion of the Serb national cause anywhere Serbs lived.[6] Milosević's nationalist rhetoric and aggressive policies in Croatia, where he launched a full-scale war following that country's declaration of independence in 1991, convinced Bosnian elites that coexistence with Serbia would be impossible.

Bosnia's declaration of sovereignty was followed by a referendum on independence in February 1992. The referendum achieved a voter turnout of 64%, with 98% of votes cast in favor of independence, but was boycotted *en masse* by the Serb population. Full-scale hostilities started in April, when Bosnian Serbs, supported by Milosević, tried to partition the republic along ethnic lines, to join Serbia, and thus to form a "Greater Serbia." Bosniak-dominated government forces fought to defend and preserve Bosnia with the same borders it had enjoyed when it was part of Yugoslavia. In response, Bosnian Croats, with the support of the Croatian nationalist government in Zagreb, launched their own land grab in April 1993. Under heavy American pressure, in March 1994 Bosniaks and Croats signed an agreement creating a joint federation. The Serbs were eventually forced to negotiate a settlement by extensive NATO bombing and Bosniak-Croat advances in Northwest Bosnia.

This brief outline of Bosnia's descent into war reveals the heart of the country's political problems. It is the nature and very existence of the Bosnian state that has been in question since the process of Yugoslav dissolution began. Profound differences about the territorial boundaries of the political community and the rights of citizenship divide the three main national groups. Bosniaks fought to preserve and consolidate the state as their best avenue to political and national survival. Although sections of the Bosniak leadership have, at times, flirted with the possibility of partitioning the country to create a small Bosniak state, they are generally in favor of maintaining the country in its internationally recognized borders. By contrast, both Croats and Serbs fear a Bosniak-dominated government in Sarajevo. The Bosniaks' relative majority in the country, they warn, could lead to the imposition of Bosniak political, cultural, and religious views on the rest of the population. Instead, both Croats and Serbs prefer extensive local autonomy and close links with Croatia and Serbia, respectively. These different views have given rise to a "stateness" problem: "the more the population of the territory of the state is comprised of plurinational, lingual, religious, or cultural societies, the more complex politics becomes because an agreement on the fundamentals of a democracy will be more difficult."[7] In late 1995, the international community, led by the American administration, imposed such an agreement—to which I now briefly turn.

THE PEACE SETTLEMENT AND ITS LIMITS

In November 1995, the Dayton Agreement concluded three-and-a-half years of war. The agreement attempted to strike a balance between the main groups' preferred institutional options. Bosnia was maintained as an independent state, with a multiethnic and democratic government with limited functions in foreign, economic, and fiscal policy. Internally the country was divided between two entities with extended sovereign prerogatives: a Croat-Bosniak Federation (called the Federation of Bosnia and Herzegovina, a designation that scarcely helps to distinguish it from the bigger Republic of Bosnia and Herzegovina of which it is a part), covering 51% of the territory, and a Serb-led *Republika Srpska* (Serb Republic), covering the remaining 49%. The federation was further divided into ten cantons, each with its own constitution, an assembly directly elected by federation voters, a prime minister, and ministries. Each entity was allowed to establish special relations with neighboring Croatia and Serbia.[8] A NATO-led peacekeeping force of 60,000 troops was mandated to prevent hostilities and to monitor the military aspects of the agreement. The Office of the High Representative (OHR) was established to monitor the implementation of the civilian aspects of the settlement; the High Representative was to be appointed in accordance with provisions drawn up by the UN Security Council. Over time, the OHR acquired increasing legislative and political powers, most notably the authority to remove local elected officials.

The Dayton Agreement has been described as a "classical example of consociational settlement," since it requires political elites to share power, in addition to prescribing proportionality in government and guaranteeing mutual veto rights and communal autonomy.[9] It created a complex institutional structure, composed of one state, two entities, three peoples, an estimated 3.9 million citizens, and five layers of governance led by 14 prime ministers and governments, making Bosnia the state with the highest number of presidents, prime ministers, and ministers per capita in the entire world. Even taking into account the very real constraints of negotiating a peace settlement in the course of bloody, ongoing war, which prevented the assessment of the long-term implications of the peace deal, it is hard to disagree with the judgment that the agreement's midwives created a "Frankenstein constitution."[10]

This institutional monster, however, succeeded in transferring the conflict from the military to the political realm, and in reestablishing much-needed conditions for civil coexistence. Since the agreement was signed, more than a million people (out of about 2.2 million displaced by the war) were able to return home, many of them in areas under the control of another ethnic group. The state has been considerably strengthened. To the original three central ministries, six more were added over time, including the Ministry for European Integration, the Ministry for Human Rights and Refugees, the Ministry of the Treasury, the Ministry of Justice, the Ministry of Defence, and the Ministry of Communication and Transportation. Many indicted war criminals have been arrested and tried. The process of reconstruction is widely considered as successful. Sarajevo's construction industry is booming—particularly in the Serb-dominated part of the town known as Eastern Sarajevo. Over the last few years, the Bosnian economy has grown at a healthy 6%–7% a year. Last, and perhaps more importantly, Bosnia has begun her first steps towards membership in the EU. In June 2008, Bosnia signed a Stabilisation and Association Agreement with the EU—a remarkable achievement in light of the state of the country at the end of the war in 1995.

Yet the process of implementation of the Dayton Agreement has drawn attention to two major problems, both of which have deepened after 2006 and have led to the apocalyptic assessments mentioned above.[11] First, consociational institutions are frequently in a state of deadlock. Nationalist elites maintain zero-sum views of each other. Reversing Clausewitz, politics in Bosnia is the continuation of war by other means. The consociational system, while necessary in 1995 to convince the fighting parties to lay down their weapons, has created conditions for a centrifugal competition that severely limits interethnic compromise in the post-Dayton period. Politicians are elected into office as representatives of their respective ethnic groups and have no incentive to make any cross-ethnic appeals. Without incentives for cooperation, they can win popularity by defending their national group and by portraying the others as enemies. Under these conditions, effective governance is very difficult to achieve.

Second, the entire institutional system is based on ethnicity, which is precisely what divides the Bosnian peoples. The Dayton Agreement recognizes the three main ethnic groups as "constituent peoples," makes political representation dependent upon ethnic belonging and thus discriminates against individuals who do not identify themselves ethnically or, even if they do, might not be able to exercise a variety of rights because they reside in an area where they constitute a minority. Instead of creating conditions for softening ethnic identities, the agreement entrenches them by making ethnicity integral to constitutional design. Unsurprisingly, civil society remains fragmented and alternative non-nationalist projects find difficulty in establishing themselves. Frustrated by years of deadlock, nationalist corruption and international rule by decree, citizens expect little from the political process and rarely mobilize to place demands on politicians.

THE FAILURE OF CONSTITUTIONAL REFORM

The limits of the constitutional structure established at Dayton forced the issue of reform onto the agenda from almost the beginning of the peace process. Local politicians' views of the agreement changed slightly over the course of more than a decade of peace implementation, reflecting the ups and downs of the peace process and changing electoral fortunes but, since Dayton was an effective compromise, nobody's interests were ever satisfied fully. Currently, few political leaders in Bosnia are wholeheartedly committed to the Dayton Agreement, with the exception of the Bosnian Serbs, who obtained most from the peace settlement, and thus remain in favor of the status quo. The agreement recognized Serbs' military gains by granting them territory they had conquered during the war through extensive ethnic cleansing of the non-Serb population. In addition, it recognized the Serbs' right to govern their entity without external interference on crucial issues ranging from the privatization of state companies to policing and education.

The Bosniaks have frequently condemned the existence of the Serb Republic, which they consider as an entity created through genocidal policies, and have called for its abolition in favor of a stronger, unified government in Sarajevo. The Bosnian Croats also have deep grievances. Unlike the Serbs, Bosnian Croats do not have a territorial unit they can govern autonomously. Moreover, within the Bosniak-Croat Federation they are outnumbered (and often outvoted) by the numerically stronger Bosniaks. Even in Mostar, the most populous and politically significant city with a numerical majority of Croats, they are unable to secure a political majority in the city council. The city statute, imposed in 2004 by the OHR, limits the ethnic majority to a minority of council seats.[12] Bosnian Croats have reacted by demanding the creation of a territorial unit with a Croat plurality (a sort of Croat version of the Serb Republic), a request they voiced for the first time in 2001. The Bosnian Croats' demographic decline has further contributed to this group's fears of being outnumbered. Since no census has been carried out in postwar Bosnia, numbers are necessarily speculative, but most estimates agree on a drop from about 820,000 Croats living in Bosnia before the war to less than 500,000 today.[13]

Thus, both Bosniaks and Bosnian Croats are in favor of constitutional reform—although they disagree on the exact shape such reform should take.[14] It is an irony of Bosnia's political life that the major attempt so far at reforming the constitution ultimately failed because of the opposition of certain Bosniak and Croat political parties. In 2006, eight major political parties, prodded by American involvement, tentatively agreed on a number of reforms.[15] The most important changes involved the strengthening of the Council of Ministers and the creation of two new state ministries, one for agricultural policy and one for science, technology, and the environment. The entities would retain their place in the constitution, but the Council of Ministers would be allowed to negotiate, to adopt, and to implement all measures necessary for compliance requirements set out in the process of European integration. This package of constitutional reforms was discussed by the Bosnian Parliament in April 2006 but narrowly failed to reach the two-thirds majority necessary for its adoption. Most "no" votes came from the Bosniak-dominated Party for Bosnia, which argued that the reform package would consolidate the existence of the Serb Republic. The other negative votes were cast by a small Croat party demanding the creation of a third (Croat) entity. For both parties, the decision to turn down the reform package was motivated both by principled reasons and by electoral posturing in the run-up to the October 2006 elections.

The failure of the constitutional reform package highlights two major shortcomings of the liberal peacebuilding framework. First, as often noted,[16] the election process exposes and accentuates the existing political divisions. Political parties are tempted to increase the nationalist rhetoric to improve their electoral chances by denouncing any interethnic compromise as a "sell-out." In Bosnia, this dynamic has been very visible since the beginning of the peace process, as Bosnians have been frequently called to the polls for elections at the national, entity, cantonal, and municipal levels. In April 2006, when the reform package was under discussion, the electoral cycle was in full swing, contributing making compromises among political parties unappealing and the timing of the reforms less than ideal.[17] Moreover, it is likely that some parties, especially the Party for Bosnia, decided to maintain their maximalist position, hoping that the international community would in the future intervene to impose a solution more favorable to their views. The frequent use throughout the Bosnian peace process of illiberal means, particularly the "Bonn powers," lent credit to this belief. Second, the heavily securitized and institutionally oriented liberal peacebuilding approach has done little to favor citizens' engagement. The constitutional reform package was initially developed in secret, as international officials did not trust Bosnian citizens to be politically mature enough to consider the advantages and disadvantages of the proposed reforms. As a result, misinformation about the issues under discussion was extensive, no sense of ownership among the general public was ever created, and, not surprisingly, no vocal reaction was heard when the parliament rejected the package.

THE INTERNATIONAL MISSION

In the absence of a compromise among the major local political parties, for a great deal of the post-Dayton period the Office of the High Representative has played a key role in pushing through much-needed political and economic reforms. In late 1997, the High Representative was granted the so-called "Bonn powers," whereby he could take actions against persons "in violation of the legal commitments made under the Peace Agreement or the terms of its implementation."[18] Successive High Representatives have used these powers more than 800 times, probably overstepping the original intention of ensuring the functionality of the Council of Ministers. The High Representative and his office have sacked elected politicians and imposed laws, thus transforming the international mission from one of providing assistance to the local parties into an undeclared protectorate. Political accountability was effectively detached from policy making, as international officials could impose policy on Bosnian citizens but were neither accountable to them nor responsible for the consequences of their decisions.[19]

Political and Constitutional Issues

The attempt to create a liberal democracy through illiberal means produced several short-term successes. Most notably, the creation of a common currency set the foundation for stronger economic growth, the design of a car plate not revealing the town of origin (and probable ethnic identity of the driver) greatly improved freedom of movement, and the imposition of a set of property laws proved indispensible in favoring the process of property repossession and the postwar return home of refugees and displaced persons. While initially not widely accepted, changes imposed by the High Representative have become part of the everyday life of Bosnian citizens.[20]

Yet, at the same time, liberal assertiveness came with considerable costs. Although useful in the short term, the High Representative's decisions reduced the local parties' incentives to reach political compromise. Liberal interventionism has allowed Bosnian politicians to free ride on international initiatives. Politicians could raise unrealistic expectations among their constituencies in order to gain popular support, knowing that decisions that could bankrupt domestic institutions would be overturned. Moreover, they could maintain an intransigent attitude, aware that the political costs of compromise would be assumed by the High Representative.[21] On occasion, as with the "Prud Agreement" (see below), Bosnian leaders have reached a compromise on issues of interest to the international community but dragged their feet on the implementation process. Overall, international activism has contributed blocking the domestic political process by making Bosnians' mutual intransigence less costly, while creating an impression of progress.[22]

Moreover, the top-down imposition of policies in the name of short-term efficiency has been compounded by a lack of attention to local knowledge, talents, and aspirations.[23] Liberal peacebuilders have dedicated much time and effort to developing Bosnian civil society, but their attention has focused squarely on those individuals and groups that conform, or appear to conform, to the Western view of nongovernmental actors. Spurred by the availability of funding, thousands of nongovernmental organizations (NGOs) have arisen to implement changing international priorities. Since 2000, when international support began to be scaled back, most of these organizations have disappeared, leaving in their wake the same social vacuum that, according to international officials, motivated their establishment.[24] At the same time, throughout the peace process any local variation of society not in conformity with the broader precepts of the liberal peace was ignored. This tendency to remove local voices from involvement in the peace process has prevented domestic actors from taking ownership of their political, economic, and social development and from trying to shape existing structures. Unsurprisingly, each assertive intrusion of international peacebuilders into Bosnian affairs has raised questions about the sustainability of an intervention model that turns Bosnians into objects of international initiatives instead of agents with legitimate views and aspirations.

These limits of liberal peacebuilding have been most clearly exposed from 2006 onwards. Christian Schwarz-Schilling, a veteran German politician, became the fifth High Representative in February 2006. While he maintained the same prerogatives granted to his predecessors, he refused to use his

powers to impose legislation on the Bosnian Parliament. After a decade of
international interventionism, the Peace Implementation Council (PIC), an
international body composed of 55 representatives of the international community and tasked with appointing the High Representative and providing
him with strategic direction, judged that the time for transition to local ownership was ripe.[25] This assessment was due as much to an evaluation of
the progress Bosnia had made since the signing of the Dayton Agreement
as to the declining interest among those involved in international intervention. However, throughout Schwarz-Schilling's tenure little progress towards
state-building and European integration was achieved. The reasons for this
setback cannot be conclusively ascertained.[26] Bosnian and international observers in favor of strong, illiberal intervention privilege an explanation that
reveals lack of trust of Bosnian leaders and a preference for continuing
international supervision. However, equally and perhaps even more plausible is the suggestion that some of the failures were due to a delayed
backlash against the interventionist policies during the mandate of Paddy
Ashdown, Schwarz-Schilling's predecessor (2002–06).[27] From the point of
view of Bosnian political actors, the frequent use of illiberal means prior to
Schwarz-Schilling's appointment could be interpreted as a willingness to use
similar means in the future—should the domestic situation reach a dangerously unstable point. Be that as it may, a new High Representative, Miroslav
Lajcak, replaced Schwarz-Schilling in June 2007 and attempted, though unsuccessfully, to set the reform process on a new course.

The Police Reform Impasse

A confrontation between the High Representative and the Serb Republic
over police reform has effectively eroded the little influence the international community could count on. The controversy began in February 2005,
when the European Commission endorsed the recommendations put forward
by the OHR-established Police Restructuring Commission, requiring Bosnia
to reform its police force in order to conclude a stabilization and association agreement.[28] Bosnia was asked to meet three criteria: all budgetary and
legislative policy making on police matters should be transferred to state-
level institutions; police districts should be drawn on technical, not political
grounds, thus allowing police units to cross the interentity line according to
necessity; and policing should be free from political interference. When Lajcak took on his post as new High Representative, police reform represented
the main stumbling block on Bosnia's road to the EU, and he made it his
priority. The new Bosnian Serb Prime Minister, Milorad Dodik, who came to
power in 2006 as a result of a realignment in politics in the Serb Republic
following the failed constitutional reform and continuing disagreement over
police restructuring, blocked the attempt to transform the separate entities'

police forces into one national force. Lajcak reacted by using his sweeping powers to change the voting procedures and to make it more difficult for the entities to block decision making at the national level. The changes were immediately interpreted by politicians in Banja Luka, capital of the Serb Republic, as an unacceptable attack on the autonomy and integrity of their entity.[29] Dodik temporarily withdrew Serb ministers from the Council of Ministers and threatened to quit his job.[30] Russia openly sided with the Serb Republic and encouraged the Bosnian Serbs in their intransigence.[31]

The Peace Implementation Council and its member states did not give the High Representative the kind of support he would have needed to overcome Bosnian Serb resistance. Because the height of the confrontation occurred in 2007–08, when most diplomatic attention was focused on settling the problem of Kosovo's final status, few had any interest in pushing confrontation with the Serb Republic authorities and risking political instability. Moreover, the EU never fully identified with the police reform pursued by the High Representative. As a result, Lajcak accepted a weak compromise. Fearing a complete loss of influence, the EU followed suit and decided to sign a stabilization and association agreement with Bosnia in June 2008—despite Bosnia's apparent failure to meet the required conditions. Although the international community presented the agreement on police reform as a reasonable middle ground between two hard-to-reconcile positions, in reality the Serb Republic succeeded in forcing on international actors the acceptance of one major point: no cross-entity police regions were established. Having backtracked from his principled decisions and having failed to secure political support from the Peace Implementation Council, the High Representative's executive powers, already weakened by Schwarz-Schilling's timid approach during his tenure, have been eroded further and are unlikely to be revived. As Lajcak blatantly put it, politically the international community in Bosnia is a "dead horse."[32] This erosion of international influence, and in particular that of the OHR, is alarming to those international officials who have been accustomed to rely on short-term, top-down measures to push the peace process forward, but at the same time it could represent an opportunity to open a new phase of international engagement in the country, as argued below.

THE PURSUIT OF A POSTSETTLEMENT SETTLEMENT

The decline of international influence in Bosnia coincides with an awareness of the need for improving the functionality of domestic institutions. Most domestic and international actors acknowledge that the structure created at Dayton demands reform. As it stands, Bosnia does not possess many of the capacities to implement what is required in order to join the EU—a goal shared by Bosnian citizens and the political class alike. The lack of a

Ministry of Agriculture is perhaps the most visible shortcoming of the current form of the Bosnian state, negatively affecting both farmers' livelihood and more broadly Bosnia's political prospects. Without a food certification process, which within EU states is normally conducted by the Ministry of Agriculture, Bosnian farmers cannot export their products anywhere into the European Union. Furthermore, given the centrality of agricultural issues within European politics, it is unlikely that the EU will ever grant Bosnia a fast-track association process without major reforms in this policy area. Paradoxically, while a much-needed Ministry of Agriculture is missing, the Bosnian state spends huge resources to preserve a far-from-indispensible bureaucratic giant. About 56% of the state budget is allocated to finance the various administrative units, from the national to the local level, and even this amount of resources often fails to meet Bosnian citizens' needs.

Positive prospects for reform suddenly materialized in late 2008. On 8 November, the leaders of the three main political parties, each representing one of the three main groups, reached the Prud Agreement, named after the village in northern Bosnia were it was concluded. The agreement, which was defined by its signatories as a "historic compromise" and took most observers by surprise, addressed a number of issues aimed, above all, at strengthening the state in order to make it more efficient and capable of meeting the criteria for joining the EU.[33] As for constitutional reform, the agreement recognized the need to change the structure of the state and identified the creation of "four units" between the central state and the municipal level as a way to simplify the current institutional structure. Although the agreement created hopeful expectations among international officials that a viable domestically led process of constitutional reform was finally under way, it soon appeared to be another instance of a step taken by local actors to appease international pressure.[34] The parties maintained different views about what the "four units" should consist of. Each side preserved its preferred solution: the Serbs considered the Serb Republic one of the units, the Croats saw the agreement as a way to carve out a Croat-dominated entity, while the Bosniaks hoped to redraw the political map to cut across existing ethnic lines.[35]

Not surprisingly, in early 2009 the talks broke down. Sulejman Tihić, leader of the (Bosniak) Party of Democratic Action, was heavily criticized from within his own community for compromising with former enemies. Bosniaks were split between those, such as Tihić, who are willing to recognize that the Serb Republic is there to stay, and those, such as Haris Silajdžić and his Party for Bosnia, who are committed to an ethnically blind "state of the citizens." Despite these differences, Bosniaks are united in lobbying the OHR and Western diplomats to impose those constitutional changes they cannot achieve in the process of negotiation with the other ethnic groups. Bosnian Croats are also internally divided. Croats in central Bosnia live in relative harmony with the Bosniak majority, while those in Herzegovina share political and economic links with neighboring Croatia and are aggrieved by the impossibility of running local institutions autonomously. In general Croats, while benefiting from a third of power at the state level with a population of less than a fifth, would consider favorably an institutional restructuring granting them more exclusive power at the local level.

Bosnian Serbs represent the most determined supporters of the status quo. They remain in favor of maintaining and possibly strengthening the existence of their semi-independent republic. Their Prime Minister, Milorad Dodik, has repeatedly called for a halt to the transfer of responsibilities from the entities to the state. In spring 2009 the National Assembly of the Serb Republic issued a declaration containing a list of 68 powers that the Bosnian state had "stolen" from the Serb Republic, including control of the judiciary, the power to collect customs duties, and management of foreign trade.[36] Occasionally, in particular following the independence of Montenegro in 2006 and that of Kosovo in early 2008, Bosnian Serbs have also threatened to hold their own referendum on independence.[37] According to international analysts in the country, Dodik, who has been under investigation for corruption, might be tempted to call for such a referendum to deflect attention from his own judicial problems.[38] If held, the referendum would trigger a reaction from the Bosniaks, who would probably fight a new war to prevent the dismemberment of the country, as they did during the 1992–95 period. Militarily a war could be made possible by the structure of the Bosnian Army. Although currently counting only about 10,000 troops and operating under a unified command and with a single defense budget since January 2006, the Army still maintains nine ethnically based infantry battalions.

As mentioned at the beginning of this article, some policy makers and international analysts fear that these mutually incompatible political views are pushing the country dangerously backwards. However, these fears might be overstated. Although the political climate has clearly deteriorated, this could also represent a sign of progress of a kind. As most Bosnian leaders privately recognize in their dealings with international officials, the Dayton constitution needs revisions to make local institutions more functional and rational.[39] Local leaders' maximalist views could be an expression of the inevitability of reform as much as of the intransigence of local politicians. For example, Serbs' threat to hold a referendum is not based on a realistic assessment of the likelihood that such a referendum could lead to independence. As Bosniaks are fond of saying, there are only 75,000 Serbs living between Sarajevo and the Drina River (Bosnia's eastern border with Serbia).[40] These could not resist Bosniaks' military advance. Rather, the Serbs' position is a bargaining one aimed at securing their real political goal in entering discussions on constitutional reforms: the preservation of their semi-independent Serb Republic.

It is impossible to know what changes, if any, local parties might ultimately accept. Throughout the post-Dayton period, various international agencies, analysts, and donors have put forward their own proposals for

reform and/or assessed existing ones.[41] Interestingly, all of these proposals endorse some variation of Dayton's basic compromise: a common state,
constitutional protection for the three constituent groups, and extensive individual human rights provisions to ensure that no one living in an area
controlled by a different ethnic group would be discriminated against. With
no apparent irony, some of these proposals are even presented as "Dayton
II." Conspicuously absent from the discussion is a realistic articulation of
Bosnians' own views. Several political parties have formulated policy ideas
about constitutional reform, but these reflect the parties' maximalist positions mentioned above.[42] An interesting out-of-the-chorus voice is that of
the Serb Mayor of Foca, Zdravko Krsmanović, who has put forward a radical
plan based on the establishment of only two levels of governance—state
and municipal.[43] In Krsmanović's view, the municipalization of the country
would improve Bosnia's institutional efficiency, transparency, and accountability. Krsmanović cites the experience of Foca, once considered as a hotbed
for extremism, as an example of how local level government can better provide for the needs of Bosnian citizens and can reduce ethnic tensions and
insecurities. Yet, although the mayor's proposal could be considered as a
sensible response to the constitutional impasse, it remains politically unrealistic and is unlikely to be adopted because of the opposition of the leadership
of the Serb Republic. The fact that its Prime Minister, Dodik, tried to engineer
an unsuccessful recall referendum for Krsmanović testifies to the resistance
to this plan.

    In this polarized environment, it is by no means clear what reforms
might be politically feasible. Yet, it may still be possible to identify the
broad outline of such reforms. As mentioned above, the post-Dayton peace
process has brought to light two main problems: the lack of functionality
of Bosnian institutions, and the marginalization of Bosnian citizens who, in
turn, have grown increasingly disillusioned with the political process. No
reform is likely to succeed in the long term unless it addresses these issues.
In practice, this would require three important adjustments. First, the current
institutional structure would need to be simplified to meet citizens' needs and
to comply with the requirements set by the process of European integration.
Such a simplification requires not only streamlining governance between the
state and the municipalities but also limiting the groups' veto rights (which
are integral to consociational institutions) in order to allow for more efficient
decision making.[44] Second, political and social space for nonethnic identities
would need to be opened and developed. Currently, citizens are identified
by their ethnic belonging—which is precisely what divides them. Those
Bosnians who identify themselves in civic, not ethnic, terms are discriminated
against and unable to put forward a political and social alternative. Third,
the top-down, state-based interventionist approach needs to be rethought.
The use of illiberal means such as the "Bonn powers" has contributed to the
securitization of political life, turned the domestic political process into the

problem, not the solution, of the Bosnian conundrum and failed to mobilize individual and collective resources in shaping social reality. The manner in which the international community could support these changes is the question addressed in the next section.

TOWARDS A NEW INTERNATIONAL STRATEGY?

The formulation of a new international strategy capable of supporting and sustaining the reform process over time is complicated by lack of attention and conflicting interests among key international players, as well as differing assessments of the situation on the ground. To begin with, most of the countries that comprise the 55-strong Peace Implementation Council are politically disengaged. In the first few post-Dayton years, council meetings were attended by prime ministers and foreign ministers, later replaced by political directors of foreign ministries. Currently, international officials appointed to serve as council members have Bosnia as only one of the many items on their agenda. In the summer of 2009 Canada, a council member, closed its embassy in Sarajevo, a clear indication of lack of concern, and indicated that it is in favor of closing the OHR as well. Among the other council members only Turkey maintains Bosnia on the list of its top ten foreign policy priorities: it considers the Western Balkans as its own "near abroad" and is determined to influence political developments in the region, in particular by preventing the creation of an Islamic state.

The other members of the Peace Implementation Council do not give Bosnia the same level of attention. Most notably, since the 11 September 2001 attacks, the United States has displayed a low strategic interest in Bosnia, limited to a narrow concern for the possible presence of al-Qaeda cells. Only after the election of President Barack Obama has a more proactive attitude been noticeable, with Vice President Biden visiting Sarajevo in spring 2009. Paradoxically, however, this renewed interest could also represent an obstacle in moving international intervention towards a new phase. If the OHR closes down in favor of a reinforced EU mission, as discussed below, the United States would lose a direct channel to influence developments on the ground. Currently the United States appoints the Deputy High Representative, a high-ranking position that would be impossible to secure within an EU-led operation. Because of this, the United States does not want to use its influence to accelerate OHR closure—particularly at a time when the situation on the ground has been deteriorating.

Thus, the lack of attention and of a clear strategy among key players, divergences between the United States and the EU, and a politically difficult situation in Bosnia have all combined to postpone early plans to restructure the international mission in the country. The Peace Implementation Council began in June 2006 to plan OHR closure. A reinforced EU engagement to fill the political vacuum that would be left by the end of the Office's mandate was anticipated, while integration into Euro-Atlantic bodies was expected to proceed apace.[45] As noted, however, since then conditions in the country have progressively deteriorated. In June 2007, the council reviewed the situation and decided to put off closure by one year due to a "severe deterioration in the political atmosphere" and a "near total deadlock in peace implementation and the delivery of reforms."[46] In February 2008, it abandoned a specific timeline, indentifying instead five objectives and two conditions, commonly referred to as the "five plus two" requirements, in order to endorse closure. The five objectives are resolution of state property issues, resolution of defense property, establishing the legal relationship of Brčko District to the state, fiscal sustainability, and entrenchment of the rule of law. The two conditions include the signing of an association and stabilization agreement with the EU and a positive assessment by the Peace Implementation Council Steering Board on "full compliance with the Dayton Peace Agreement."[47] As of mid-2009, none of the objectives have been fully met, although some limited progress has been recorded.[48]

How strictly the international community will monitor further progress remains unclear. On the one hand, a soft attitude towards the "five plus two" requirements might allow the speedy closure of the OHR and might solve one of the contradictions of liberal interventionism. The OHR was created to monitor the implementation of the Dayton Agreement, but in fact it has supported the strengthening of the central institutions at the expense of the entities, justifying these centralizing efforts as required by the process of European integration. Since 2002 the High Representative has also worn a second hat as European Union Special Representative. With OHR closure, a new High Representative appointed by the EU could focus squarely on the task of helping Bosnia to meet the criteria for EU integration—and not just on monitoring the implementation of an outdated agreement. At the same time, lowering standards might negatively affect the EU's future ability to use conditionality. All too often the international community has declared high principles but then, faced by domestic opposition, retreated and accepted cosmetic changes while, oddly, declaring victory.

On the other hand, a strict adherence to the "five plus two" criteria might postpone the transition from the OHR to a new Office of the Special EU Representative for a long time. In 2010 an election will fall due in Bosnia—perhaps not an ideal time to push for major changes to the international mission. Not only would this deferral suit American needs, as noted above, but it would also reassure the Bosniaks, who fear that Europe might be unprepared to guarantee Bosnia's stability and security. A similar scenario of marginal US interest and hopeful European involvement was not able to prevent bloodshed breaking out in Bosnia in 1992. Understandably, Bosniaks, who suffered most during the war, are wary of taking another chance.

Ultimately, the decision to close the OHR will be a political one, dependent both on an assessment of Bosnia's progress and on the EU's ability to step up to the task. The European Commission mission in Sarajevo currently maintains about a staff of about 100, the third largest such mission in the world after those in Moscow and Tokyo—a clear sign of the EU's interest in Bosnia. European officials seem confident that European institutions are ready to take up the challenge. On 31 October 2008 two senior officials, Olli Rehn and Javier Solana, presented a joint declaration arguing in favor of a new policy.[49] The paper recommended closure of the OHR and a stronger EU initiative. The identification of future European prerogatives in Bosnia was missing; in particular, it was not clear whether a strengthened EU representative would continue to hold the kind of powers that the OHR had enjoyed since late 1997. This gap in the proposal reflected the presence of different views among major EU members. The United Kingdom and the Netherlands insist on the need for continued international interventionism, while France, Italy, and Spain consider the job of international agencies concluded—at least in their current form. Although Rehn and Solana did not take a clear stand on the "Bonn powers," it is very likely that any future EU mission will not hold them, since they appear incompatible with the democratic beliefs guiding EU foreign policy.

In principle, the EU has the potential to overcome some of the major flaws in the liberal peacebuilding approach implemented since the signing of the Dayton Agreement.[50] The EU shares with liberal peacebuilders a general commitment to the promotion of democracy, human rights, the rule of law, and free market principles. However, the EU's major potential advantage vis-à-vis previous international involvement lies in the attractive force that the prospect of EU integration casts over prospective EU member states. Rather than enforcing reform through illiberal means, the EU can favor a process of domestic change without the blatant and problematic use of the "Bonn powers." The recent experience of Central and Eastern European states, which in a few years successfully reformed their political and economic institutions and were able to join the EU collectively in 2004, suggests that the EU integration process can be crucial, committing all major political forces to the goal of EU membership.[51] By so doing, the domestic political process could be revitalized and indigenous resources mobilized. The presence of a "silent majority" in the country committed to EU integration and constitutional change is a hopeful indication of the viability of this approach.[52]

Whether the EU will be able to steer a new course, and how it might do so, is a matter of debate.[53] The EU integration process is often seen as being too insubstantial and long term to provoke much enthusiasm among Bosnian politicians and citizens. Most notably, the delay in adopting the Lisbon Treaty poured cold water on prospective EU members. Pending adoption of the new EU Constitutional Treaty the enlargement process was stalled, effectively undermining the EU's conditionality powers and the reforming force of the

European integration process. Lack of an open commitment on the part of the EU to the process of European integration contributes to explaining Bosnia's limited attention to European issues. For example, between mid-2008 and mid-2009 the position of Minister for European Integration has been vacant, apparently because the local parties did not see any reason to agree on a new appointment at a time when the process of EU enlargement has come to a halt. As for constitutional reform, the EU has refrained from indicating its preferred outcome. The 27 EU members have vastly different institutional arrangements, hindering the adoption of a template for reform. So far, the EU has only demanded compliance with the European Convention on Human Rights, not with any particular constitutional principles. It has been reluctant to identify which reforms it favors because of concerns about imposing a sort of "Dayton II" from the top down with little domestic support.

This attitude has fomented speculation among the parties involved. The Bosnian Serbs in particular fear that the EU might eventually come out in support of the abolition of the Serb Republic. By remaining on the fence, the EU has left the initiative to those who favor the status quo, or who are willing to accept only cosmetic changes. An alternative, wiser approach would lead the EU to identify the reforms it does not want, leaving the local parties the task of sorting out a new constitutional structure within defined limits. As Judy Batt aptly put it, the EU's effort in mediating the constitutional reform process "does not mean imposing any new blueprint, but assuring the quality of the process."[54]

CONCLUSION

There is little doubt that the Bosnian peace process has reached a difficult stage. The liberal interventionist approach, often pursued through illiberal means, has marginalized the domestic political process, has ignored local resources and has prevented Bosnians from shaping political, economic, and social life. Paradoxically, the unsustainable nature of this approach has been most evident with the 2006 failure of the constitutional reform package, when local political parties enjoyed unprecedented room for maneuvering to reach their own solutions but continued to reason that future international intervention could replace domestic agreement. Eventually the failure of the reform effort led to a further deterioration of the domestic political situation and to the postponement of OHR closure. At the time of writing in late 2009, it is not known whether and when international intervention will be refocused away from peace implementation and towards European integration. The lack of agreement between international actors (particularly American and European ones) on the future role of the OHR contributes to hold Bosnia back in her transition process towards Euro-Atlantic institutions.

A speedy transition from the OHR to the EU is likely to improve a dangerously unstable situation. The EU does possess the potential to overcome some of the limits of earlier assertive interventionism. The reform of state institutions can probably not be imposed without a backlash, and the EU is well placed to stimulate a process of domestic change without the blatant use of illiberal and undemocratic means. Ultimately, however, Bosnian political and social actors will have to assess their prospects and take responsibility for their choices. Only Bosnians' commitment to a meaningful political process can ground Bosnia's future on more solid foundations.

NOTES

1. Paddy Ashdown and Richard Holbrooke, "A Bosnian Powder Keg," *The Guardian*, 22 Oct. 2008, p. 28.

2. Patrice C. McMahon and Jon Western, "The Death of Dayton," *Foreign Affairs*, Vol. 88, No. 5 (2009), p. 69.

3. Kurt Bassuener, James Lyon, and Eric A. Witte, *Sliding Toward the Precipice: Europe's Bosnia Policy*. Democratization Policy Council, 7 Nov. 2008; www.democratizationpolicy.org (accessed 1 Sept. 2009).

4. Insightful histories of Bosnia and its peoples include Noel Malcolm, *A Short History of Bosnia* (New York: Columbia University Press, 1996); Robert J. Donia and John V. A. Fine, *Bosnia-Herzegovina: A Tradition Betrayed* (New York: Columbia University Press, 1994); Ivan Lovrenović, *Bosnia: A Cultural History* (London: Saqi Books, 2001); Marko Attila Hoare, *The History of Bosnia from the Middle Ages to the Present Day* (London: Saqi Books, 2007).

5. Among the many accounts of Bosnia's descent into war, see Steven L. Burg and Paul S. Shoup, *The War in Bosnia-Herzegovina: Ethnic Conflict and International Intervention* (Armonk, NY: M. E. Sharpe, 1999).

6. V. P. Gagnon, *The Myth of Ethnic War: Serbia and Croatia in the 1990s* (Ithaca, NY: Cornell University Press, 2004).

7. Juan J. Linz and Alfred Stepan, *Problems of Democratic Transition and Consolidation: Southeastern Europe, South America and Post-Communist Europe* (Baltimore: Johns Hopkins University Press, 1996), p. 21.

8. For further details on Bosnia's constitutional structure, see Florian Bieber, *Post-War Bosnia: Ethnicity, Inequality and Public Sector Governance* (Basingstoke, UK: Palgrave, 2006).

9. Sumantra Bose, *Bosnia After Dayton: International Intervention and Nationalist Partition* (Oxford, UK: Oxford University Press, 2002), p. 216.

10. James Lyon, "Will Bosnia Survive Dayton?", *Current History*, Vol. 99, No. 635 (2000), p. 112.

11. This paragraph draws from Roberto Belloni, *State Building and International Intervention in Bosnia* (London and New York: Routledge, 2007), pp. 50–3.

12. Since late 2008 this situation has prevented the election of a city mayor and effectively deadlocked local governance; see International Crisis Group, *Bosnia: A Test of Political Maturity in Mostar*, Crisis Group Europe Briefing No. 54, 27 July 2009; www.crisisweb.org [accessed 1 Sept. 2009].

13. Ibid., p. 7.

14. Belloni, *State Building*, pp. 54–8.

15. For an analysis of the 2006 attempt at constitutional reform, see Sofia Sebastian, *Leaving Dayton Behind: Constitutional Reform in Bosnia and Herzegovina*, Madrid: FRIDE, Working Paper 46, Nov. 2007; www.fride.org [accessed 10 June 2009].

16. See, for example, Roland Paris, *At War's End: Building Peace After Civil Conflict* (Cambridge, UK: Cambridge University Press, 2004).

17. Sofia Sebastian, "The Role of the EU in the Reform of Dayton in Bosnia-Herzegovina," *Ethnopolitics*, Vol. 8, Nos. 3–4 (2009), pp. 346–7.

18. Peace Implementation Council, *Bosnia and Herzegovina 1998: Self-Sustaining Structures*, Bonn, Germany, Peace Implementation Council, ch. 11, para. 11, 9–10 Dec. 1997; www.ohr.int/pic/default.asp?content_id=5183 [accessed 10 Jan 1998].

19. David Chandler, *Empire in Denial: The Politics of Statebuilding* (London: Pluto Press, 2006).

20. Florian Bieber, "After Dayton, Dayton? The Evolution of an Unpopular Peace," *Ethnopolitics*, Vol. 5, No. 1 (2006), p. 15.

21. Marcus Cox, *State Building and Post-war Reconstruction: Lessons from Bosnia* (Geneva: Center for Applied Studies in International Negotiation, 2001), p. 14.

22. Roberto Belloni, "A Dubious Democracy by Fiat," *Transitions Online*, 22 Aug. 2003, www.tol.cz [accessed 22 Aug. 2003].

23. A uniquely reflective account of the myopic attitude of international interveners can be found in Mark W. Huddleston, "Innocents Abroad: Reflections From a Public Administration Consultant in Bosnia," *Public Administration Review*, Vol. 59, No. 2 (1999), pp. 147–60.

24. For an analysis of the international civil society building efforts see Roberto Belloni and Bruce Hemmer, "Bosnia-Herzegovina: Constructing Civil Society Under a Semi-Protectorate," in Thania Paffenholz (ed.), *Civil Society and Peacebuilding: A Critical Engagement* (Boulder, CO: Lynne Rienner, forthcoming).

25. The Peace Implementation Council was established in Dec. 1995. Its formal composition has not changed since then; although its meetings have been attended by a fluctuating number of observers.

26. See, for example, Colin Woodward, "Debate Surrounds International Community's Role in Bosnia," *Christian Science Monitor,* 2 Feb. 2007, p. 7.

27. Thanks to an anonymous reviewer for drawing my attention to this point.

28. Police Restructuring Commission, *Final Report on the Work of the Police Restructuring Commission of Bosnia and Herzegovina* (Sarajevo: Police Restructuring Commission, 2004). The rationale for police reform and the manner in which the High Representative attempted to introduce it in Bosnia is analyzed in Thomas Muehlmann, "Police Restructuring in Bosnia-Herzegovina: Problems of Internationally-led Security Sector Reform," *Journal of Intervention and Statebuilding*, Vol. 2, No. 1 (2008), pp. 1–22.

29. Letter to the EU Parliament from Milorad Dodic, Prime Minister of Republika Srpska, 20 Sept. 2007; www.wmin.ac.uk/sshl/pdf/JISB [accessed 10 Dec. 2008].

30. A good, short account of this escalation can be found in International Crisis Group, *Bosnia's Incomplete Transition: Between Dayton and Europe*, Europe Report No. 198, 9 Mar. 2009, pp. 4–5; www.crisisweb.org [accessed 10 June 2009], pp. 11–14.

31. Tomas Valasek, *Is Russia a Partner to the EU in Bosnia?*, London: Center for European Reform, Policy Brief, 19 Mar. 2009; www.cer.org.uk/pdf/pb_tv_bosnia_19march09.pdf [accessed 1 July 2009].

32. Srecko Latal, "Western Bodies in Bosnia 'Dead Horse'—Lajcak," *Balkan Insight*, 2 Feb. 2009; www.balkaninsight.com/en/main/news/16352 [accessed 10 June 2009].

33. International Crisis Group, 9 March 2009.

34. Confidential interview with European Commission Official, Sarajevo, Sept. 2009.

35. "BiH Main Parties Announce New Decentralisation Agreement," *SE Times*, 29 Jan. 2009; www.setimes.com/cocoon/setimes/xhtml/en_GB/features/setimes/features/2009/01/27/feature-01 [accessed 1 Sept. 2009].

36. After a stand-off between international and Serb officials, the High Representative used his Bonn powers to abolish the declaration; see Anes Alic, "Bosnian Serbs vs Inzko," *International Relations and Security Network*, 23 June 2009; www.isn.ch [accessed 1 Sept. 2009].

37. Dan Bilefsky, "Tensions Rise in Fragile Bosnia as Serbs Threaten to Seek Independence," 27 Feb. 2009, *The New York Times*, p. 11.

38. Interview with Kurt Bassuener, independent political analyst, Democratization Policy Council, Sarajevo, Sept. 2009. See also Kurt Bassuener, *How to Pull Out of Bosnia-Herzegovina's Dead-End: A Strategy for Success*, Democratization Policy Council, 19 Feb. 2009; www.democratizationpolicy.org [accessed 1 Sept 2009].

39. Confidential interview with EU Official, Sarajevo, Sept. 2009.

40. James Lyon, "Halting the Downward Spiral," *New York Times,* 24 Feb. 2009; www.nytimes.com/2009/02/24/opinion/24iht-edlyon.1.20395827.html [accessed 1 Sept. 2009]

41. Belloni, *State Building*, pp. 160–66.

42. For a discussion of the current state of the constitutional debate, see Kenneth Morrison, *Dayton, Divisions and Constitutional Revisions: Bosnia and Herzegovina at the Crossroads* (London: Defence Academy of the United Kingdom, Research and Assessment Branch, 2009).

43. Vanja Filipovic and Kurt Bassuener, "Mayor with a Plan," *Transitions Online*, 25 July 2007; www.tol.cz [accessed 1 Sept. 2009].

44. For a discussion of institutional arrangements that protect group interests but do not entrench ethnic vetoes, see Florian Bieber, "Challenge of Democracy in Divided Societies: Lessons

from Bosnia—Challenges for Kosovo," in Florian Bieber and Džemal Sokolović (eds.), *Reconstructing Multiethnic Societies: The Case of Bosnia-Herzegovina* (Aldershot, UK: Ashgate, 2001), pp. 109–22; Benjamin Reilly, *Democracy in Divided Societies* (Cambridge, UK: Cambridge University Press, 2001).

45. Peace Implementation Council Steering Board, "Towards Ownership: From Peace Implementation to Euro-Atlantic Integration," Sarajevo: PIC, 23 June 2006; www.ohr.int/pic/default.asp?content_id=37503 [accessed 1 July 2009].

46. "Declaration by the Steering Board of the Peace Implementation Council," available at: www.ohr.int/pic/default.asp?content_id=39997 [accessed 1 July 2009].

47. "Declaration by the Steering Board of the Peace Implementation Council," 27 Feb. 2008; www.ohr.int/pic/default.asp?content_id=41352 [accessed 1 July 2009].

48. "Communiquè of the Steering Board of the Peace Implementation Council", 30 June 2009; www.ohr.int/pic/default.asp?content_id=43665 [accessed 1 July 2009].

49. Summary note on the joint report by Xavier Solana, EU High Representative for the CFSP, and Olli Rehn, EU Commissioner for Enlargement, on "EU's policy in Bosnia and Herzegovina: The Way Ahead," (10 Nov. 2008) Brussels, S367/08; www.eu2008.fr/webdav/site/PFUE/shared/import/1110_cagre_defense/EU_policy_in_bosnia_and_Herzegovina_joint_report_solana_rehn_en.pdf [accessed 1 July 2009].

50. For an assessment of the EU's role, actual and potential, in the Western Balkans, see Roberto Belloni, "European Integration and the Western Balkans: Lessons, Prospects, and Obstacles," *Journal of Balkan and Near Eastern Studies*, Vol. 11, No. 3 (2009), pp. 313–31.

51. European Stability Initiative, *The Helsinki Moment: European Member-state Building in the Balkans, Berlin/Brussels/Istanbul: ESI*, Feb. 2005; www.esiweb.org [accessed 3 May 2006].

52. United Nations Development Programme, *Silent Majority Speaks*, Sarajevo: UNDP, May 2007; www.undp.ba/index.aspx?PID=3&RID=43 [accessed 13 Oct. 2008].

53. See Edward P. Joseph and R. Bruce Hitchner, *Making Bosnia Work: Why EU Accession is not Enough*, Washington DC: United States Institute of Peace, USIP Peace Briefing, June 2008; Megan Chabalowski and Michael Dziedzic, *Bosnia and Herzegovina: Parsing the Options*, Washington DC: United States Institute of Peace, USIP Peace Briefing, Sept. 2009; both reports at www.usip.org [accessed 10 Sept. 2009]; International Crisis Group, 2009.

54. Judy Batt, *Bosnia and Herzegovina: The International Mission at a Turning Point*, FRIDE Policy Brief, p. 4, 9 Feb. 2009; www.fride.org [accessed 10 June 2009].

6

Cyprus: Domestic Ethnopolitical Conflict and International Politics

JOSEPH S. JOSEPH

University of Cyprus

This article provides an essential background to the domestic setting of the conflict in Cyprus and some of its international repercussions. In doing so, emphasis is placed on the geographical, historical, social, cultural, institutional, and political roots of the conflict. The presentation and analysis of these aspects aims at examining the relationship between political division along ethnic lines and the generation and internationalization of the conflict. It places some emphasis on the factors that contributed to the maintenance and reinforcement of ethnic cleavages in a bicommunal society and the failure of the political system to counteract divisive forces.

INTRODUCTION

In recent decades, the Cyprus problem has gone through three phases. Until 1960, it was a colonial issue that was settled with the declaration of independence and the establishment of the Republic of Cyprus. From 1960 to 1974, the problem was essentially an internal dispute between the Greek Cypriots and the Turkish Cypriots in which external powers became involved —primarily Greece, Turkey, and Britain, the guarantor powers of the independence of Cyprus under the 1960 settlement, but also, during the second phase, the United States and the Soviet Union, by virtue of their superpower status. The third phase covers the period from 1974 to the present: following the Greek coup and the Turkish invasion of Cyprus in 1974, the dominant element of the problem has been the de facto division of the island and the continuing occupation of its northern part by Turkey.

This article deals mainly with the period of ethnopolitical conflict from 1960 to 1974. Its purpose is to provide a basic context and an analysis of the political developments that followed the declaration of independence in 1960. In doing so, emphasis is placed on the geographical, historical, social, cultural, institutional, and political roots of the conflict on the island. The role of Greece and Turkey (the motherlands) during that same period is also examined. The three middle sections look at the operation of the 1960 blueprint in the early years of the Republic of Cyprus: its constitutional content, its political operation, and its ultimate failure. Finally, the article also looks at the efforts towards and prospects for a settlement, especially now that Cyprus is a member of the European Union.

BACKGROUND TO THE CONFLICT

Geographical and Historical Setting

Three geographical characteristics of Cyprus have determined much of its fate: location, size, and the fact that it is an island. It is located at a strategic position in the eastern Mediterranean at the crossroads of three continents. Its long exposed coastline and relatively small size (9,851 square kilometers) always made it an attractive and easy target for outsiders. Its historical and demographic records reflect the ebb and flow of peoples and powers in the region. As Alan James aptly points out, "[t]hroughout recorded time, its political experience has reflected the interlocking impact of two utterly basic geographic factors: size and location. From their influence the island has been wholly unable to escape."[1] In the course of its long history, Cyprus has been conquered by most of the major powers that had an interest in, or sought control of, the Middle East. The list of its successive rulers includes the Egyptians, Greeks, Phoenicians, Assyrians, Persians, Ptolemies, Romans, Byzantines, Franks, Venetians, Ottoman Turks, and British. It gained its independence from Britain in 1960.

Among these rulers, only the Greeks and the Turks had a significant and lasting demographic impact on Cypriot society. The Greeks settled on the island during the second half of the second millennium BC. The Turks settled in Cyprus following the Ottoman occupation of the island in 1571. Under the Cyprus convention, which was signed at the Congress of Berlin in 1878, the sultan ceded Cyprus to Britain, which was to administer the island in exchange for a promise to help Turkey defend itself against Russian expansion. In 1914, at the onset of the Second World War and after Turkey had joined forces with the Central Powers, Britain declared the 1878 convention null and annexed Cyprus. With the 1923 peace treaty of Lausanne, Turkey officially recognized the annexation of Cyprus by Britain and the island was proclaimed a colony of the British crown in 1925.

By 1878, when the British took control of the island, the bicommunal character of Cypriot society had been formed and consolidated. During the 82 years of British rule no major demographic change took place on the island. In 1960, its population was approximately 570,000, consisting of roughly

80% Greeks and 20% Turks.[2] There were purely Greek, purely Turkish, and mixed settlements in all regions of the island. There were (and still are) also small ethnic groups of Armenians, Maronites, and Latins living in Cyprus.[3]

Roots of Sociopolitical Differentiation

The Greek Cypriots and the Turkish Cypriots have been divided along linguistic, ethnic, cultural, and religious lines. The Greek Cypriots speak Greek and identify with the Greek nation, Greek culture, and the heritage of classical Greece and the Byzantine Empire. Almost all of them are members of the Orthodox Church of Cyprus, which is an autocephalous member of the Greek Eastern Orthodox Church. The Turkish Cypriots speak Turkish and identify with the Turkish nation, Turkish culture, and the heritage of the Turkish Ottoman Empire. Virtually all of them are Muslims of the Sunni sect.[4]

Despite four centuries of coexistence and considerable physical intermingling, the two communities remained separate and distinct ethnic groups. It should be recalled that the current spatial distribution of the two groups was to come later: a partial physical separation of the two communities took place with the eruption of intercommunal violence in 1963 and an almost complete separation came into effect after the Turkish invasion of Cyprus in 1974, with the result that by the end of 2009 there are only a few hundred Greek Cypriots living in the Turkish occupied part and about a thousand Turkish Cypriots in the south. During the period of Ottoman and British rule, certain factors contributed to the preservation of the linguistic, ethnic, cultural, and religious characteristics of the two communities and the creation of a political cleavage along ethnic lines.

The Orthodox Church, which maintained a dominant position among the Greek Cypriots, helped them preserve their religious, ethnic, cultural, and political identity. When the Ottomans conquered Cyprus from the Venetians in 1571, they destroyed the Roman Catholic Church and elevated the Greek Orthodox Church to a position of supremacy in the island. The autonomy of the Orthodox Church was confirmed and the archbishop was recognized as the religious and political leader of the Greek Cypriot community.[5] For the Greek Cypriots, the church became a symbol of political and ethnic unity. Most of their political, social, cultural, and intellectual life was associated with religious activities and institutions. The church continued to be the most prominent institution of the Greek Cypriots under British rule.

The Ottoman *millet* administrative system distinguished the two communities on the basis of religion and ethnicity.[6] According to this system, which was applied throughout the Ottoman empire, each religious ethnic group was treated as a distinct entity. Taxes were imposed on a denominational basis and administration was carried out with the help of the various religious institutions. The Ottoman conquerors restored the Orthodox Church of Cyprus with this aim in mind. The administrative separation of the Greek

Cypriots and the Turkish Cypriots helped them maintain their ethnic identity, but it also contributed to the politicization of ethnicity. When the British took control of Cyprus, the *millet* system was not completely abolished. A modern bureaucratic administration was established, but the two ethnic groups retained control in matters of religion, education, culture, personal status, and communal institutions.

The divisive educational system perpetuated ethnic distinctiveness by transferring conflicting ethnic values from generation to generation. The two communities had separate schools that were, to some degree, controlled by their respective religious institutions. Throughout the Ottoman period and the early years of British rule, Orthodox and Muslim priests were also school teachers. During the period of British rule, the curricula of the Cypriot schools were similar to those in Greece or Turkey. They placed emphasis on religion, national heritage (of Greece and Turkey respectively—not of Cyprus), ethnic values, and the long history of Greek-Turkish rivalry.

The two Cypriot communities had antagonistic loyalties to Greece and Turkey. Each community honored the national holidays, played the national anthem and used the flag of its mother country. Cypriots from both ethnic groups fought as volunteers on opposite sides during the 1912–13 Balkan wars, the First World War, and the Greek-Turkish war of 1919–23. Attachment to two rival and often belligerent countries promoted ethnic distinctiveness and served as an instrument for the transplantation of the wider Greek-Turkish confrontation into Cyprus.

The two ethnic groups held conflicting views about the political future of the island. Throughout the British period, *enosis* (union of Cyprus with Greece) was the most persistent and rigid goal of the Greek Cypriots.[7] It could be seen as part of the wider Panhellenic movement of *megali idea* (great idea) that aimed at reconstruction of the Byzantine Empire. On the Turkish side, the idea of *taksim* (partition of Cyprus into Greek and Turkish sections) was advanced as a counterforce to *enosis*. Both movements were supported by Greece and Turkey, respectively. Attachment to the conflicting goals of *enosis* and *taksim* led to a political polarization between the two ethnic groups.

The British colonial policy of "divide and rule" maintained and reinforced the ethnic, administrative, and political separation inherited from the Ottoman period. The British administration made no effort to create a unifying Cypriot political culture. The two communities were treated as separate groups for administrative purposes and antagonism between them was stirred.[8] The maintenance of a psychological and administrative gap between the two ethnic groups was instrumental in securing British control over Cyprus.

The above factors—church dominance, *millet* system, fragmented ethnic education, antagonistic national loyalties, political polarization, and the British policy of "divide and rule"—contributed to the preservation of the

ethnic identity of the two Cypriot communities and the generation of a political schism between them. Four centuries of geographic proximity and
physical intermingling did not produce intercommunal bonds strong enough
to counteract the divisive effects of religious, administrative, educational,
social, and cultural distinctiveness. Communal segregation was further reinforced by mutual suspicion, fear, and uncertainty "for which one might coin
the term 'postjudices,' since they are based upon close observation and not
ignorant misconception."[9] It was on these fragmented historical and social
foundations that an independent bicommunal Cypriot state was built in 1960.

POLITICAL INSTITUTIONS IN INDEPENDENT CYPRUS

Establishment of the Republic of Cyprus

Britain granted independence to Cyprus in 1960, giving way to pressure
from three different directions. First, there was a bloody Greek Cypriot anticolonial revolt, which lasted from 1955 to 1959, causing much trouble for
the British authorities and making the administration of the island a difficult and costly task. The revolt, which took the form of a guerilla war, was
spearheaded by the Orthodox Church under the leadership of Archbishop
Makarios and the underground National Organization of Cypriot Fighters
(*Ethnike Organosis Kyprion Agoniston* [EOKA]) under the leadership of its
founder General George Grivas Dighenis. The revolt was carried out in the
name of *enosis* and had the support of Greece. Turkey and the Turkish
Cypriots, on the other hand, were demanding partition. Some incidents of
ethnic violence occurred and further tension was generated between Greece
and Turkey.[10]

Second, there was global pressure resulting from the internationalization
of the Cyprus issue, especially at the UN, in the context of the broader
anticolonial movement and decolonization process that were sweeping the
world in the 1950s. The issue was taken to the UN General Assembly in
five consecutive years, from 1954 to 1958.[11] Appeals to the UN were made
by Greece, asking for application of the principles of equal rights and self-
determination in Cyprus. The Greek appeals were supported by the Eastern
(Soviet) bloc and the third-world countries. Greece also asked for *enosis* "in
view of the repeatedly and solemnly expressed will of the overwhelming
majority of the people of Cyprus for union with Greece, which they regard
as their mother country."[12] The General Assembly made a recommendation
for a peaceful solution of the Cyprus colonial problem in accordance with
the principles of the UN Charter.

Third, American pressure was applied to Britain, Greece, and Turkey
to seek a solution to the Cyprus problem and to heal the Greek-Turkish
"festering sore" within NATO. The United States was concerned with the
mounting Greek-Turkish tension that threatened to paralyze the southeastern

flank of the Western alliance. American concern over Cypriot developments was manifested in unsuccessful initiatives in 1957 and 1958 aiming at a settlement of the problem within NATO.

As a result of the above pressures, a solution to the colonial problem of Cyprus was sought through diplomacy. Early in 1959, tripartite talks were held in Zurich between Britain, Greece, and Turkey and an agreement was reached for the establishment of an independent Cypriot state, the Republic of Cyprus. Final agreements were signed in London on 19 February 1959, by Britain, Greece, Turkey, and the two Cypriot communities, although the latter did not participate in the negotiations. The problem was, in effect, settled on a bilateral basis between Greece and Turkey under British auspices. Factors and considerations emanating from the ethnic, historical, linguistic, cultural and religious ties of the two Cypriot ethnic groups with their respective motherlands defined the context and content of the settlement.

The London and Zurich Agreements

The London and Zurich agreements consisted of a series of treaties that laid the foundations of the political structure of the new state. These treaties were the Treaty of Establishment, the Treaty of Alliance, the Treaty of Guarantee, and the agreement on the basic structure of the Republic of Cyprus that contained the key provisions of the constitution that was drafted later. The treaties and the constitution were officially signed on 16 August 1960, in Nicosia, and went into effect immediately.[13]

The Treaty of Establishment was aimed at safeguarding British military interests in Cyprus. It provided for two sovereign British military areas of 99 square miles (256 square kilometers). The Treaty of Alliance was a defense pact between Greece, Turkey, and Cyprus. It provided for the permanent stationing of Greek and Turkish contingents in Cyprus, comprising 950 and 650 men, respectively. With the Treaty of Guarantee Cyprus undertook to "ensure the maintenance of its independence, territorial integrity and security" and to prohibit "any activity likely to promote, directly or indirectly, either union with any other State or partition of the Island."[14] Britain, Greece, and Turkey were named guarantor powers of the Republic and were granted the right to take action, jointly or unilaterally, toward "reestablishing the state of affairs created by the present Treaty" in the event of its breach.[15] The Treaty of Guarantee was primarily aimed at mutual abandonment of the conflicting ethnopolitical goals of *enosis* and partition.

The Constitution of Cyprus

The agreement on the basic structure of the Republic of Cyprus contained the key provisions of the constitution that was drafted later and put into effect when the republic officially came into being. The constitution was based on communal dualism. It provided for the establishment of a bicommunal state and aimed at regulation and protection of the interests of the two communities as distinct ethnic groups. It identified and recognized the two communities by reference to their ethnic origin, language, cultural traditions, and religion.[16] It gave them "the right to celebrate respectively the Greek and Turkish national holidays"[17] and to use "the flag of the Republic or the Greek or Turkish flag without any restriction."[18] The two communities were also granted the right to establish separate special relationships with Greece and Turkey on educational, religious, cultural, and athletic matters.

The constitution institutionalized communal dualism in all spheres of government activity. In the executive branch, it provided for a presidential regime, the president being Greek Cypriot and the vice-president Turkish Cypriot, elected separately by the two communities. The council of ministers was composed of seven Greek Cypriots and three Turkish Cypriots. The president appointed the Greek Cypriot and the vice-president the Turkish Cypriot ministers. Decisions by the council of ministers were taken by absolute majority, but the president and the vice-president had the right to veto, jointly or separately, decisions on foreign affairs, defense, and security.

According to the constitution, legislative power was exercised by the House of Representatives and two communal chambers. The House was composed of 35 Greek Cypriots and 15 Turkish Cypriot representatives, elected separately by the two ethnic groups.[19] The president of the House was Greek Cypriot and the vice-president Turkish Cypriot. Laws in the House were passed by simple majority, except in the cases of "any modification of the Electoral Law and the adoption of any law relating to the municipalities and of any law imposing duties or taxes," where a separate simple majority of the representatives of the two communities was required.[20] The two communal chambers were independent legislative bodies elected separately by the two communities. They had exclusive legislative power in relation to their respective ethnic groups in the following areas: all religious matters; all educational, cultural, and teaching matters; personal status; administration of justice dealing with civil disputes relating to personal status and religious matters; and in matters where the interests and institutions were purely of a communal nature, such as charitable and sporting institutions. The two chambers could also impose personal taxes and fees on their communities in order to finance communal activities and institutions. Division of the legislative branch meant, in effect, that each ethnic group could run its own affairs independently and in contrast to the interests of the other community.

Communal dualism was also institutionalized in the judicial system. The composition of the lower courts, both civil and criminal, was determined by the communal membership of the disputants. If the plaintiff and the defendant belonged to the same community, the court was composed of judges belonging to that community. The Supreme Court was composed of a Greek Cypriot, a Turkish Cypriot, and a neutral judge. The neutral judge was the president of the court and could not be a citizen of Cyprus, Greece, Turkey, or Britain. Needless to say, the transplantation of ethnic fragmentation into the administration of justice, which was partly inherited from the colonial period, could undermine the very concept of justice. In an ethnically and politically divided society, ethnic considerations could influence the operation of the courts and result in an undermining of the administration of justice.

The constitution provided for the establishment of separate municipalities: "separate municipalities shall be created in the five largest towns of the Republic. . . . The Council of the Greek municipality in any such town shall be elected by the Greek electors of the town and the Turkish municipality in such towns shall be elected by the Turkish electors of the town."[21] It is worth mentioning that despite the existence of Greek and Turkish quarters, there was some intermingling of the population in the five towns. Application of this provision could result in some movement of people, who would be inclined to relocate following the letter and spirit of "creating separate municipalities."

A disproportional communal ratio of participation in the public service, the police, and the armed forces was fixed by the constitution. Although the Greek-Turkish population ratio was roughly 80:20, the public service and the police would be composed of 70% Greeks and 30% Turks; the ratio in the army was 60:40. The provisions for disproportionate participation of the Turkish Cypriots in the public sector left an opening for a negative reaction among the Greek Cypriots, given its departure from the principle of equal treatment of all citizens.

Finally, the constitution provided that provisions incorporated from the Zurich and London accords could not "in any way be amended, whether by way of variation, addition, or repeal."[22] All the constitutional features presented above were among the "basic articles," and so were the treaties of alliance and guarantee that were integral parts of the constitution. In other words, the political framework was not only awkward and unworkable but also rigid and unalterable. It excluded any adaptation or evolutionary political process through which the two groups could negotiate, could adjust their positions and could seek common ground for reconciliation and a settlement. As a political analyst put it, "it was a constitutional straitjacket precluding that adaptation essential to the growth and survival of any body politic."[23]

It should also be noted that the Republic of Cyprus came into being as a result of international agreements that were reached in the absence of the Cypriot people. The constitution of the new state was imposed on the population; it was never submitted to a referendum. A series of treaties set limitations on the independence, sovereignty, and territorial integrity of the republic. Foreign powers were granted the right to station military forces on its territory and to interfere in its domestic affairs.

THE CONSTITUTION IN OPERATION

The Dysfunctional State

One of the primary tasks of the first government of the republic was to build the state institutions provided for by the constitution. This, however, proved to be a difficult task. The Greek Cypriots were not enthusiastic about the implementation of some of the constitutional provisions that they regarded as unjust and unrealistic. The Turkish Cypriots, on the other hand, insisted on full implementation of the constitution, especially the provisions regarding their safeguards and privileges. A series of incidents revolving around "basic articles" of the constitution undermined the entire process of state building. After three years of simmering tension and fruitless efforts to establish constitutional order and a working state, a complete constitutional breakdown and eruption of violence occurred in December 1963. The major sources of constitutional tension included the provisions for the 70:30 ratio in the public service, the separate majority vote in the parliament, the establishment of separate municipalities, and the right of the president and vice-president to veto decisions of the council of ministers and the parliament.

The 70:30 ratio in the public service was in discordance to the 80:20 ratio of the population. The Greek Cypriots felt that this provision was arbitrary, unjust, and discriminatory, and that, therefore, it should not be implemented. The Turkish Cypriots, on the other hand, argued that the 70:30 ratio was a restoration of equity in the public service, which had been dominated by the Greek Cypriots under the British administration. Efforts made by President Makarios and Vice-President Kutchuk to find a compromise solution failed and the issue was never settled. From 1960 to 1963, a large number of appointments in the public service were disputed on communal grounds and taken to court. The court, however, could not make any progress toward a settlement of the conflict because it was also paralyzed by ethnic fragmentation and polarization. Its neutral president, German jurist Ernst Forsthoff, found himself caught amidst ethnically polarized factions and resigned in May 1963. Since the conflict was more ethnopolitical than legal in nature, the question of the 70:30 ratio was never resolved. As a consequence, the public service could not become fully operational.

The provision for separate majorities in the parliament was another source of ethnically based political tension. The Greek Cypriots felt that the provision violated democratic principles and gave the Turkish Cypriot minority a powerful obstructive weapon. The Turkish Cypriots argued that with the separate majority vote they could protect themselves from Greek Cypriot domination. The confrontation over the separate majority provision led to a communal polarization in the legislative process. As a result, basic laws badly needed for the smooth operation of the state could not pass. This may be illustrated by the case of tax legislation. When the republic came into being, there was a need for legislation on income tax. The government introduced a bill in parliament to address this, but the Turkish Cypriot representatives used their separate majority right to block it. They justified their position by referring to a delay in the implementation of other constitutional provisions, especially the 70:30 ratio in the public service and the establishment of separate municipalities. Finally, the two communal chambers intervened separately and passed communal laws imposing taxes on their respective ethnic groups. With this development, the two groups moved further apart and the unity of the state and the economy suffered a heavy blow. Taxes were, in effect, imposed on an ethnic basis and used to finance separate communal institutions, projects, and services. The lack of central control or regulation of public financial affairs led to chaos and disarray in the economic life of the new state. Economic paralysis in the public sector had, in turn, a negative impact on the economy and well-being of both communities.

The provision for separate municipalities also caused much trouble and gave rise to problems that were never resolved. The Greek Cypriots criticized this provision and resisted its implementation. They looked at it with suspicion because it had partitionist connotations and could be seen as a first step toward partition. Needless to say, the handling of the municipal affairs of a city by two potentially competing councils would be inoperable. The issue was brought to the parliament, where separate majority votes confirmed the deadlock. Thereafter, the two sides followed different courses of action. The president, backed by the Greek Cypriot dominated council of ministers, issued an executive order calling for the appointment of unified municipal boards. The Turkish Cypriot communal chamber responded by passing a communal law legitimizing separate Turkish municipalities. Both acts were ruled unconstitutional and void *ab initio* by the supreme court. In both instances the vote of the opposite communal judge decided the case. The two sides, however, insisted on their positions, and a settlement on the issue was never reached. The result was chaos and disarray in the municipal affairs of the five largest towns of the island. Diana Markides accurately writes that "[t]he municipal issue, as manifested during this period, was in effect a microcosm of the Cyprus problem. It represented a method of maintaining Turkish political control within the island. Simultaneously, it would give the Turkish Cypriots the element of autonomy they needed to avoid assimilation and discrimination as an impotent minority."[24]

The right granted to the president and vice-president to veto certain decisions of the government and the parliament led to a deadlock in the executive branch. The frequent exercise of the veto right in the government led to disturbing controversies and immobilization of the entire governmental machinery, with destructive effects on the functioning of the state and interethnic relations. A major crisis occurred when a decision was made by the council of ministers for the formation of an army on a mixed basis. The vice-president vetoed the decision and asked for the establishment of an army based on separate communal units. He argued that soldiers with linguistic, cultural, religious, and ethnic differences could not be quartered together, and, therefore, the army should be ethnically separated. The president reacted by questioning the applicability of the right of veto of the vice-president in that particular case. Then, he went further to declare that under the circumstances there was no need for the creation of an army. The crisis in the government was never resolved and an army was never established as provided by the constitution. A destructive consequence of that deadlock was the emergence of underground military groups, types of "private armies," on both sides. These groups were largely controlled by aspiring political leaders who did not report to any authority. The emergence of private ethnic armies revived old fears, suspicions, and uncertainty among the two communities. Both sides began to realize that they could not rely on an inoperative state for their security and proceeded to take measures for their own protection.

In sum, the institutional framework of the Republic of Cyprus reflected the divided past and antagonistic loyalties of the two ethnic groups. The disproportional rights and privileges granted to the minority did not counterbalance the dynamics of majority-minority dynamics and relations. As Anna Jarstad points out, "although the agreements including the ethnic quota system did imply strong guarantees for ethnic rights, they were in practice insufficient for providing safety for the Turkish Cypriots. Rather, the discrepancy between formal and real power was great and the grievances increased."[25] The two communities were treated as distinct, self-contained political units, and political boundaries were established between them parallel to the ethnic cleavage. The political institutions of the state formalized and reinforced ethnic differences through political structures and practices. Ethnic fragmentation and political segregation of the two communities had a negative effect on the newborn republic. Political separation along ethnic lines prevented the two communities from participating and interacting in a common political arena. The coincidence of linguistic, ethnic, religious, cultural, and political cleavages eliminated any chance of cross-cutting political activities, overarching loyalties, and shared political culture supportive of the state. The two communities remained ethnically and politically distinct and looked upon each other as ethnopolitical antagonists, without distinguishing ethnicity from politics. Rather, ethnicity dominated politics and it was natural for both sides to seek to ethnicize the state in their favor. As a result, Cypriot politics was heavily colored by ethnicity and turned into an implacable ethnic struggle, rather than a fair political game. In sum, the ethnopolitical polarization inherited from the past, the structural inadequacies of the new state, the lack of experience in self-government, and the absence of a consensual political leadership that could transcend ethnic differences were the major factors that contributed to the generation of an open ethnic confrontation and the collapse of the Cypriot state in 1963, three years after its establishment.

Ethnic and Social Fragmentation at the Grassroots Level

The legal controversies and political polarization that paralyzed the state and the political process were merely the "superstructure" of a similarly ethnically polarized and potentially explosive "infrastructure" inherited from the past. Socially, the two ethnic groups remained largely divided. The epitome of their social segregation was the absence of intermarriage and limited participation in joint social and cultural events. Greek and Turkish social activities were closely related to distinct religious beliefs and practices, ethnic holidays, and cultural traditions. Therefore, there was not enough common ground for social interaction. Intermarriage was extremely rare, since it carried with it a social and religious stigma. In effect, marriage of a Greek Orthodox with a Turkish Muslim was prohibited under the separate family laws of the two communities.

In the professional field and party organization, the two communities were largely self-sufficient and self-contained. They had separate political parties, professional organizations, and labor unions with mostly uniethnic membership. The major Greek Cypriot political parties at the time of independence were the pro-*enosis* Patriotic Front and the pro-independence communist party, Anorthotikon Komma Ergazomenou Laou, the Progressive Party of the Working People (AKEL). The major Turkish Cypriot parties were the Turkish Cypriot People's Party and the National Front. Both held propartition views. The ethnically based division of political parties was partly due to the ethnopolitical division provided by the institutional framework of the state. The absence of common parties and organizations articulating the economic interests of the two ethnic groups across ethnic boundaries further widened the gap between the two sides.

The segregation of education inherited from the colonial era was preserved and reinforced. The two communal chambers, acting separately and in accordance with the constitution, passed legislation that to a large extent established educational unity of the two communities with their motherlands. The curricula and textbooks used in Cypriot elementary and high schools were mostly imported from the two mainlands. Ethnic and political controversies also undermined early efforts at the establishment of a badly needed university. The first state-supported University of Cyprus was established by law only in 1989 and began operating in 1992. The limited communal interaction in the educational and intellectual fields sustained one-sided "ethnic ways" of thinking within the two communities. The result was a growing gap in the perceptions held by the two sides about each other.

The two communities also had their own newspapers and other publications, which mostly presented biased ethnic views and conflicting positions. Besides the local press, publications imported from Greece and Turkey emphasizing Greek-Turkish antagonism enhanced mutual fears and biased perceptions.

Despite the declaration of Cypriot independence, the two communities continued celebrating the national holidays of Greece and Turkey, which were mostly directed against each other. It should be recalled that the celebration of Greek and Turkish national holidays was allowed, if not encouraged, by the constitution. These celebrations—which as a rule included pompous parades, pageants, and flying of flags—cultivated mutually negative sentiments at the grassroots level. The Greek and Turkish national anthems and flags were used during these celebrations (Cyprus has no national anthem of its own to the present day). These ethnic celebrations quite naturally reminded the people on the two sides of the ethnic line that their ethnic roots and loyalties extended to Greece and Turkey, and that the Cypriot state did not fulfill their national aspirations. As a result, any prospects for the development of a supportive political culture and mass legitimacy for the new state were undermined.

Perhaps the most destructive element in interethnic relations was the fact that the two communities failed to abandon their old conflicting ethnopolitical goals of *enosis* and partition. This was manifested in the attitudes of the communal elites, who missed no opportunity to deliver intensely patriotic speeches reaffirming their continuing commitment to the achievement of those goals. In effect, the creation of an independent state was viewed by the two sides as an interim phase for materialization of *enosis* or partition.

Proposal to Revise the Constitution

Repeated ethnically colored legal and political deadlocks caused tensions that led ultimately to a breakdown of the Zurich and London settlement. The political life of the republic was polarized along ethnic lines and the state was headed for paralysis. Under these circumstances, President Makarios took the initiative for an amendment of certain articles of the constitution. In November 1963, he made a proposal of 13 points to Vice-President Kutchuk for "revision of at least some of those provisions which impede the smooth functioning and development of the State."[26] Makarios argued that a revision of the constitution was necessary because "one of the consequences of the difficulties created by certain Constitutional provisions is to prevent the Greeks and Turks of Cyprus from cooperating in a spirit of understanding and friendship, to undermine the relations between them and cause them to draw further apart instead of closer together, to the detriment of the well-being of the people of Cyprus as a whole."[27] The proposed amendment addressed mainly constitutional deadlocks. The most important of them were the following: abolition of the veto right of the president and the vice-president; abolition of the separate majority votes in parliament; establishment of

unified municipalities; unification of the administration of justice; participation of the two communities in the public service in proportion to their
population; and abolition of the Greek communal chamber.

Makarios's proposals were aimed at the establishment of a unitary state
with majority rule. This would mean elimination of some of the privileges and
safeguards of the minority. Vice-President Kutchuk rejected the proposals as
completely unacceptable and of a sweeping nature aimed at the destruction
of the republic and attainment of *enosis*. He insisted that Cyprus should
remain a bicommunal state, or complete separation of the two ethnic groups
should come into effect through partition of the island.

THE COLLAPSE OF THE CONSTITUTION

Flare-up and Internationalization of the Problem

Constitutional crises, political immobilization, ethnic passion, mutual mistrust, suspicion, fear, uncertainty, limited bicommunal interaction, and the
emergence of underground military groups paved the way for an open communal confrontation. Both communities had already begun stockpiling arms
since the declaration of independence. The inevitable came in December
1963, when heavy fighting broke out in the capital city of Nicosia and soon
spread to other parts of the island.

The outbreak of hostilities brought about a breakdown of intercommunal relations. A process of physical separation of the two communities
began in December 1963. The Turkish Cypriots moved into armed enclaves
that emerged in various parts of the island. The Turkish Cypriot leadership
and public servants withdrew from the government and set up a separate
administration (it was only in 1974 that the separation was completed, when
the Turkish invasion of Cyprus resulted in the creation of two ethnic zones
by forced movement of population).

In essence, from 1960 to 1964 the Cyprus issue went through a transformation. As James points out, "the crisis of 1963–64 changed the political
character of Cyprus in a truly fundamental way."[28] The troubled colonial relationship with Britain came to an end and domestic ethnic conflict emerged
as the dominant problem. After taking the form of open armed confrontation
it entered a course of internationalization.

Cyprus was now an independent state and, therefore, an autonomous
unit within the international system. It could pursue its own foreign policy
and interact directly with other states and international organizations. The
young republic sought to establish itself in the international arena by becoming a member of international organizations and establishing relations
with other countries. It became a member of the United Nations, the Council
of Europe, the Commonwealth of Nations, and other international organizations. It joined the Non-Aligned Movement and established diplomatic

relations with several countries. Membership in the world community linked Cypriot developments to the web of international politics. Cyprus was no longer a colonial problem that could be contained within the jurisdiction of the imperial power. Outside parties could now interact directly with the new state and with the parties involved in the conflict.

The complicated treaty structure by which the Cyprus Republic was bound at birth also established channels of external interference in Cypriot affairs. The treaties of establishment, alliance, and guarantee gave Britain, Greece, and Turkey the right to station forces in Cyprus and to intervene, jointly or unilaterally, in Cypriot affairs. Any change of the status quo created by the London and Zurich accords could cause intervention from outside.

The power vacuum created by the British withdrawal from Cyprus was another factor conducive to the internationalization of the ethnic conflict. With the removal of British administration and the declaration of independence, Cyprus became a *terra nullius* in superpower politics. Both superpowers had an interest in influencing developments on the island, and the means to do so. The United States could use its junior allies—Britain, Greece, and Turkey—to influence the course of events and to seek a settlement safeguarding Western interests in Cyprus. The Soviet Union could use AKEL, the powerful Greek Cypriot communist party, to influence Cypriot politics and future developments. President Makarios had already established a political alliance with AKEL and friendly relations with Moscow. The outbreak of communal hostilities presented an opportunity and a challenge to both superpowers to fish in troubled waters and to promote their goals.

Ethnic ties between the two Cypriot communities, on the one hand, and Greece and Turkey, on the other, were especially instrumental in causing foreign involvement in Cypriot affairs. They provided a basis for the establishment of close relations between the two local ethnic groups and their mother countries. The Cypriots looked upon Greece and Turkey as their protectors and counted on their diplomatic, military, economic, and moral support. Greece and Turkey viewed the two Cypriot communities as parts of the Greek and Turkish nations and considered the Cyprus issue as their "national issue." Cyprus carried a heavy load of national pride and honor and had a great appeal in domestic Greek and Turkish politics. Geographic proximity and strategic considerations added another dimension to Greek and Turkish interests in Cyprus.

Attachment of the two ethnic groups to two rival states, which have been at sword's edge for centuries, prevented the generation of common patriotic bonds or overarching loyalties supportive of the newborn Cypriot state. The "suspicion syndrome" dominating Greek-Turkish relations and perceptions was transplanted into Cyprus, and it eliminated any hope of constructive interaction among the Cypriots. It was in this setting of national polarization and cross-boundary ethnic alliances that intercommunal violence erupted in

1963. The communal flare-up provided an opportunity for the mainlands to come in support of their local ethnic groups and become involved in Cyprus and part of the Cyprus problem.

The 1967 Crisis

The already tense Greek-Turkish relations deteriorated further with the ascent to power of a Greek nationalist right-wing military junta in April 1967. Seven months later, in November, another short but sharp crisis made Cyprus a flashpoint in international politics and brought Greece and Turkey again to the brink of war. The United States urgently intervened diplomatically to manage the crisis and to prevent its escalation. President Johnson hastily dispatched former Secretary of Defense Cyrus Vance to the troubled region with the succinct instruction: "Do what you have to to stop the war. If you need anything let me know."[29]

The American envoy was successful in resolving the crisis by exercising pressure on the Greek military regime, which was largely responsible for the crisis, and satisfying most of the Turkish demands. One of the Turkish demands that was met was the withdrawal of the 10,000 Greek troops that had infiltrated into Cyprus in 1964.

Although the 1967 crisis was eventually resolved, a settlement of the broader ethnopolitical conflict never came within sight. The United States could exercise considerable influence on Greece and Turkey, but that was not enough for the promotion of a final and comprehensive solution. President Makarios, with Moscow on his side, showed no interest in negotiating such a settlement with Western powers. Therefore, the problem remained and so did the prospects for another flare-up and more bloodshed.

The 1974 Crisis and its Aftermath

The strong antipathy towards Makarios shared by Washington and the military regime in Athens provided the impetus for a new round of violence and bloodshed in 1974. Following a seven-year period of tension and hostility with Makarios, the Greek military regime attempted to overthrow him. On 15 July 1974, the Greek forces stationed on Cyprus and the Greek-controlled Cypriot national guard staged a bloody coup against the Cypriot president that brought to power an extremist pro-*enosis* puppet regime.

Turkey reacted fiercely to the military intervention of Athens by invading Cyprus and occupying 35% of the island. The Turkish government justified its action on legal and ethnic grounds. It argued that the Greek coup was a step toward annexation that was prohibited by the 1960 Treaty of Guarantee. It also claimed that the Treaty of Guarantee had established a responsibility and a right for Turkey to intervene and protect the Turkish Cypriots. According to the Turkish argument, the nationalist policies and behavior of the Greek military regime posed a direct threat to the Turkish community on the island.

The coup and the invasion of 1974 once again brought Greece and Turkey to the brink of war and necessitated outside diplomatic intervention. The United States, deeply concerned over the prospects of a catastrophic escalation of the crisis, offered to mediate to prevent an "unthinkable" war from happening. Secretary of State Henry Kissinger dispatched Undersecretary for Political Affairs Joseph Sisco to the troubled region two days after the coup, while Turkey was preparing for the invasion. Sisco failed to prevent the invasion and a second diplomatic initiative was taken by Britain to contain the crisis and its consequences. A peace conference was held in Geneva under the chairmanship of the British Foreign Minister James Callaghan, but without success.

The 1974 confrontation brought to Cyprus destruction and demographic changes unique in its history. Following the diplomatic failures of Sisco and Callaghan, Turkey launched a second massive attack on Cyprus, completing its control of 35% of the island and bringing about an exchange of populations by force. The Greek Cypriots living in the north were forced to move to the south and the Turkish Cypriots living in the south were transferred to the north. This exchange of populations, which made one-third of the Cypriots refugees in their own country, brought into effect a physical separation of two communities that had been living together for four centuries. The forceful creation of two separate ethnic zones demarcated by the heavily fortified "Attila line" and a buffer zone controlled by UN forces eliminated any interaction between the two sides and made the reunification of the island a difficult task.

SEARCHING FOR A SETTLEMENT

Role of the United Nations

Several initiatives and attempts to devise a solution made so far by the UN, or in the name of the UN, did not lead anywhere. The most recent one, which lasted four years, culminated in the submission of a comprehensive plan for a settlement (known as the Annan Plan after the UN Secretary General, Kofi Annan) in 2004 but almost immediately ended in failure. The Greek Cypriots and the Turkish Cypriots played a major role in negotiating the plan. Greece and Turkey also played some role in assisting this effort. The United Nations, in close cooperation with the European Union, the United States, and Britain, also played a role, and made a contribution in shaping the Annan Plan. In March 2004, the plan was finalized by the UN Secretary General who "filled in the gaps" during a hasty conference in Switzerland and presented it to the leaders of Greece, Turkey, the Greek Cypriots, and the Turkish Cypriots. In finalizing his Plan, the UN Secretary General used his discretion "to fill in the blanks" and he completed the text on issues on which the two sides failed to reach an agreement. The Plan was not exactly and fully the result of negotiation, but rather a compromise on several key issues reflecting external involvement and an urgency to overcome long-standing deadlocks and to settle the problem a few days before Cyprus's accession to the EU. It provided for the establishment of a new state of affairs on the island based on a loose bizonal, bicommunal federal political system.[30] It was a huge text, comprising a federal constitution of about 250 pages, a constitution for each of the two constituent states, and about 9,000 pages of laws for the new United Republic of Cyprus.[31]

On 24 April 2004, the two Cypriot communities held separate, simultaneous referenda on the Annan Plan. Voters in the two communities were asked to answer "yes" or "no" to the following question: "Do you approve the Foundation Agreement with all its Annexes, as well as the constitution of the Greek Cypriot/Turkish Cypriot State and the provisions as to the laws to be in force, to bring into being a new state of affairs in which Cyprus joins the European Union united?"[32]

A majority of the Greek Cypriots (75.8%) voted "no" and a majority of the Turkish Cypriots (64.9%) voted "yes." The Greek-Cypriot rejection of the Annan Plan evoked a negative reaction from the international community, especially the UN, the EU, the United States, and Britain. As the UN Secretary General put it, it was "another missed opportunity to resolve the Cyprus problem."[33] Apparently, a majority of the Greek Cypriots believed that the Plan was neither fair nor functional. In particular the provisions on security, the Turkish settlers (who moved to Cyprus after the Turkish invasion of 1974 and today outnumber the Turkish Cypriots), the gradual withdrawal of the Turkish army, the exchange of properties, and the return of refugees made Greek Cypriot voters especially unhappy. There were also serious questions about the implementation and viability of the Plan that created feelings of uncertainty and insecurity among Greek Cypriots.[34]

The results of the referenda and the accession of Cyprus to the EU a week later created a new political setting. The Greek Cypriots joined the EU, but at least temporarily lost some of the international support they had enjoyed for decades. The Turkish Cypriots and Turkey, on the other hand, gained some political benefits. Turkey, however, which started accession negotiations with the EU in 2005, continues to face difficulties in its European policy because of the Cyprus dispute.

Role of the European Union

Since the accession of Cyprus on 1 May 2004, the EU, in cooperation with the United Nations, has been in a unique position to play a role on Cyprus and in the region. The parties involved are either part of the EU or have special relations with it and can, therefore, appreciate and support a European contribution or initiative on Cyprus. Greece is a member-state while Turkey is as close to the EU as a nonmember-state can be, following the commencement of accession negotiations in October 2005. Britain, a major partner in the EU and a guarantor power of the independence and unity of Cyprus under the 1960 settlement of the colonial issue, is in a privileged position to play a constructive role within and outside the EU context. The United States is also concerned with Cyprus because the Eastern Mediterranean is a region of vital geopolitical importance to it, Turkey is an "important strategic partner," and Greece is an "old good friend."

The EU favors a settlement that will reunite the island and its people under a bizonal bicommunal federation not unlike the Annan Plan. Such a solution would, of course, have to guarantee the civil, political, economic, and cultural rights of all Cypriots without any restriction or discrimination, and the security of all Cypriots in each and every respect—and not only in military terms. The institutions, legal order, principles, and policies of the EU—the *acquis communautaire*—have the capacity to provide a conducive framework in the search for a solution on Cyprus. A settlement based on the law, policies, and practices of the EU could provide a sound basis for peaceful coexistence and prosperity for all Cypriots, given the role of the European integration process, for half a century, in bringing states and peoples together under conditions of interdependence and peaceful coexistence. The dynamics of the single market and the advent of economic and monetary union have taken over in strengthening the conditions for peace, as the free movement of people, goods, services, and capital reduces the risks of intercommunal conflict.

Under the circumstances, it is not surprising that the most widely canvassed settlement is one based on a bizonal and bicommunal form of federation where all citizens would enjoy universally accepted rights and opportunities all over the island. Given the realities of Cyprus—geography, economy, size, distribution of natural resources, demography, and the political failures of the past—a federal solution seems to be the only pragmatic way out of the stalemate.

Looking at the broader impact that European integration may have on the triangle of Cyprus, Turkey, and Greece, it could be argued that the EU provides a new context within which the relations of the three countries can improve. In recent years, Greek-Turkish relations have improved considerably and Greece's policy towards Turkish accession is a positive one, but this cannot always be taken for granted as it depends on the political barometer in Europe as well as over the Aegean and Cyprus. The fact that Turkey does not recognize the Republic of Cyprus—a full member of the EU—may lead to political complications, especially in the context of accession negotiations, but by resolving the Cyprus problem Turkey can expect major political benefits from Europe.

CONCLUSION

In general, a settlement of the Cyprus problem may have a catalytic effect on Greek-Turkish relations and may generate a momentum for addressing other bilateral issues. Moreover, it cannot go unnoticed that Cyprus is not only a source of Greek-Turkish tension but also a major economic burden for the two countries that traditionally included the island in their defense doctrines and strategies. For Turkey the burden is much higher because it maintains a sizable army on the island (about 30,000) and also provides extensive financial support to the Turkish Cypriots. The failure of the Annan Plan, the accession of Cyprus, and the ongoing accession negotiations between Turkey and the European Union have created a new reality, additional urgency, and a promising prospect. A new momentum is also emerging for the reunification of the island, which is too small to remain divided, but big enough to accommodate all its people as a reunited EU member-state.

NOTES

1. Alan James, *Keeping the Peace in the Cyprus Crisis of 1963–64* (London: Palgrave, 2002), p. 3.

2. According to the 1960 census, the population of Cyprus was 572,707, distributed as follows: Greek Cypriots 447,901 (78.20%); Turkish Cypriots 103,822 (18.13%); Other (mainly Maronites, Armenians, and Latins) 20,984 (3.66%).

3. For detailed statistics and an extensive analysis of the demography of Cyprus at the time of independence, see L. W. St. John Jones, *The Population of Cyprus* (London: Maurice Temple Smith, 1983).

4. For a variety of perspectives and insightful analyses on the history, culture, and demography of Cyprus, see the collective volume Vangelis Calotychos (ed.), *Cyprus and Its People: Nation, and Experience in an Unimaginable Community, 1955–1997* (Boulder, CO: Westview Press, 1998).

5. By the seventeenth century the archbishop became recognized as the *ethnarch* (ethnic political leader) of the Greek Cypriot community. Thus, the religious leader also became *ex officio* political leader. That practice remained unchanged until Cyprus became independent in 1960. This explains, to some degree, why it was easy for Archbishop Makarios to win the first presidential elections and become the first president of Cyprus.

6. The word *millet* is of Arabic origin. It appears in the Koran with the meaning of religion. In the Ottoman Empire it came to mean ethnic/religious group. For remarks on the application of the *millet* system in Cyprus, see H. D. Purcell, *Cyprus* (New York: Praeger, 1968), pp. 169–75.

7. The idea of *enosis* dates back to the creation of the modern Greek state in 1830. It became a political issue when the British took control of Cyprus in 1878. Under Ottoman rule its propagation was not allowed. The Greek Cypriots saw the change from Ottoman to British rule as a first step toward the achievement of *enosis*. For accounts on the emergence of the idea of *enosis* and the evolution of the *enosis* movement see Anita Walker, "Enosis in Cyprus: Dhali, a Case Study," *Middle East Journal*, Vol. 38, No. 3 (1984), pp. 474–94; and Michael Attalides, *Cyprus: Nationalism and International Politics* (New York: St. Martin's Press, 1979), pp. 22–35.

8. Two measures illustrating the segregationist character of British policy may be given as examples. First, the Greek and Turkish members of the legislative council were elected separately by the two communities. Second, during the Greek Cypriot revolt against British colonial rule (1955–59), a special police consisting primarily of Turkish Cypriots was set up by the colonial administration to fight the Greek Cypriot guerillas.

9. Purcell, *Cyprus*, p. 245.

10. For detailed accounts on domestic and international developments during the period 1955–59, see Robert Holland, *Britain and the Revolt in Cyprus* (Oxford, UK: Clarendon Press, 1998); and Nancy Crawshaw, *The Cyprus Revolt: An Account of the Struggle for Union with Greece* (London: Allen and Unwin, 1978).

11. For a standard work on the Greek appeals to the UN and other developments in the international diplomacy see Stephen Xydis, *Cyprus: Conflict and Reconciliation, 1954–1958* (Columbus, OH: Ohio State University Press, 1967).

12. UN doc. A/2703, letter dated 16 Aug. 1954, from the Greek prime minister to the secretary-general requesting the inclusion of the Cyprus issue in the agenda of the General Assembly.

13. For extensive analyses and interpretations of the legal and political aspects and consequences of the 1960 founding treaties see R. St. J. Macdonald, "International Law and the Conflict on Cyprus," *Canadian Yearbook of International Law,* Vol. 29 (1981), pp. 3–49; and Thomas Ehrlich, *Cyprus, 1958–1967: International Crises and the Role of Law* (New York: Oxford University Press, 1974).

14. Treaty of Guarantee, art. 1.

15. Ibid., art. 4.

16. Art. 2 of the Constitution identified the two communities as follows: "(1) the Greek Community comprises all citizens of the Republic who are of Greek origin and whose mother tongue is Greek or who share the Greek cultural traditions or who are members of the Greek-Orthodox Church; (2) the Turkish Community comprises all citizens of the Republic who are of Turkish origin and whose mother tongue is Turkish or who share the Turkish cultural traditions or who are Moslems."

17. Constitution, art. 1.

18. Ibid., art. 4.

19. In 1985 these figures were changed to 56 Greek Cypriots and 24 Turkish Cypriots, although, because of the de facto partition of the island, Turkish Cypriots representatives have not been serving in the parliament.

20. Constitution, art. 78.

21. Ibid., art. 173.

22. Ibid., art. 182.

23. Glenn D. Camp, "Greek-Turkish Conflict over Cyprus," *Political Science Quarterly,* Vol. 95, No. 1 (1980), p. 49.

24. Diana Weston Markides, *Cyprus 1957–1963, From Colonial Conflict to Constitutional Crisis: The Key Role of the Municipal Issue* (Minneapolis: University of Minnesota, Minnesota Mediterranean and East European Monograph No. 8, 2001), pp. 187–88.

25. Anna Jarstad, *Changing the Game: Consociational Theory and Ethnic Quotas in Cyprus and New Zealand* (Uppsala, Sweden: Uppsala University, Department of Peace and Conflict Research, Report No. 58, 2001), p. 165.

26. Memorandum submitted by President Makarios to Vice-President Kutchuk on 30 Nov. 1963 under the heading "Suggested Measures to Facilitate the Smooth Functioning of the State and Remove Certain Causes of Intercommunal Friction." This is a widely cited document. The entire document can be found in *Facts about Cyprus* (Nicosia, Cyprus: Cyprus Chamber of Commerce and Industry, 1964); reproduced in Halil Ibrahim Salih, *Cyprus: The Impact of Diverse Nationalism on a State* (Tuscaloosa, AL: University of Alabama Press, 1978).

27. Ibid.

28. James, p. 179.

29. Quoted in Cyrus Vance, *Hard Choices: Critical Years in American Foreign Policy: Memoirs* (New York: Simon and Schuster, 1983), p. 144.

30. For an extensive account of the developments that led to the shaping of the Annan Plan and its failure, see the "Report of the Secretary General on his Mission of Good Offices in Cyprus," UN doc. S/2004/437, 28 May 2004.

31. The Annan Plan was submitted in five versions during the period from Nov. 2002 to April 2004. As indicated by its official title, it aimed at "The Comprehensive Settlement of the Cyprus Problem."

32. The question was included in the Annan Plan, *Annex IX: Coming into being of the New State of Affairs,* art. 1.

33. "Report of the Secretary General on his Mission of Good Offices in Cyprus," UN doc. S/2004/437, 28 May 2004, p. 18.

34. An elaborate account of the Greek Cypriot positions on the weaknesses and rejection of the Annan Plan was presented in a long letter by the President of the Republic of Cyprus to the UN Secretary General dated 7 June 2004. For an insightful analysis and useful information on the background, context and failure of the Annan Plan, see David Hannay, *Cyprus: The Search for a Solution* (London: I. B. Tauris, 2005).

7

Lebanon: From Consociationalism to Conciliation

SIMON HADDAD

Lebanese-American University

This article seeks to interpret recent developments in Lebanon in the light of a well-known theory, consociationalism, which presents itself as a model for the government of deeply divided societies. It therefore begins by looking at the character of this particular approach to government, describing the main features of consociationalism. The next section explores the historical background to contemporary Lebanese politics, from the pre-independence period to the 2005 crisis. This is followed by a discussion of events since 2005, and of the changing dynamics of Lebanese politics. The last section seeks to interpret these events, returning to the question of consociationalism and questioning its relevance in understanding the Lebanese conflict.

INTRODUCTION

On 7 May 2008, sectarian strife broke out in Lebanon reminiscent of the earlier civil war, causing severe human and property loss and threatening theessential fabric of Lebanon's fragile confessional democracy. Before the outbreak of these events, Lebanon's consensual democracy had suffered a fully-fledged political stalemate in the form of a vacant presidential office, a government whose constitutionality was questioned by a considerable part of the population, and a parliament that failed even to convene. The conflict was fought between two alliances dating from the 2005 assassination of premier Rafik Hariri: the conservative March 14 Bloc, aiming at the preservation of the status quo, and the March 8 Alliance, striving for the application of three essential consociational features entailing a more equitable share in power. These were a more representative governmental coalition, a veto right, and legislative elections under a fair law. As will be shown, the conflict was mitigated through unconventional conflict-resolution methods—through conciliation and not through institutional procedures.

This article seeks to interpret recent developments in Lebanon in the light of a well-known theory, consociationalism, which presents itself as a model for the government of deeply divided societies. It therefore begins by looking at the character of this particular approach to government, describing its main features. The next section explores the historical background to contemporary Lebanese politics, from the pre-independence period to the 2005 crisis. This is followed by a discussion of events since 2005, and the changing dynamics of Lebanese politics. The last section seeks to interpret these events, returning to the question of consociationalism and questioning its relevance in understanding the Lebanese conflict.

CONSOCIATIONALISM IN LEBANON

Consociationalism refers to a fragmented but stable political system, where the elites undertake institutional and procedural measures to maintain communal stability. These measures are presumed to provide equitable representation for all groups. Consociationalism also assumes pluralism and frequent intercommunal dialogue. Arend Lijphart identifies consociational democracies as fragmented but stable political democracies that seek to elide the problem of majority rule altogether by requiring the inclusion of all groups in government.[1] As is well known, the consociational approach is essentially a regime of guarantees and proposes the following principles:

- Proportional inclusion: Political elites participate in a governing grand decision-making coalition (cabinet) in proportion to their numbers as determined by election results conducted under a proportional representation system. This implies that opposition is located inside the government. Both moderates and extremists are to be represented proportionally in cabinets.
- Mutual vetoes: Major political decisions in cabinet or parliament are consensual and can be challenged by a minority that includes a prespecified proportion of cabinet or parliamentary votes.
- Segmental autonomy: Each community runs its own internal affairs autonomously. The elites representing different communities, therefore, should keep their communities under tight control. This control is achieved by discouraging intercommunal relations.

In a critique of the consociational approach, Horowitz warns that this model suffers from at least three deficiencies. First, it does not place the abolition of ethnic conflict on its agenda. It accepts the existence of ethnic cleavages and attempts to manage their effects by guaranteed representation and outcomes, or by various regimes of incentives to moderation, cooperation, or fragmentation. Second, it assumes that a majority ethnic group, where one exists, will be willing to exchange the complete power it could gain through the polls for a frustrating system of power sharing, including minority vetoes. Third, proportional representation has a polarizing effect that increases the distance between voting blocs in societies that already possess some degree of polarized identities.[2]

Horowitz fairly remarks that in severely divided societies the recent record of consociational constitutions (or the presence of some consociational features) shows that they have more or less succeeded in containing violence, but where consociational arrangements are reached between a variety of armed factions, as in Lebanon, peace is volatile, whether because the factions cannot be integrated as a single armed force, or because the arrangement is merely tactical, or because the presence of arms makes leaders willing to take direct action at the first signs of a breach.[3] Surprisingly, Horowitz does not mention Lebanon as a model of consociationalism, despite the consensual nature of its political arrangement under the Ta'if Accord. He maintains that, although Lebanon's system contains consociational aspects (including grand coalition government and political vetoes), it is at best a hybrid, since the electoral system is centripetal or incentive based: multimember constituencies and reserved seats but common and not communal electoral rolls.[4]

Despite the presence of some elements of consociationalism, then, Lebanon does not fit this model fully. Lebanon is not a pluralist society; it is a plurality of peoples who do not have enough in common to warrant the establishment and maintenance of a viable state.[5] According to Barakat, the social structure of Lebanon is a mosaic, characterized by the following features:[6]

1. *Lack of consensus on fundamentals.* Despite Muslims' recurrent demands, the Maronites refused to grant them any concession in the area of political representation until the proclamation of the Ta'if Accord in 1989, even during 15 years of civil war. The Maronites clung to their political supremacy based on what they saw as an immutable National Pact.
2. *Absence of open dialogue.* Elite communication is essential to spare the country tension and instability and to resolve disputes. In general, institutional procedures do not solve problems (in such areas as the police, the army, and the judiciary); these are normally resolved through direct elite intervention.
3. *Lack of loyalty to the country.* A general assumption about the Lebanese communities is that the Christians have always been seeking partition or federalism and that Sunni Muslims wanted to be incorporated in a larger Arab Muslim state. While these ideas have been dismissed following the Ta'if Accord, the ideological debate shifted in the aftermath of Syria's

withdrawal: the Shi'ites manifested allegiance to Syria and Iran while the Druze, Sunnis, and part of the Christians expressed attachment to the West. More recently, the Druze leader Walid Jumblat, a pioneer of the March 14 Movement, took a more neutral stance and restated his attachment to Arabism and Syria.

4. *Geographical representation of the different religious communities.* During the civil war, the Maronites and Druze enjoyed de facto control of different parts of the country while the Sunnis and Shi'ites were opposed to the authority of the state. The country risked being partitioned. This was highlighted by large waves of displaced persons who were forced to migrate from heterogeneous areas.

5. *A strong link between religion and the state (segmental autonomy).* Communal transactions such as marriage, divorce, baptism, and civil laws and rights are confined to religious authorities independent of the state apparatus. This amounts to a nonterritorial federation where autonomy exists inside each community without being confined to a specific region, as in Lebanon there are rarely homogenous regions with a concentration of a specific minority.

6. *Conflicting reference groups.* The primary allegiance of Lebanese people is to their sect. For the Lebanese, the religious community is the nation; that is the people to whom one belongs, and with whom one identifies.[7] Membership in the sect serves mainly as a reference in regard to the world at large. It follows that the different confessional groups perceive themselves in the first place along confessional lines as Maronites, Sunnis, Druze, and so on. They do not perceive themselves as Lebanese.[8] The notion of citizenship is weak and there is a lack of a unified national identity.

7. *An educational system that reinforces the stratified social mosaic.* The Lebanese undergo different socialization processes: parochialism infiltrates the media. Television, radio, and newspapers are diverse, and each follows a particular communal orientation. Christians make use of some, while Muslims use others. This also applies to schools and universities, which reflect the sectarian divergence in the country.

In addition, at the political level, while the system matches in certain respects the main features described in consociational theory, namely proportionality in the allocation of political posts and electoral quotas and segmental autonomy, other features, such as grand coalitions and vetoes, have been consistently missing.[9] The distorted application of consociational principles continued to characterize post-Ta'if governance, as will be seen below. Lebanon thus offers an important testing ground for consociational theory. It is appropriate now to turn to those arrangements in the past that laid the groundwork for the contemporary alignment of political forces and the set of institutional choices.

EVOLUTION OF THE LEBANESE CONFLICT

Any understanding of contemporary Lebanese politics needs to take account of its historical origin. We may see this as having passed through four phases. The first is the pre-independence period, during which the seeds of later conflicts were sown. The second is the period of over three decades of relative stability under the National Pact of 1943 that coincided with Lebanese independence. The third is the civil war period of 1975–90, with its disruptive effect on conventional politics. The fourth is the post-1989 period, during which the Ta'if Accord offered a new blueprint for government.

The Ottoman and European Legacies

Confessionalism in the Lebanese system was introduced by the Ottoman Turks, who first emphasized group differences in the Arab East generally, and particularly in what is now Lebanon, by compartmentalizing ethno-religious differences through the introduction of the "*millet* system." Non-Muslims were treated as second-class citizens and forced to pay a tax in exchange for protection. However, Ottoman rule over Mount Lebanon (the core of what is now Lebanon) in the sixteenth century resulted in a sequence of instability, bloodshed, and sectarian strife that culminated in the massacre of several thousand Maronites by Druze in 1860. These incidents led to intervention by European powers and the introduction of a new form of governance, the *Muttassarifyia* or organic statute arrangements, in 1861. Power was to be allocated on a confessional basis. The *Muttassarif* (governor) was to be a non-Lebanese Christian, assisted in running the affairs of the governorate by an advisory council of 12 elected members proportionally representing the different religious communities. This system served as a guideline for the construction of modern Lebanon in 1943. It gave influence to the ascending Maronite community, who, however, continued to express opposition to the *Muttassarif*, demanding an end to Ottoman rule and an autonomous political entity. However, the period was characterized by religious coexistence, economic prosperity, and stability until the First World War.

With the collapse of the Ottoman Empire, the Treaty of Versailles in 1919 placed Lebanon and Syria under French mandate. The French proclaimed the state of Greater Lebanon in 1920. The Muslim-populated regions of Beirut, Bekaa, Saida, and Tripoli were added to the predominantly Christian Mount Lebanon to form a heterogeneous state. None of the regions contained a denominationally uniform population, and no community formed a majority of the population. The last official census to ascertain the confessional proportions dates from 1932: it was found that Christians exceeded non-Christians by a ratio of 6 to 5 (Maronites 29%, Sunnis 22%, and Shi'ites 20%).[10] The newly independent entity faced problems of legitimacy and political integration as two culturally different groups with politically divergent views were incorporated into Greater Lebanon. The Maronites, under French patronage, sought to obtain political supremacy in political offices, while Muslims resented the emerging state and looked for incorporation into the larger Arab world. In 1941, Lebanon was occupied by allied forces, and the Free French promised the Maronites independence; this was eventually achieved in 1943 and given expression in the National Pact of that year.

The National Pact, 1943

The conflict that generated the 1943 pact was essentially one between Maronites and Sunnis, with other groups on the sidelines. The National Pact, an unwritten agreement between the two main communities, attempted to promote stability through accommodation, co-optation, and representation. First, it was meant to reconcile opposing views within the country over matters of identity and foreign policy: the Maronites would sever their relations with France, and the Muslims would dump their aspirations for Arab unity, both expressing their will to live in the newly independent entity. Second, the pact would stabilize expectations among sects by defining the manner in which power was to be distributed. It would also co-opt the leadership of the various sects through a system of power sharing based on sectarian representation. Inside the parliament, seats were allocated according to a 6:5 ratio in favor of the Christians. Ministerial posts as well as other civil service appointments also followed the principle of sectarian quotas.

A tacit understanding, however, reserved the key political posts, the presidency, the premiership, and the speakership of parliament, to the Maronites, Sunnis, and Shi'ites, respectively. Being the head of the executive with a six-year mandate, the president had by far the most important function, with sweeping powers over the cabinet and parliament. Despite Muslim demands for political reform, Christian leaders refused to make any concession regarding the allocation of political representation.

The Civil War, 1975–90

Over the three decades that followed independence, Christians were asked to give concessions to Muslim demands for greater participation in political power commensurate with their increased demographic weight.[11] Muslim calls for an adjustment in the proportional allocation of posts were countered by fierce Maronite reaction claiming that "a leading Maronite role is the only guarantee to preserve the security of the community."[12] Maronite domination of key political and military positions was seen as an important guarantee against pan-Arab nationalism and served to calm Maronite worries concerning the country's independence. This eventually led to civil strife in 1958, demonstrating the feebleness of the internal equilibrium and further deepening Christian-Muslim cleavages.

In the 1960s, the resurgence of Arab nationalism and the repercussions of the Arab-Israeli conflict further challenged the pact. Expedited by a massive Palestinian military build-up in the country, Lebanon's religious, social, economic, and ideological tensions ultimately exploded in a protracted civil war (1975–90). This war was fought over a number of issues, including the balance of power in government, the role of the armed Palestinian groups, the redistribution of wealth, and Lebanon's foreign policy orientation. The conflicting attitudes held by Christians and Muslims over the Palestinian presence in the country revealed the precariousness of the Lebanese political system and the degree to which the Lebanese were not genuinely integrated.

The pact allowed the country to proceed to independence and contributed to its relative stability during the next three decades. However, the fragmentation of the Lebanese system along ethno-religious or communal lines, characterized by negligible social contact and very limited integration, has led some political scientists to classify Lebanon as a consociational democracy until 1975, when the civil war broke out, leading to the collapse of the system.

The Ta'if Accord

The "Ta'if Accord," charted by Lebanese parliamentary deputies in 1989 under Arab sponsorship, ended the conflict and hypothetically established internal conditions for peace. Basically, although not all parties consented to the accord, its imposition as a solution in the form of a communal contract was made possible because no party or community emerged victorious during the war, and also because no party or community could claim to be a majority (in terms of demographic weight). Maintaining the peace, therefore, was and continues to be a matter of maintaining a balance of sharing power and of preserving the rights of communities that view themselves as the bedrock on which the Lebanese state is constructed.[13]

The Ta'if Accord attempted to achieve intercommunal equilibrium by embracing a consensual, sectarian logic. It dictated procedures for distributing public offices among the various communities and provided communities with a veto power to facilitate regulation of conflicting sectarian interests. Essentially, the agreement wrought a change in the political structure to take account of the new power balances among the communities: the decline of the Maronites and the advance of the Sunnis and the Shi'ites. A gap exists, however, between what is prescribed in texts and actual practice. The implementation of the accord turned out to be selective and controversial, leading to an increase in discord in a highly segmented Lebanese society.

Though Lebanon still has a Christian president, his authority no longer towers over the Sunni prime minister or the Shi'ite speaker of parliament. The agreement speaks of a distribution of power among all communities based on parity between Christians and Muslims. In accordance with this, the council of ministers became an autonomous authority, exerting all the prerogatives taken from the president. On the other hand, the increase in the mandate of the speaker of the parliament to four years gave him an important role in the election of the president, the formation of cabinets, and the control of government activities.[14] Similarly, the agreement prescribes a veto power in order to reinforce consociational practice and to enable minorities to challenge decisions that harm their interests. However, in practice, the blocking veto was granted to pro-Syrian majorities and never to Christian opposition or independent ministers, ensuring that Syrian priorities would face no objection inside the council of ministers. In relation to this, an innovation of the new constitutional arrangements was that major policy issues and resource allocation have been subjected to intercommunal consensus among the top three offices (the president, premier, and speaker), as representatives of their respective communities (the Maronites, the Sunnis, and the Shi'ites). A three-way understanding replaced the Maronite-Sunni covenant of 1943.

However, the accord did nothing to curtail Syrian influence in Lebanon, which continued to increase until April 2005, a process of steady growth that may be dated back to the late 1980s. An intricate system of Syrian control ensured official Lebanese compliance with Syrian guidelines. This combined military and intelligence ubiquitousness, economic penetration, a sizeable Syrian civilian presence, control of the Lebanese military command, and meticulous screening of domestic office aspirants in a pervasive patronage system, where political appointments and personal loyalties appeared to coincide.[15] Few political decisions were made without the involvement of Damascus, and it was widely understood that Syria routinely intervened in all affairs of the Lebanese government. Local decisions were tailored to suit Syrian preferences, and no decision was made that would have even the remotest likelihood of offending Damascus.

Parliamentary elections failed to ensure political normalization and prepared inadequately for the national reconciliation and integration that was envisaged. Electoral laws were tailored to fit specific political purposes, to the benefit of those who approved of full cooperation with the ruling class and to the disadvantage of those who might be expected to resist. Designed to consolidate Syrian influence, elections succeeded in depriving important segments of genuine representation, in marginalizing all opposition and in preparing the ground for pro-Syrian governments in the post-civil war period. Political alienation resulted also from appointing militia leaders to governmental positions, contributing to the malfunctioning of the institutions and thus of the political system more generally, and severely constraining the state's ability to function in an autonomous manner.

The Ta'if Accord ended sectarian violence in Lebanon but disrupted the political equilibrium between the communities, replacing the hegemony of one community (the Maronites) by that of another (the Shi'ites and Sunnis). Conflict regulation was confined to the allies of Syria, who controlled every facet of Lebanon's political life, ensuring that the government in Beirut remained responsive to Damascus.

NEW FORMS OF POLITICS

The fragile architecture of the Ta'if Accord was ill designed to withstand the new tensions that beset Lebanon in the late twentieth and early twenty-first centuries. These included a new set of political relationships, as the character of inter-bloc alliances was redefined, and the relationship with Syria was challenged more profoundly than at any time since the 1970s. They also included new realities in the disposition of power, with the rise of Hezbollah (the Party of God), demonstrated most strikingly in the 2006 conflict with Israel and related political events. These changes led to a revisiting of the Ta'if Accord, resulting in a revision that was given effect by the Doha Agreement of 2008. We consider these three matters in turn.

A Bipolar Party System

With the assassination of Prime Minister Rafik Hariri in Feb. 2005 and the ensuing retreat of Syrian forces from the country, where they had been installed since 1976, Lebanon's sociopolitical life regrouped in the form of two rival factions. Up to this point, Lebanon's fractured party system had consisted of a set of parties representing in varying degrees particular confessional groups. This multiparty configuration now consolidated itself into two alliances deriving their labels from crucial events in 2005 (March 8, when the largest pro-Syrian demonstration was held, and March 14, the date of the "Cedar revolution," in which Syria was expelled from Lebanon). The boundaries of the new alliances cut across traditional religious ones. On one side was the March 8 Alliance, composed of Hezbollah, Amal, and other pro-Syrian factions; on the other was the March 14 Bloc, comprising basically the Hariri Future Current, the Progressive Socialist Party headed by Walid Jumblat, the Lebanese Forces and Phalangists, and, later, the Free Patriotic Movement headed by General Michel Aoun. Rivalry between the two took the form of mass demonstrations and counterdemonstrations for and against the Syrian military presence in the country. As Abu Khalil puts it, "No more is the classic Christian-Muslim divide relevant; nor the narrow Sunni-Maronite divide, which dominated the squabbles of the Lebanese political elite in pre-war Lebanon. The two new camps have crystallized along lines that are rather new to the history of the Lebanese conflict."[16] Following the 2005 parliamentary elections, Aoun's Free Patriotic Movement, which emerged as the major Christian bloc, joined the March 8 Alliance.

The Ta'if Accord had incorporated into the political system a confessional schism, allocating public offices among confessional groups according to demographic and political weight, with the proportion of Muslims to Christians in the legislature coming to parity. Accordingly, the formation of the various post-Ta'if governments and parliaments took account of this constitutional principle. The 128 seats in the parliament were divided equally between Muslims and Christians, as were seats in the cabinet. Applying the Ta'if principle to the period under study (from 2005 onwards) would produce a government in which the Shi'ites would be entitled to 5 ministers out of the 24 (the total number of cabinet ministers after 2005). Even if they were all to resign, the cabinet would still be able to meet and take decisions by a two-thirds majority vote. This reflected neither Hezbollah's demographic strength nor its big political force on the ground. Since Hezbollah decided to participate in the political system in its current form, its only possibility of gaining the upper hand required it to participate in alliances based on negotiations, bargaining, and compromises.

Following the 2005 election, the March 8 Alliance possessed 59 MPs out of a total of 128, thus controlling 44% of the parliament. This would imply, theoretically, that this Hezbollah-led group would be entitled to more than 13 ministers out of the 30 of the future national unity cabinet. Aiming at obtaining veto power, it requested 11 ministers. Thus, after its alliance with the Free Patriotic Movement, the balance of power was tilted in Hezbollah's favor.[17]

The balance of power in the top political offices in the three most important institutions (presidency, government, and parliament) was already tilted to the advantage of the March 8 Alliance as incumbent President of the Republic Emile Lahoud (in office until 24 Nov. 2007) and Speaker of Parliament Nabih Berri both sided with the opposition. Therefore, the March 8 Alliance needed the veto power to lay their hands on the remaining crucial institution: the executive. As a result of the March 14 Bloc's reluctance to concede on all three demands, the opposition took to the streets until the incumbent government headed by Seniora acquiesced. On another level and in order to resolve the differences between the March 8 Alliance and the March 14 Bloc (ranging from relations with Syria to disarming Hezbollah), a sequence of sessions dubbed the "National Dialogue" attended by all 14 key communal representatives of the two blocs was held at the Parliament by speaker Berri from March to June 2006 to try to appease growing intercommunal tensions in the country. The talks stalled before the Israeli campaign in 2006.

The Israeli Campaign and its Consequences

The Hezbollah victory by default over Israel in 2006 had devastating consequences for Lebanon's internal political life. In the wake of Israel's war on Lebanon and stimulated by its own victory over Israel, Hezbollah and its allies in the opposition demanded (1) the implementation of the one-third veto power in the Council of Ministers specified in the Ta'if Accord, (2) the formation of a representative national unity government, and (3) the holding of early legislative elections based upon a more representative election law that all the Lebanese would agree upon, preferably one based upon proportional representation and small electoral districts.

Meanwhile, the two Hezbollah ministers, along with their three Amal colleagues and a pro-March 8 Alliance Greek Orthodox minister suspended their participation in the government on 11 November. This came after the cabinet was asked to endorse a proposal outlining the establishment of an international court to try the perpetrators of Hariri's assassination. Hezbollah and Amal objected to the decision because it was taken on the basis of a majority vote rather than consensus. The resignation of the six ministers did not lead to the collapse of the incumbent government, since eight would have to resign for this to occur.[18]

In the wake of these tensions, the assassination of Pierre Jemayyel, a prominent minister, took place on 21 November 2006. Since six ministers had already resigned, the resignation or assassination of one more would be a fatal blow to the Seniora Cabinet. Tensions subsequently erupted to a new high and a political deadlock took hold of Lebanese political life. The Speaker, Nabih Berri, refused to convene the parliament for more than 10 months following the resignation of the six ministers. As a goodwill gesture, he called for a parliamentary session on 25 September 2007 in order to elect a new president, but, since the two-thirds quorum was not met, Berri called for another session on 23 October 2007, which was again postponed to 12 November. The current president has also taken the view that the cabinet is unconstitutional following the November 2006 resignations, and refused to ratify any bill submitted to him by it.

Despite deteriorating security conditions,[19] on 1 December 2006 the Lebanese opposition undertook a sit-in, living and sleeping in hundreds of tents in the Beirut city center surrounding the prime minister's headquarters in an attempt to pressurize the government to resign. In a symbolic gesture that underlines the intensity of the Shi'ite-Sunni discord—Sunnis supporting the government headed by a Sunni, and a Shi'ite attempting to topple the cabinet—the Grand Mufti of Lebanon held a Friday prayer publicly in the office of the prime minister. Another symbolic gesture came from Saudi Arabia, as King Abdullah made telephone calls to the remaining ministers in the Grand Serail (the prime minister's headquarters) to express public support for the government.

Unable to score any political victory as a result of the sit-in in the Beirut business district, the opposition called for a general strike, associated with active blocking of main roads and incidents of violence. The short-lived civil unrest reached an unprecedented level of political violence as demonstrators resorted to the use of gunfire and the destruction of property and cars, with a toll amounting to 4 killed and 300 wounded. Fearing an uncontrolled escalation that could plunge the country into civil war, the Hezbollah leader called his men off the streets.

On 9 May 2008, Hezbullah and Amal militiamen (Shi'ites), aided by a few guerrillas belonging to the March 8 Alliance, but not including Aoun's (Christian) Free Patriotic Movement, launched a series of armed assaults in Beirut, pitching a few Lebanese regions into intersectarian battles much like the 1975–90 civil war. In a carefully calculated and coordinated operation, Hezbollah managed to take over the Sunni sector of Lebanon's capital after surrounding and isolating the part of the Southern Mount Lebanon region controlled by Walid Jumblat. Only the residences of Sunni leader Saad Hariri and of Jumblat, in Koraytem and Clemenceau respectively, were spared.[20]

The Doha Agreement

The Hezbollah led their armed uprising against the Siniora government in May 2008 ("Hezbollah's coup attempt"), in objection to the government's decision to investigate Hezbollah's phone network and to transfer an airport security chief with an alleged link to Hezbollah from his position. The result of this uprising was not only the killing and injuring of dozens of Lebanese citizens from all groups but also deeper distrust between the March 14 Bloc and the March 8 Group, in general, and the Sunnis and Shi'ites, in particular.[21] The political fallout was also significant. In a speech on 8 May, Sayyed Hassan Nasrallah, Hezbollah's secretary general, denounced the Lebanese government's decisions and interpreted them as synonymous to a declaration of war. His party, he said, would "cut off the hand" that dared to touch his organization's arms.[22] After two weeks of sectarian fighting across the country, the government offered to defer the two decisions to the Lebanese army command.

Hezbollah's military showdown came at the expense of Sunnis and to a lesser extent to the detriment of the main Druze faction, the Progressive Socialist Party. While the Druze combatants were able to resist and even to repel the Hezbollah offensive against their regions, the Sunni community in Beirut was heavily intimidated and repressed by Shi'ite factions and their allies. In a rare act of retribution, Sunni militiamen in the Northern Akkar region massacred eight Syrian Socialist Nationalist Party activists on 11 March in order to avenge the suppression of their counterparts in Beirut.

In spite of the Hezbollah-led actions, the Western-leaning government led by Prime Minister Fouad Siniora continued to function and withstood all the pressures aimed at toppling it. Within a few days, and under the Aegis of the Arab League, what is known as the Doha Agreement was signed in Doha, Qatar, on 21 May 2008 by the Lebanese political leaders participating in the conference. Welcomed by the United States, Saudi Arabia, Iran, and Syria, this deal brought a new head of state to Lebanon, revised the country's electoral formula, reactivated its parliament and other state institutions and gave its severely worn-out economy a prospect of recovery. The agreement called for the election of a consensus president, the commander-in-chief of the army, General Michel Suleiman. It stipulated also that a new cabinet would be made up of 16 ministers from the March 14 Bloc, the majority, 11 from the opposition, and 3 nominated by the president. Eleven ministers (one-third plus one) are all it takes for the opposition to block any government decision to which it is opposed. On the other hand the agreement called for adopting the *caza* (smaller district) as a constituency in conformity with the 1960 law.[23]

INTERPRETING THE LEBANESE MODEL

The Ta'if Accord was essentially intended to end the political stalemate in the country, which characterized the first republic (1943–89), and to reconcile the Lebanese to a program of internal reforms. If properly handled, the Ta'if political process would have provided an appropriate agenda for constitutional alteration—a more accommodating political setting and a more balanced functioning of the constitution instead of a selective interpretation, which alienated a major sector of the population. We may consider first some general interpretations of conflict resolution in Lebanon and then seek to identify the factors that have made the most significant contribution to this process more recently.

Consociational Perspectives

The challenge that the consociational model offers in Lebanon is considerable. For example, Rigby finds that while power sharing is the only practical solution in Lebanon "there is no shared sense of what it is to be Lebanese ... and that there is little hope for the eventual establishment in Lebanon of a secular democratic state which promotes citizenship without reference to communal or religious identity."[24] In similar fashion, Bieber, who studied civil wars in Lebanon and Bosnia, concluded that "in Lebanon confessional identity does not preclude coexistence with other confessions in one state."[25] The existing lack of confidence radically strengthens confessional identities and correspondingly constrains the propensity for intergroup cooperation without, however, completely hindering it. There is also an important external aspect. Seaver, for instance, emphasizes the regional dimension: the influence of Lebanon's neighbors on the political system and on the durability of institutional arrangements.[26] She warns that "a majoritarian system cannot replace the existing power-sharing arrangement but would only exacerbate tension and the probability of civil strife."[27] In a rather similar fashion, Kerr's comparative analysis of power-sharing agreements and peace processes in Northern Ireland and Lebanon concludes that dependence on outside powers governs conflict regulation and the success of consociationalism in both countries.[28]

In addition, various studies have emphasized the deficiencies of this power-sharing system and the endemic fragmentation of Lebanon's political culture. Jaafar, for instance, notes that consociationalism did not end Lebanon's problem.[29] The flaws that led to the collapse of the 1943 pact were maintained: the reinforcement of sectarian identity, the weakening of the state, the proliferation of alternative power centers, the prevalence of the inert nature of government and its failure to absorb new social forces, and the incapacity of this rigid political organization to adapt to a changing demographic environment. Choueiry notes that throughout Lebanon's political history each civil war was launched and settled under similar conditions: first, the absence of an adequate political formula; second, the emergence of a new sectarian configuration demanding representation; third, the imposition of a new settlement by outside forces, or through their mediation; and fourth, no Lebanese civil war has come to an end as a result of direct and unmediated negotiations by the parties concerned.[30] Beydoun goes further to say that "we believe the reasons behind violence in Lebanon do not lie within the previous wars but within the peace settlements that were adopted in Lebanon."[31]

The consociational model was successful in some small European states, such as the Netherlands and Switzerland, but its application in Lebanon is profoundly challenging in the light of the country's realities. Obviously the Lebanese civil war of 1975 and the recent political upheaval in the country have indicated that Lebanon does not meet all the requirements for a successful consociational democracy. True, the Lebanese system is characterized by distinct lines of cleavage: the Maronite-Sunni antagonism in the pre-civil war era, and the Sunni-Shi'ite intercommunal struggle more recently. Polarization also takes on an ideological aspect, with the Christians looking to the West and Sunnis to the Arab environment under the 1943 Pact, and the current conflict reflected in competition between the two multicommunal alliances, the pro-Western March 14 Bloc and the pro-Syria and pro-Iran March 8 Alliance. In prewar Lebanon, there was no consensus on the meaning of external threats or enemies. The Sunni Muslims used to perceive Israel as the enemy while Christians perceived Syria, the Palestinians, and Nasserism as a threat to the country's sovereignty. To the Maronite Christians nationalism meant "Lebanonism"; to the Muslims Lebanon was not a final entity. They conceived it as part of a larger Arab nation. Recently, from 2005 on, the Sunnis joined the Christians in perceiving Lebanon as a final arrangement and in viewing Syria as a common enemy.[32]

Paths Toward a Settlement

From the process of resolution of this particular dispute, one can draw a number of broad conclusions. These may be described as follows.[33]

First, as regards the procedural aspects of the crisis, it is clear that conflicts in Lebanon cannot be solved between and among the warring parties by themselves but necessitates intervention by a third party. In 1989, agreement was made possible through the convening of Lebanese MPs on Arab soil in Ta'if, Saudi Arabia, and because of intense pressures by Saudi Arabian leaders under the auspices of the Arab League. History repeated itself in Doha, where a settlement was reached on another Arab country's territory, Qatar, and due to personal and insistent intervention by the Qatari leadership. The analogy is important, as it shows on the one hand the intensity of intercommunal tensions inhibiting a meeting between Lebanese communal factions inside Lebanon and on the other hand it emphasizes also the third-party connectedness to these disputes.[34]

Second, the conflict resolution process tends to produce only a short-term end to the conflict, which may erupt once again later on. Each side is asked to make once-off concessions. In 2008, for example, the opposition was granted two of its demands—the one-third veto power in government and change in the electoral law. The progovernment coalition was accorded the possibility of electing its candidate for the presidency. In addition, they continue to head the government, to assume a majority inside it, and to maintain Seniora in office, despite the opposition request to replace him.

Third, in Lebanon a low-scale dispute can rapidly degenerate into a large-scale comprehensive conflict, which may become a serious threat, potentially disruptive to the normative order and requiring to be settled quickly if serious degeneration is to be avoided. Because the group, not the individual, is the central locus of action, the hostilities may spread from one region to another relatively quickly. The assault by the Shi'ites on the Sunnis in Beirut in 2008, for instance, shifted the dispute from a localized one in Beirut to a more general one involving Shi'ites and Sunnis in the Bekaa area of Taalabaya, and also in Northern Lebanon clashes erupted between Sunnis and Alawis in Tripoli and the Akkar region.

Fourth, the initiation and implementation of Arab mediation are based on the social norms and customs inherent in Arab society. Arab values of *oukhoua* ("brotherhood"), *solha* ("conciliation"), and so forth are referred to by Arab negotiators as a way to pressure sides to the conflict. Thus, Qatari mediators advocated settlement accords compatible with notions of justice that are accepted in their societies and are less concerned with lasting settlements in the very different context of Lebanon. They are emotionally involved in the dispute and have an interest in its settlement, since the Qatari leadership aims at an influential regional role similar to that of Saudi Arabia. On the other hand, because the Qatari mediators are very powerful and highly respected by the disputants, the disputants will try to maintain good relations with them. Therefore, authority to resolve a dispute is typically relinquished to Qatari leadership. As such, none of the outcomes of the agreement addresses the roots of the conflict: the need to establish viable political relations, to overcome communal and religious stereotypes and prejudice, and to rectify the imbalance of power between the communities. The mediators did not intend to handle the political consequences of the dispute. The settlement outcome did not deal with the future implications of the dispute or relationships between the parties. On the contrary, it relates to the dispute as a crisis situation and on an immediate basis as if no conflict exists between the two groups.

Fifth, the army commander was the main beneficiary of this political compromise, though the army remained throughout the conflict a neutral umpire setting the rules of the competitive game without having to step into the fray forcibly when the rules were violated and civil peace was thereby jeopardized. It is true that the military have been deployed with quite conscious attention to the communal composition that will be politically optimal for the nervous central government, but they have been keen not to intervene effectively to stop the bloodshed when needed. The compromise between the warring parties was placed on hold given the military's neutral position.

CONCLUSION

The first and most important lesson to be drawn from the conflict analyzed above is that pacts are not effective tools for accommodating tensions and mediating disputes in multicommunal societies such as Lebanon. In a brilliant study, Widner concludes that

> High hopes often attend efforts to write new constitutions. "Success" has many dimensions. A common aspiration includes the achievement of a durable agreement, an arrangement that will not be disregarded or suspended lightly and within a short period. More immediately and perhaps more importantly, people often hope for a reduction in violence and an increase in civility. The degree to which a constitution or a constitution-writing process displaces conflict from the streets and into institutions is an important measure of success.[35]

She adds that "whether a country has implemented the terms of a new constitution five years out from ratification may also capture an important dimension of the success of a process."[36] The Ta'if Accord has not reduced the likelihood of violence in the country, nor did the Lebanese implement the remaining provisions. Instead, the accord has sparked tension and violence more often than not, even over the interpretation of these provisions. At the same time it has set the stage for two army commanders to be elected as presidents of the republic (out of three presidents in all). In justifying their condoning of military generals occupying the presidency, politicians frequently concede that army commanders are chosen for their integrity, loyalty to the country, disposition to preserve the constitution and equal distance from all parties, and for their role in ensuring intercommunal integration among their troops, in the hope of extending their experience to the society at large. In fact, the Lebanese Army remains one of the few symbols of national unity, if not the only one. In other terms, the Lebanese system prevents politicians from acceding to the presidency because of their expressed political tendency towards one party or another, or just because they have not been neutral and impartial. This alarming symptom in Lebanese political life should be addressed with caution as it does not appear to be transitory. In reality, consensus here is confounded with unanimity, contradicting the very essence of democracy and democratic choice. As a rule in Lebanon, confrontational and imposed choices need to be avoided in order to maintain peaceful coexistence. But moderation does not imply unanimity. For example, whenever two or more candidates compete for a certain political post, the extreme candidate is discarded and a compromise candidate is selected. But this does not mean that the different sectarian leaders approve the selection unanimously—if such a principle was to become a general rule, Lebanon's democratic system would become paralyzed and even void.

The preceding analysis has shown that neither the constitution nor the political institutions are able to resolve even minor differences; instead, foreign interference by third parties is often required to assist in problem solving and in securing the proper functioning of the Lebanese democratic model. Consociationalism has failed in its task of providing stable and properly functioning public institutions. Instead it has led to political deadlock, inviting outside interference through nonconventional conflict resolution procedures.

Political divisions in Lebanon are intense. The political nature of the Lebanese system and the difficulty in achieving national understanding over the future of the country is complex. The events of May 2008 that we have analyzed bear witness to the propensity for conflict and violence inherent in pacts. Needless to say, the Lebanese are under urgent pressure to overcome their political differences and to learn to sort out their problems inside state institutions rather than in the streets. This may well force them to abandon their narrow confessional perspectives, allowing space for constitutional reform and modern political behavior, if Lebanon is to stand a chance of political survival. A Western-type secular democracy, although difficult to envision in the current situation, may indeed offer the road to enduring stability.

ACKNOWLEDGMENTS

The author thanks John Coakley for his very helpful comments.

NOTES

1. Arend Lijphart, "Consociational Democracy," *World Politics*, Vol. 21, No. 2 (1969), pp. 207–25; *Democracy in Plural Societies: A Comparative Exploration* (New Haven, CT: Yale University Press, 1977).

2. Donald Horowitz, "Conciliatory Institutions and Constitutional Processes in Post-Conflict States," *William and Mary Law Review*, Vol. 49, No. 4 (2008), pp. 1213–49, in particular, p. 1216.

3. Horowitz, "Conciliatory institutions," p. 1218.

4. Communication with the author, 8 Dec. 2008.

5. Hilal Khashan, *Inside the Lebanese Confessional Mind* (Lanham, MD: University Press of America, 1992), p. 1.

6. Halim Barakat, "Social and Political Integration in Lebanon: A Case of Social Mosaic," *Middle East Journal*, Vol. 27, No. 3 (1973), pp. 301–18.

7. Ralph E. Crow, "Electoral Issues: Lebanon," in Jacob M. Landau, Ergun Ozbudun, and Frank Tachau (eds.), *Electoral Politics in the Middle East* (London: Croom Helm, 1980), p. 40.

8. A. Ghossein, "Geography in the Study of the Lebanese Structure and Crisis," *Halyyat*, No. 25 (1980), pp. 28–9.

9. Some cabinets have been restricted to as few as four members, making inclusion of multiple groups all the more difficult.

10. Ghassan Salameh, "Small Is Pluralistic: Democracy as an Instrument of Peace," in Ghassan Salameh (ed.), *Democracy without Democrats: The Renewal of Politics in the Muslim World* (London: I. B. Tauris, 1994), pp. 84–111, at p. 89.

11. Hani Faris, "The Failure of Peacemaking in Lebanon: 1975–1989," in Deidre Collings (ed.), *Peace for Lebanon? From War to Reconstruction* (Boulder, CO: Lynne Rienner, 1994), pp. 18–30.

12. Mahmood Ayoub, "Lebanon between Religious Faith and Political Ideology," in Collings, *Peace for Lebanon?*, pp. 241–248.

13. Joseph Maila, "The Ta'if Accord: An Evaluation," in Collings, *Peace for Lebanon?*, pp. 31–44.

14. Ibid., p. 37.

15. Hilal Khashan and Simon Haddad, "The Coupling of the Syrian-Lebanese Peace Tracks: Beirut's Options," *Security Dialogue*, Vol. 30, No. 2 (2000), pp. 201–14.

16. As'ad Abukhalil, "The New Sectarian Wars of Lebanon," in Nubar Hovsepian (ed.), *The War on Lebanon: A Reader* (Northampton, MA: Olive Branch Press, 2008), pp. 358–67, at p. 360.

17. Mathematically, the number of parliamentary seats gained by the opposition would entitle them to 13 cabinet ministers. However, one should bear in mind that the president of the republic retains a share in any cabinet. Currently, in a cabinet of 30 ministers, the president has three ministries, the March 14 Bloc 16, and the opposition 11.

18. Joseph Alagha, "The Israeli-Hizbullah 34-Day War: Causes and Consequences," *Arab Studies Quarterly*, Vol. 30, No. 2 (2008), pp. 1–22.

19. On a few occasions the Lebanese Army fired on Shi'ite Hezbollah demonstrators, killing several militiamen. The last of these events occurred in Dec. 2006, when Lebanese army troops opened fire against demonstrators in Shi'ite slums, killing 11 and wounding some others.

20. Abbas William Samii, "Shi'ites in Lebanon: The Key to Democracy," *Middle East Policy*, Vol. 13, No. 2 (2006), pp. 30–38.

21. Samar El-Masri, "The Hariri Tribunal: Politics and International Law," *Middle East Policy*, Vol. 15, No. 3 (2008), pp. 80–93.

22. Bilal Saab, "Rethinking Hezbollah's Disarmament," *Middle East Policy*, Vol. 15, No. 3 (2008), pp. 93–107.

23. Despite various attempts to modify the election law, to render it fairer through the introduction of proportional or semi-proportional electoral formulas, the government ratified a law that satisfies most Lebanese parties. In particular, Christian politicians favor small electoral districts where they would be able to improve their political representation because they are a minority in many regions but a majority in a number of small districts.

24. Andrew Rigby, "Lebanon: Patterns of Confessional Politics," *Parliamentary Affairs*, Vol. 53, No. 1 (2000), pp. 169–80.

25. Florian Bieber, "Bosnia-Herzegovina and Lebanon: Historical Lessons of Two Multireligious States," *Third World Quarterly*, Vol. 21, No. 2 (2000), pp. 269–81, at p. 279.

26. Brenda Seaver, "The Regional Sources of Power-Sharing Failure: The Case of Lebanon," *Political Science Quarterly*, Vol. 115, No. 2 (2000), pp. 247–71.

27. Ibid., p. 244.

28. Michael Kerr, *Imposing Power-Sharing: Conflict and Coexistence in Northern Ireland and Lebanon* (Dublin: Irish Academic Press, 2006).

29. Rudy Jaafar, "Democratic System Reform in Lebanon: An Electoral Approach," in Youssef Choueiri (ed.), *Breaking the Cycle: Civil Wars in Lebanon* (London: Stacy International, 2007), pp. 285–306.

30. Youssef Choueiri, "Explaining Civil Wars in Lebanon," in Choueiri, *Breaking the Cycle*, pp. 21–46.

31. Ahmad Beydoun, "Movements of the Past and Deadlocks of the Present," in Choueiri, *Breaking the Cycle*, pp. 3–20.

32. It is worth noting that while the ideology of the Lebanese army, whose confessional composition reflects the country's sectarian demographic weights, continues to perceive Israel as Lebanon's enemy, the Internal Security Forces, whose makeup and leadership is heavily Sunni concentrated, perceive Syria as the enemy.

33. These conclusions are very much inspired by Mohammed Abu-Nimer, "Conflict Resolution Approaches: Western and Middle Eastern Lessons and Possibilities," *American Journal of Economics and Sociology*, Vol. 55, No. 1 (1996), pp. 35–52.

34. For instance, to take another dispute, say the Arab-Israeli one, Norway, which was the party to receive the Arab and Israeli negotiating teams in Oslo, was completely external to the conflict.

35. Jennifer Widner, "Constitution Writing in Post-Conflict Settings: An Overview," *William and Mary Law Review*, Vol. 49, No. 4 (2008), pp. 1513–42.

36. Ibid., p. 1516.

8

South Africa: The Long View on Political Transition

ADRIAN GUELKE

Queen's University of Belfast

The article revisits South Africa's unexpected transition to majority rule during the early 1990s. It underscores how surprising this development was by recalling the range of possibilities that appeared to exist at the time of apartheid's demise. The course of events that led to the African National Congress's achieving its objective of one person one vote in an undivided country is briefly explained, while the longer term trends that helped to make such an outcome possible are also identified. The manner in which the country has managed without the political devices commonly associated with the governance of deeply divided societies is analyzed.

INTRODUCTION

In the late 1980s it was common for South Africa to be compared with other cases of intractable conflicts, most notably the Israeli-Palestinian conflict and the troubles in Northern Ireland. Thus, in September 1989 a conference in Bonn on the comparison of these three cases under the auspices of the Friedrich Naumann-Stiftung heard a keynote address by a distinguished British professor of politics, Bernard Crick, that underlined the theme of intractability and made stark assumptions about the limited possibilities of progress (thus drawing attention to the degree to which developments in the three societies in the course of the 1990s were unexpected):

> I call the three problems "insoluble" for two formal reasons: (i) that no internal solution likely to guarantee peace can possibly satisfy the announced principles of the main disputants and (ii) that any external imposed solution or enforced adjudication is likely to strengthen the desperation and self-righteousness of the threatened group.[1]

In this context, Crick notes that he first encountered the expression "*laager* mentality," commonly used in South Africa, to describe the siege mentality of the dominant community in Northern Ireland. It is worth underlining how surprising South Africa's transition to democracy in the first half of the 1990s appeared to most observers, to the extent that it was widely dubbed a miracle.[2] This invites comparison with parallel processes elsewhere, and it is the purpose of this article to suggest both similarities and differences with other cases. To facilitate the analysis, this article begins by discussing an influential categorization of approaches to the conflict. This is followed by an analysis of how a negotiated settlement was reached and how longstanding predictions that apartheid would end in a racial bloodbath were thereby confounded. The next section examines the basic structural factors that contributed to the country's negotiated revolution. The last section looks at the formidable challenges remaining, challenges that demand answers from the country's political institutions and are likely to continue doing so for the foreseeable future.

INTERPRETING THE SOUTH AFRICAN CONFLICT

The articulation of alternatives to apartheid that ran directly counter to the National Party's plans to reverse the erosion of segregation through ambitious social engineering began in tandem with the implementation of the party's policies. In this context, the process of decolonization in the rest of Africa that began in the 1950s encouraged a belief among the National Party's enemies that apartheid could not survive for long and that the wind of change in the rest of the continent would reach South Africa. However, developments during the 1960s, when apartheid did not merely survive but the country enjoyed high economic growth rates that liberals had predicted could not be achieved under the stultifying influence of apartheid, forced the government's adversaries to abandon the assumption that majority rule was simply inevitable. As a consequence, other alternatives began to receive serious consideration.[3] The possibilities multiplied still further during the 1980s when it became clear that the National Party itself had lost confidence in apartheid as a blueprint for the country's future and was ready to consider other options.

A useful framework for interpreting this terrain is provided by Donald Horowitz's 1991 book on the subject of the constitutional choices then facing the country. Its first chapter (appropriately entitled "The Conflict and the Conflict about the Conflict") opens with the words:

> There is a conflict in South Africa that has something to do with race. That is about as far as agreement runs among many of the participants and interpreters of the conflict. Beyond that, there is disagreement over

the extent to which the conflict is really *about* race, as opposed to op-
pression merely in the guise of race, or about nationalism among groups
demarcated by race, or about contending claims to the same land.[4]

He goes on to set out 12 different positions on South Africa's future.[5] These
are worth considering further and may be summarized as follows:

1. *An Official View*. This equates to what Giliomee and Schlemmer dubbed
   "reform-apartheid."[6] It departed from the original Verwoerdian blueprint
   for apartheid by combining partition with a form of power sharing with
   the Coloured and Indian communities, a system dubbed "sham consociationalism" by its critics, who included the originator of consociationalism
   as a political concept, Arend Lijphart. It presumed the continuation of
   the policies of authoritarian reform that had taken place during the presidency of P.W. Botha.
2. *A Charterist View*. The Charter referred to was the Freedom Charter
   adopted by the Congress of the People in 1955. This proclaimed that
   "South Africa belongs to all who live in it, black and white."[7]At the same
   time, the Freedom Charter acknowledged the existence of a number of
   national groups that were entitled to equal rights.
3. *An Alternative Charterist View*. In contrast to the stance above that acknowledged the plural nature of South Africa, this view contended that
   South Africa could develop as a common society. From this perspective,
   the country's divisions had been artificially exacerbated by apartheid,
   and a normal, nonracial democracy could take its place.
4. *A People's Democracy View*. This lay to the left of the views just discussed
   but shared some of their assumptions about the artificiality of racial
   divisions. In Horowitz's formulation, what was most striking about this
   perspective was its emphasis on grass roots control and its rejection of
   representative democracy as inadequate.
5. *An Africanist View*. To Africanists, the central issue was that South Africa
   was a colonial society in which the fundamental divide was between
   settlers and natives.
6. *A Black Consciousness View*. The focus of this perspective was slightly
   different. Color was the fundamental divide for the Black consciousness
   movement, thus pitting Whites against the rest—Africans, Coloureds, and
   Indians in the colloquial racial terminology of the society.
7. *A Racial Self-Assertion View*. Here, Horowitz has in mind groups and
   individuals whose vision of the future envisaged a reversal of the existing
   racial hierarchy. While the Black consciousness movement argued that
   people of color needed to be self-reliant and proud of their own worth,
   the ultimate aim was the creation of an equal society. It was possible
   to envisage going beyond that, though such a view never achieved any
   significant political traction.

8. *A Two-Nationalisms Partitionist View.* This enjoyed a following in the 1960s when even significant international figures saw it as a potential alternative to apartheid. This was because its advocates argued that it would entail a much fairer division of the land than under apartheid, under which the areas reserved for African ownership amounted to only 13% of the country. Typically, proponents of partition envisaged the roughly equal division of the land between Whites and Blacks. It was advocated as the only realistic way forward in a situation in which Whites possessed the capacity to resist majority rule. However, by the 1980s, this perspective had few followers except on the far right in South Africa. This was because it was no longer viewed by any credible international figure as a solution that Blacks would be willing to accept, and without such support it seemed likely to be a transitional arrangement, at best, that would not fundamentally change the country's pariah status.

9. *A Two-Nationalisms Accommodationist View.* This position was advocated by those who saw White opposition to majority rule as an insuperable obstacle to the establishment of a normal liberal democracy. It proceeded from the assumption that at the heart of the conflict lay a struggle between African and Afrikaner nationalism for political supremacy and stressed the need for a binational solution.

10. *A Consociational View.* This was in a similar vein to the "two-nationalisms accommodationist" view. It was also premised on a negotiated settlement of the South African conflict, but its advocates saw South Africa as a land of minorities and consequently attributed a major role for the elites of a number of different groups in fashioning a power-sharing solution along the lines described by Arend Lijphart in his writings.[8]

11. *A Modified Consociational View.* By contrast to the consociational view, Horowitz had in mind the objections that a number of liberals had raised to a fully fledged consociational settlement, where the operation of minority vetoes would enable Whites to prevent necessary socioeconomic reforms, hence making necessary a modification of some aspects of the consociational model as applied to South Africa. Otherwise, its effect might be to freeze in place the inequalities that had been imposed under the system of apartheid.

12. *A Simple Majoritarian View.* From this perspective, the basis of the South African problem was simply undemocratic government, and the straightforward answer would be the establishment of a normal liberal democracy. Horowitz characterizes the stance of advocates of this position as reflecting the view that "whether South Africa is or is not a severely divided society is irrelevant."[9] On the face of it, there seems to be little difference between this position and the "Alternative Charterist View" described above.

While it might be argued that Horowitz tends to multiply the number of categories unnecessarily both though fine distinctions among quite similar positions and the inclusion of positions with little political credibility, his setting out of what he calls the meta-conflict over South Africa's future does convey how relatively open the possibilities appeared to be at the start of the transition.

THE PURSUIT OF A SETTLEMENT

By the time of the publication of Horowitz's study, the country had already firmly embarked on the path to the creation of a new dispensation. President de Klerk's announcement in February 1990 that he was lifting the ban on the African National Congress (ANC), Pan-Africanist Congress, and South African Communist Party and that he was releasing Nelson Mandela from gaol is generally taken as the first step in South Africa's transition, because, although there had been movement before this in the direction of opening a dialogue with the ANC, this was the first irreversible commitment by the government to the objective of a negotiated settlement.

The opening round of negotiations between the government and the ANC took place in May 1990, and a further set in August 1990. At this point the ANC agreed to suspend all armed actions. Ironically, this coincided with a massive upsurge in political violence linked to the launch of a Zulu traditionalist party, the Inkatha Freedom Party, which received covert government backing for its offensive against ANC supporters. The violence soured relations between the ANC and the government, delaying the start of formal multiparty negotiations to December 1991 in a body named the Convention for a Democratic South Africa (CODESA).

The violence was by no means the only obstacle to the start of formal negotiations. The National Party and the ANC disagreed fundamentally on how a new dispensation should be brought about. The National Party wanted agreement on the institutions of the new order to be reached by consensus among the political parties ahead of democratic elections, while the ANC insisted that the constitution of the new dispensation should be determined by a democratically elected constituent assembly. Throughout the CODESA process, which finally broke down in May 1992, the National Party government remained wedded to the notion of finding some way of entrenching group rights in any future constitution.

The breakdown of CODESA was followed by ANC-led mass action and another upsurge in violence. As a consequence of the violence and the interpretation placed on it, there was a further weakening of the National Party's position both inside the country and internationally. The unwillingness of the United States to support the concept of a minority veto was important in this context. Ultimately, President de Klerk concluded that there was no alternative to a deal with the ANC and this was clearly signalled with his signing of "The Record of Understanding" with Nelson Mandela in September 1992. The content of the accord was far less significant than its implication that the government had finally abandoned the strategy of attempting to weaken the ANC by all the means at its disposal, including arming the movement's enemies, before the holding of elections.

A new body for the formal negotiations was established, the Multi-Party Negotiating Forum (MPNF). It first met in April 1993. Its main achievement was the transitional constitution adopted in December 1993 but subsequently amended to facilitate the Inkatha Freedom Party's participation in the elections in April 1994. Though frequent reference was made to best international practice during the course of the South African negotiations, it was an internal process confined to South Africans; a bewilderingly large and fluctuating number of delegations (comprising both representatives of political parties and administrations) participated in both CODESA and the MPNF. Walkouts were common. However, it was widely understood that on fundamental points the consent of both the National Party and the ANC was required and that "sufficient consensus" would be forthcoming for any proposal that did enjoy the support of both parties.

Giliomee has strongly criticized President de Klerk for his readiness to accept a staged process that enabled the ANC in the fullness of time to establish a majoritarian constitution.[10] What President de Klerk did secure through his concessions to the ANC was the preservation of legal continuity between the old and the new order, arguably a significant constraint on the behavior of future governments. In addition, the provision that the final constitution had to satisfy a series of constitutional principles and be certified by the Constitutional Court provided a further set of constraints, though this was limited, since it did not apply to any subsequent amendments of the constitution.

The transitional constitution provided for the establishment of a Government of National Unity following the country's first democratic elections in April 1994. Political parties that secured at least 5% of the national vote were entitled to be represented in this government. This provision formed part of Lijphart's claim that South Africa had adopted consociationalism in its transition from apartheid.[11] But this overlooked the fact that the commitment to power sharing in government was limited to five years and, more importantly, that representation in government was not accompanied by minority vetoes or any similar such mechanisms. In short, the majority's power to make decisions was unconstrained.

Given the overwhelming majority that the ANC enjoyed in the National Assembly and in the cabinet of the Government of National Unity, power sharing meant little more than a share in the spoils of office. So unsatisfactory was the arrangement from the perspective of the National Party that it withdrew from the government after two years. Its entitlement to hold office was not an obligation to do so, and the National Party calculated that it needed to establish its distance from the policies being pursued by the ANC, even if this meant the loss of its ministerial positions. The National Party's withdrawal from the Government of National Unity coincided with the adoption of the country's final constitution. In contrast to the transitional constitution, this was explicitly majoritarian and removed any obligation for a party commanding a majority in the National Assembly to include minor parties in the government.

Of the positions outlined by Horowitz, it is evident that the view that has prevailed is the second or "Charterist" one. The ANC, the party that has completely dominated the country since the elections of 1994, increasing its share of the vote in the elections of 1999 and 2004 and holding its dominant position in 2009, has espoused a policy of nonracialism. It has pursued this in the context of recognition of the country's divisions, reflected in commitment to help historically disadvantaged groups through affirmative-action measures. Admittedly, some of the policy positions articulated in the Freedom Charter have been discarded. In particular, in line with views on the left of the political spectrum around the world at the time, the Freedom Charter had advocated widespread nationalization.

Of the four ANC landslide election victories, that of 2009 is the most remarkable since it followed a highly divisive power struggle within the party itself. Nelson Mandela, as iconic ANC leader, had served as president during the formative years of postapartheid South Africa (1994–99) and was succeeded by Thabo Mbeki. In 2007, however, Jacob Zuma, whom President Thabo Mbeki had dismissed from his position as Deputy President in 2005 as a result of a corruption scandal, challenged Mbeki for leadership of the ANC. The allegations against Zuma arose out of the handling of arms deals that the postapartheid government had entered into, at least in part to ensure the loyalty of the armed forces to the new dispensation. It was an unusual contest insofar as Mbeki could not serve a further term as president of the country and, consequently, had he won the contest, it would have created a division between the leader of the country and the leader of its dominant political party that itself might have proved damaging and difficult to manage. As it turned out, grass-roots dissatisfaction with the government and Mbeki's style of leadership secured victory for Zuma, notwithstanding the possibility that he might be convicted of corruption.

Because of this possibility, at the time of Zuma's election as ANC President, it was by no means considered certain that he would ever become president of the country. However, unexpectedly, the situation changed dramatically when in September 2008 a judge in the Pietermaritzburg High Court threw out fresh charges of corruption against Zuma on procedural grounds. What is more, Judge Chris Nicolson also implied that there might have been political interference in the prosecution case, though that was not the basis of his decision. His judgment appeared not only to vindicate Zuma but to damn Mbeki, sealing the latter's fate. The ANC Executive, dominated since the ANC conference in December 2007 by supporters of Zuma, forced Mbeki's resignation as president in Sept. 2008.

However, there was one small consolation for Mbeki. His rival was unable at this point to take his place, as the constitution required that the choice of the president should be made from members of the National Assembly. Whereas Kgalema Motlanthe, the ANC Deputy President, had been put into the Assembly following the ANC's 2007 conference, Zuma had not. Consequently, Motlanthe was elected to serve out the rest of Mbeki's term but on the basis that Zuma would be the ANC's candidate for the presidency after the 2009 elections. Doubts about Zuma's prospects of becoming and remaining president then resurfaced when Judge Nicolson's judgement was reversed on appeal in January 2009. This enabled the prosecuting authorities to reinstate the charges against him. The implication of a conviction was that he might have to resign within months of becoming president.[12] The story then took yet another dramatic twist just two weeks before the country's elections in April 2009. Evidence in the form of taped conversations emerged that political considerations had indeed influenced the conduct of the case against Zuma. The result was a decision by the prosecution not to proceed.[13]

The humiliation of Thabo Mbeki through his enforced exit from power prior to the completion of his second term prompted a split in the ANC. Those angered by Mbeki's removal from office and distrustful of the populism espoused by Zuma in his pursuit of the ANC leadership formed a new political party, the Congress of the People (COPE), in November 2008. By choosing to name the party after the political alliance that had forged the Freedom Charter in 1955, they underlined their commitment to the Charterist position. But this was not ground that the ANC was willing to cede to any of its political opponents. The ANC went to court to contest the right of the defectors to use the name. However, the Pretoria High Court rejected the ANC's case in December 2008.

As a new political party, COPE fared relatively well in the elections of April 2009, securing 7.4% of the vote. However, the outcome did not match the party's expectations. Furthermore, in the context of the performance of both the ANC and the Democratic Alliance, its share of the vote fell far short of what the party needed if it were to have any prospect of bringing about political realignment. First, it failed to attract sufficient support to dent the ANC's majority seriously. This was in part because the ANC made up for some of the votes it lost to COPE by gains among rural Zulus, assisted by Zuma's portrayal as a "100 per cent Zulu boy," as a popular t-shirt described him.[14] Second, the Democratic Alliance achieved its best ever result. Its share of the votes (16.7%) was more than double that of COPE. One of the factors in the party's success was a large increase in its vote in the Western Cape, where Coloured voters turned against the ANC. The implication of the outcome was that the opposition to the ANC would continue to be led by a party with relatively little support among the African electorate, a circumstance likely to perpetuate the ANC's dominance.

But it is worth underlining that at the time Horowitz wrote his book at the start of South Africa's transition, the triumph of the Charterist position seemed far from assured. Its dominance now appears set to continue under Zuma, notwithstanding the political fallout from the power struggle within the ANC. Indeed, it can be argued that it was never under threat. In January 2009 the South African Institute of Race Relations profiled the positions of six leading contenders for the leadership of the country, including two of COPE's leaders. A striking feature of the quotations that were used to illustrate their stance on the issues facing the country was the frequency of their references to the Freedom Charter, as well as the closeness of their positions on major issues.[15]

EXPLAINING THE TRANSITION

Debate about South Africa's transition from apartheid to democracy tends to focus on the period between February 1990 and May 1994—from Nelson Mandela's release from prison to his inauguration as the country's president. The story between these two dates does have numerous twists and turns, but in retrospect it seems that once President de Klerk initiated the liberalization of the system and embarked on negotiations on a new political dispensation, the die was cast. It has been argued by Heribert Adam, among others, that this was not inevitable: that the National Party did not have to embark on the transition and could have clung to power for many further years, suggesting, for example, that "there is very little doubt that the Afrikaner minority as represented by the National Party could have dominated into the 21st century if it had so wished."[16]

This argument is persuasive insofar as it is evident that the ANC was in no position to mount a military challenge to the government's control of the country in 1990. So why, as the saying goes, did de Klerk do it? Part of the answer lies in the serendipity of his struggle for power with P. W. Botha during the course of 1989, which ensured F. W. de Klerk's hostility to the security establishment and his consequent rejection of the option of intensifying repression. His miscalculation of the impact of the collapse of communism in Eastern Europe on the ANC's political prospects is another. In particular, he assumed that in the light of the discrediting of communism the ANC would be damaged by its alliance with the South African Communist Party. In fact, the fall of communism meant that the ANC's links with the South African Communist Party ceased to worry Western governments.

By taking a longer view of apartheid's demise, however, it is possible to identify the more fundamental structural aspects of the shift in power that took place in South Africa during the 1990s. They include the impact of demographic change, shifts in the social structure, and the effect of economic forces, as well as attitudinal change, especially among members of the White elite.

While White racism can be traced as a factor in the politics of the region from the very beginnings of European settlement, modern South Africa and its pursuit of the policy of segregation and then of apartheid was a product less of the farmers who trekked into the African interior than of the mineral revolutions of the second half of the nineteenth century. The discovery of diamonds and gold transformed the region. It was a spur to White settlement and at the same time empowered the settlers in political terms, so much so that during the course of the first half of the twentieth century it was common to discuss South Africa as a country of two races but to confine this description to English-speaking Whites and to Afrikaners, with the latter interpreted as meaning only Whites whose primary language was Afrikaans and not the many Coloureds for whom Afrikaans was also their mother tongue. For example, in 1941 George Harold Calpin argued that the gulf between English speakers and Afrikaners, underscored by divisions over South African participation in the Second World War, was such that the views of the two communities were irreconcilable.[17]

An explanation as to why the African population appeared so powerless that its political aspirations could simply be ignored by those examining South African politics up to this point in time can be found in the demographics of South Africa as shown in the country's regular censuses. In 1911 the White population constituted 21.4% of the population of the country; it remained above 20% until 1960, when it fell to 19.3% (see Table 1). It was not just the relative size of the White and African populations that was

TABLE 1 South Africa: Population by Race, 1911–2001

Year	Africans	Whites	Coloureds	Indians	Others or unclassified	Total (thousands)
1911	67.3	21.4	8.8	2.5	—	5,973
1921	67.8	22.0	7.9	2.4	—	6,927
1936	68.8	20.9	8.0	2.3	—	9,588
1946	68.6	20.8	8.1	2.5	—	11,416
1951	67.6	20.8	8.7	2.9	—	12,671
1960	68.3	19.3	9.4	3.0	—	16,003
1970	70.4	17.1	9.4	2.9	—	21,794
1985	74.1	14.8	8.6	2.6	—	33,622
1996	76.7	10.9	8.9	2.6	0.9	40,584
2001	79.0	9.6	8.9	2.5	—	44,820

Note. All figures except those in the last column are percentages.
Sources: Herma Fogey et al., *South Africa Survey 2000/2001* (Johannesburg: South African Institute of Race Relations, 2001), p. 48, and Marco Macfarlane (ed.), *South Africa Survey 2007/2008* (Johannesburg: South African Institute of Race Relations, 2008), p. 6.

important in this context but their geographical distribution. In 1921 only a third of the total urban population was African. By this time majorities of Whites, Coloureds, and Indians lived in the urban areas. As late as the 1970 census Africans still constituted a minority of the urban population. Even by 2000, in sharp contrast to the rest of the population, only a minority of Africans lived in the urban areas.[18]

The political significance of this point derives from the fact that the ANC was widely perceived and portrayed as an urban movement. This affected perceptions of the ANC's political strength, as well as its legitimacy, both inside the country and, to a lesser extent, outside the country among Western governments. It may reasonably be argued that the stereotype of the ANC as just an urban phenomenon, and one moreover confined to the fully urbanized population and excluding migrants with continuing links to the rural areas, was crude and simplistic. Nonetheless, it was the case that the main centers of opposition to the government were to be found in the urban areas. Indeed, this formed the basis of the government's approach to counterinsurgency during the 1980s, the so-called oil-spot strategy of upgrading services in selected urban areas, such as Alexandra township in Johannesburg, so as to counter the ANC's political influence.

Another aspect of the relative political powerlessness of the African population was the subordinate position of Africans in the political economy of the country. Merle Lipton's seminal work in this context explains both how the system functioned to the advantage of different sectors and why it came under increasing strain that prompted change.[19] Central to the system was influx control that treated most of the African population as temporary sojourners in the urban areas with very limited rights. As long as the economy was geared to the exploitation of cheap labor and mining and agriculture dominated the economy, there was a measure of congruence between the government's political and economic objectives. However, the growth of manufacturing and of the service sector created pressure for the establishment of a more differentiated labor force. The network of labor bureaus created to manage influx control was ill equipped to facilitate such a development. At the same time, further strain was placed on the system by developments within both the mining and agricultural sectors, in particular by mechanization. This changed the preference of employers that the Africans they hired should constitute an undifferentiated, unskilled labor force that was both cheap and readily replaceable, since working with machinery required the training of employees, an investment that needed a stable work force if it were to pay off.

These strains had become apparent as early as the 1950s. They prompted predictions by liberal economists of apartheid's demise as a result of its economic contradictions or, alternatively, ruin if the government persisted with the policy. The Sharpeville massacre in 1960, when the police killed 69 demonstrators protesting against the pass laws, which controlled the influx of Africans into the urban areas, caused a loss of confidence at the start of the decade. However, once the impact of that crisis had dissipated the South African economy entered an unprecedented period of boom, during which there was massive foreign investment attracted by the huge profits to be made by disregarding international disapproval of apartheid. This unexpected turn of events led to a challenge in the academic world to conventional liberal accounts that had stressed apartheid's incompatibility with capitalism. A new generation of scholars argued that the interests of capitalists and those of the National Party government were complementary. The lasting consequence of this challenge was a divide among South African scholars that has persisted into the postapartheid era and continues to be reflected in debates on the interpretation of the country's history. A seminal account of the debate characterized the divide as one between liberals and radicals,[20] but it has also been characterized more sharply as a debate between liberals and Marxists.[21]

The boom in the South African economy came to an abrupt end during the 1970s. The consequence has been succinctly described by the South African economist, Sampie Terreblanche:

> When the oil crisis of 1973 slowed down economic growth elsewhere, South Africa also experienced a severe recession. But in contrast with most other countries the recession deteriorated into chronic stagflation that coincided with a period of political instability and black unrest, culminating in the collapse of white political domination in the early 1990s.[22]

A time series of real per capita incomes in South Africa underlines Terreblanche's case (see Figure 1). Thus, in the year that Nelson Mandela became president, 1994, per capita incomes in real terms were below what they had been in 1966, the zenith of the boom of the 1960s. It is worth pointing out that the stagnation Terreblanche identified preceded the imposition of Western economic sanctions. This is a contentious subject on which there is by no means a consensus in the literature. But the direct impact of trade sanctions does seem to have been slight. While there is wide agreement that external pressures played a role in persuading the government to embark on the country's transition from apartheid, these pressures tend to be accorded a much greater role in external accounts of the transition than those originating inside the country.

This difference of perspective is underlined by the stance of the National Party's chief negotiator during the transition, Roelf Meyer. Meyer has been a passionate advocate of the view that one of the keys to South Africa's miracle was that the settlement was achieved by South Africans themselves with little or no input from the outside world. He has advised parties in other

FIGURE 1 South Africa: Gross Domestic Product Per Capita at Constant 1990 Prices, 1960–96. *Source*: Elizabeth Sidiropoulus, Anthea Jeffrey, Shaun MacKay, Herma Forgey, Cheryl Chipps, and Terence Corrigan, *South Africa Survey 1996/97* (Johannesburg: South African Institute of Race Relations, 1997), p. 654.

conflicts, most notably those in Northern Ireland, to do likewise and to settle their differences without reference to external mediators.[23]

Meyer overstates the case, but his view is a useful corrective to the assumption that the global antiapartheid movement and Western economic sanctions brought about South Africa's transformation in the 1990s. In particular, it is important not to discount the role that changes in the attitudes of the White population played over a period of years in preparing the ground for the transition. South African Whites saw themselves as part of Western, Christian civilization. Consequently, they were not entirely indifferent to the changes in racial attitudes within the West, a shift that was most evident in the 1960s with the civil rights movement in the United States and the virtual completion of the process of decolonization. This was most clearly reflected in acceptance by Whites of the gradual relaxation of petty apartheid in the course of the 1980s, and especially of the changes made under the rubric of multinationalism in an effort to counter the country's isolation in sport and other areas. However, the polls also showed that White resistance to political change remained strong.[24]

Thus, two of the positions outlined by Horowitz in 1991 characterizing the conflict as a clash of two nationalisms remain a valuable short-hand for the primary forces involved. On the one hand, there was Afrikaner nationalism, a nationalism centered on culture and language, but also a racially conscious nationalism that rejected the inclusion among the *volk* of people who differed only in the color of their skin. This was embodied in the National Party and its project for the long-term partition of the country to sustain White political hegemony. On the other hand, there was African nationalism, though this was given a nonexclusive interpretation through the commitment of the ANC to nonracialism. The ANC's main political objective was to achieve one person one vote in a unitary state. The advocates of the "two nationalisms" positions that Horowitz discusses did not envisage that one of these nationalisms would triumph completely over the other, as by and large it did at the political level, with the ANC making no concessions to the National Party over the issues of the entrenchment of power sharing or group political rights in general. But it did so against a global economic backdrop that facilitated continuing White prosperity under majority rule that provided a measure of compensation for the other nationalism.

POSTTRANSFORMATION CHALLENGES

The fact that the ANC achieved its main political objective through a process of negotiations and without the collapse of the apartheid state had important consequences for the future. Constitutional continuity was preserved, along with existing property rights. The ANC opted to introduce change on an incremental basis and justified the relatively slow pace of reform as necessary to the maintenance of racial reconciliation. The result has been that South Africa remains as unequal a society in terms of the distribution of income and wealth as it was before 1994. Indeed, on some measures it is even more unequal. Thus, according to one series of figures, the Gini coefficient measuring income inequality rose slightly from .68 in 1970 to .69 in 1996 and increased by a further .05 between 1996 and 2007.[25] In short, these figures indicate a further widening of inequality. At the same time, the racial distribution of income has changed markedly at the top, with the rise of the Black elite. Nevertheless, the economic disparities between the races remain very large, even by current international standards. In 1960 White personal disposable incomes were nearly 12 times those of Africans on a per capita basis, while in 2007 they were still a little over six times those of Africans on a per capita basis.[26]

The government of Thabo Mbeki encountered some opposition to the affirmative action measures it enacted to accelerate the process of upward mobility for historically disadvantaged groups, as they are described. But far more damaging to Mbeki's position was the perception that, by contrast, his government had done too little to help the vast majority of ANC supporters who lacked the skills and education to be in a position to benefit from affirmative action and who remained poor. That perception assisted Zuma in his challenge to Mbeki in 2007. The push for greater equality can be justified as necessary to the country's long-term political stability on the grounds that a system reproducing the level of inequality under apartheid is likely to prove unsustainable in the long run. But, labeled as populism, a more radical trans-formative approach can also be presented as endangering the country's eco-nomic future. In particular, it is commonly argued that policies of redistribu-tion are likely to prompt an exodus of the wealthy and of wealth creators. In this context, what has happened to Zimbabwe tends to be seen as a warning of what might befall South Africa, were the country to succumb to populism.

While the influx of economic refugees from Zimbabwe has brought home to many South Africans the negative consequences of the path Zim-babwe took under Robert Mugabe, the appeal that a populist leader might have in the absence of a more rapid improvement in the lives of the majority of the population should not be dismissed. The point is well made by an academic who was himself the victim of another populist leader. Mahmood Mamdani, exiled from Uganda in 1972 by the regime of Idi Amin when it expelled the entire Asian population of the country, wrote of his experience of returning to Uganda after Amin's fall:

> In 1979 I began to realise that whatever they made of Amin's brutal-ity, the Ugandan people experienced the Asian expulsion of 1972—and not the formal independence of 1962—as the dawn of true independence. The people of Zimbabwe are likely to remember 2000–3 as the end of the settler colonial era. Any assessment of contemporary Zimbabwe needs to begin with this sobering fact.[27]

However, there is little likelihood that Jacob Zuma will follow in the footsteps of Idi Amin or Robert Mugabe. Indeed, since his election as president, he has taken great pains to reassure members of the business community that his policies will not present a threat to their interests. That has been reflected in very positive coverage of his first hundred days as president.[28] At the same time, there have been the first rumblings of discontent from the poor in areas of high unemployment and poor service delivery.[29]

A factor in Thabo Mbeki's unpopularity, especially during his second term of office, was the apparent unresponsiveness of the political system to serious social problems that engulfed the country during the 2000s. These include the HIV/AIDS pandemic, the crime rate, and xenophobic attacks on foreigners. AIDS had a devastating impact on the country's health, so that by the close of Mbeki's rule the life expectancy of Africans in South Africa was not markedly above that of Zimbabweans. One of the highest murder rates in the world underlined the seriousness of the problem of crime, while the events of May 2008 in which more than 60 people were killed in mob violence directed against foreigners from other African countries, particularly refugees, underscored the impact of xenophobia on the society. However, while politicians debated these problems, they had no direct connection as issues to the ideologies of the parties, or to any party's primary appeal.

TABLE 2 South Africa: General Election Results, 1994–2009

Party	1994 Votes	1994 Seats	1999 Votes	1999 Seats	2004 Votes	2004 Seats	2009 Votes	2009 Seats
African National Congress	62.6	252	66.4	266	69.7	279	65.9	264
Congress of the People	—	—	—	—	—	—	7.4	30
New National Party	20.4	82	6.9	28	1.7	7	—	—
Democratic Alliance	1.7	7	9.6	38	12.4	50	16.7	67
Independent Democrats	—	—	—	—	1.7	7	0.9	4
Inkatha Freedom Party	10.5	43	8.6	34	7.0	28	4.6	18
Freedom Front Plus	2.2	9	0.8	3	0.9	4	0.8	4
Pan-Africanist Congress	1.2	5	0.7	3	0.7	3	0.3	1
African Christian Democratic Party	0.5	2	1.4	6	1.6	6	0.8	3
United Democratic Movement	—	—	3.4	14	2.3	9	0.9	4
United Christian Democratic Party	—	—	0.8	3	0.8	3	0.4	2
others	0.9	0	1.4	5	1.2	4	1.3	3
Total	100.0	400	100.0	400	100.0	400	100.0	400

Note. New National Party includes the National Party, Democratic Alliance the Democratic Party, and Freedom Front Plus the Freedom Front in earlier elections.
Source: www.elections.org.za.

Furthermore, policies to address these problems did not lend themselves easily to political mobilization along ethnic or racial lines. In any event, a basic assumption of the political parties seeking to challenge the ANC's dominance (see Table 2) was that ethnic and racial identification as a basis for generating support constituted a losing strategy. Thus, all the political parties have sought to extend their appeal across racial and ethnic divisions, though with limited success. The paradox of South African politics is that the rhetoric of the parties belies the reality of the continuing electoral importance of race and ethnicity, at least as a basis for analyzing how people voted. Admittedly, the correlation between race and voting behavior might also be interpreted as a rich-poor divide, since the categories overlap substantially. In 2009 the ANC's claims to represent the poor of the society were stronger than ever as a result of its gains in KwaZulu Natal, while, by contrast, its losses in the Western Cape also underscored the economic divide, as members of better-off communities abandoned the party.

The narrow ground of political debate among the parties contending for office in South Africa stands in marked contrast to the scale of the country's problems. A striking example is the fact that all the leading political figures in the country have fundamentally continued to endorse the neo-liberal macroeconomic framework known as GEAR (standing for growth, equity, and redistribution) that was put in place in 1996 when Mandela was president.[30] Remarkably, what has been called the Washington consensus still holds in South Africa at the policy-making level, notwithstanding its unpopularity with the trade unions and others that helped Zuma in his campaign against Mbeki, and also notwithstanding the fact that neo-liberal economic policies have been in retreat elsewhere. Even the global economic downturn has not shaken the parties' acceptance of this strategy.

A common assumption of much of the literature on deeply divided societies is that they require special mechanisms for their governance so that the interests of minorities are not disregarded. The argument is that without some special provision for minorities, their disaffection is likely to destabilize the political system. The South African case runs directly counter to this assumption. Thus, it is virtually unimaginable that the very large inequalities of wealth and income that continue to characterize this society would be politically tolerable except under a majoritarian system, another paradox of the South African transition.

It may be considered fortuitous in this context that the major shift in power in South Africa occurred at a moment of an unprecedented degree of tolerance within the global political economy for a widening of economic inequalities within and between countries. If that moment passes, it may have a considerable impact on the character of South African politics. This adds another dimension to the uncertainty over the country's political future and seems likely to prove rather more important in the long run than the personal rivalries that have beset the country's ruling and dominant party in the last few years. There is little basis for arguing that isolation from trends in the rest of the world is or has been responsible for the character of the country's politics. But external influences are filtered through the local circumstances that shape their impact.

CONCLUSION

As a legacy of apartheid, political mobilization along ethnic or racial lines remains in disrepute, and this has helped to prevent the explicit political exploitation of a number of potential fault lines. Admittedly, a number of the political parties in the South African system, including the Inkatha Freedom Party and some of the minor parties on the far right of the political spectrum, can be characterized as ethno-nationalist ones. But ethno-nationalism creates a niche for these parties rather than offering them the basis for expanding their appeal.

Ethnicity played a role in the 2009 elections, largely to the benefit of the ANC. Thus, Jacob Zuma's Zulu identity enhanced the ANC's appeal in KwaZulu Natal and was a factor that cut into support for the Inkatha Freedom Party. By contrast, COPE was damaged in the run-up to the elections by rows over the party's leadership that took on an ethnic coloration.[31] Despite evidence that the country's ethnic and racial fault lines are reflected in how people vote, the assumption that parties are damaged by any appearance of ethnic or racial favoritism remains a disincentive to any party wishing to present itself as a national party from seeking to capitalize on ethnic or racial differences.

From a comparative perspective, the legacy of apartheid in dampening racial and ethnic political competition may limit the relevance of the South African example in achieving and sustaining both constitutional and majoritarian government in a plural society. Where there are no taboos on political mobilization by ethnically exclusivist parties, the case for mechanisms to ensure fair treatment of minority groups may be a much stronger one. Consequently, South Africa's institutions are not necessarily a suitable model for other deeply divided societies. However, the South African experience should not be seen as unique. Indeed, it is sometimes too readily assumed in ethnically divided societies, or even in simply multiethnic societies, that ethnic cleavages are of such overriding importance that they need to be given priority in the design of the society's political institutions, to the neglect of other pressing issues. In particular, in the South Africa case, it seems improbable that consociational or other devices conventionally employed to defuse ethnic antagonisms would have made it any easier for government to tackle the challenges facing postapartheid South Africa—indeed, on the contrary.

ACKNOWLEDGMENTS

My thanks are due to John Coakley, Merle Lipton, and two anonymous referees for their comments on an earlier draft of this paper.

NOTES

1. Bernard Crick, "The High Price of Peace," in Hermann Giliomee and Jannie Gagiano (eds.), *The Elusive Search for Peace: South Africa, Israel and Northern Ireland* (Cape Town: Oxford University Press, 1990), p. 265.

2. See, for example, Patti Waldmeir, *The Anatomy of a Miracle: The End of Apartheid and the Birth of the New South Africa* (London: Viking, 1997).

3. See, for example, F. van Zyl Slabbert and David Welsh, *South Africa's Options: Strategies for Sharing Power* (Cape Town: David Philip, 1979).

4. Donald L. Horowitz, *A Democratic South Africa? Constitutional Engineering in a Divided Society* (Cape Town: Oxford University Press, 1991), p. 1.

5. Ibid., p. 3. The "twelve South Africas" are set out on pp. 3–8.

6. Hermann Giliomee and Lawrence Schlemmer, *From Apartheid to Nation-building* (Cape Town: Oxford University Press, 1989), pp. 114–49.

7. From text of the Freedom Charter quoted in Thomas Karis and Gwendolen Carter (eds.), *From Protest to Challenge: A Documentary History of African Politics in South Africa 1882–1964*, Thomas Karis and Gail M. Gerhart (eds.), *Volume 3: Challenge and Violence 1953–1964* (Stanford, CA: Hoover Institution Press, 1977), p. 205.

8. See, for example, Arend Lijphart, *Democracy in Plural Societies: A Comparative Exploration* (New Haven, CT: Yale University Press, 1977); Arend Lijphart, "Consociational Democracy," *World Politics*, Vol. 21, No. 2 (1969), pp. 207–25; and of special relevance in this context, Arend Lijphart, *Power-Sharing in South Africa* (Berkeley, CA: Institute of International Studies, University of California Berkeley, 1985).

9. Horowitz, *A Democratic South Africa?*, pp. 7–8.

10. Hermann Giliomee, *The Afrikaners: Biography of a People* (Cape Town: Tafelberg, 2003), p. 645. Joe Slovo famously described ANC's acceptance of the staged process as agreement to "sunset clauses."

11. Lijphart claimed that "the newly founded democracy is clearly a consociational democracy"; Arend Lijphart, "Prospects for Power Sharing in the New South Africa," in Andrew Reynolds (ed.), *Election '94 South Africa: The Campaigns, Results and Future Prospects* (London: James Currey, 1994), p. 222.

12. For an account of these events, see Joshua Hammer, "Jacob Zuma: Will He Rule South Africa?", *New York Review of Books*, Vol. 56, No. 2 (12–25 Feb. 2009), pp. 28–31.

13. See Richard Lapper and Tom Burgis, "ANC Backers Jubilant as Zuma Case Dropped," *Financial Times*, 7 April 2009.

14. See Donna Bryson, "Back-to-Tribal-Roots Move Sparked by Zuma?", *Independent online* (South Africa), 18 Jan. 2009, available www.iol.co.za.

15. See "Profiles of the Top Six," *Fast Facts* (Johannesburg: South African Institute of Race Relations, Jan. 2009), pp. 2–11.

16. Heribert Adam, Frederik Van Zyl Slabbert, and Kogila Moodley, *Comrades in Business: Post-Liberation Politics in South Africa* (Cape Town: Tafelberg, 1997), p. 53.

17. G. H. Caplin, *There Are No South Africans* (London: Thomas Nelson and Sons, 1941).

18. See John Kane-Berman (ed.), *South Africa Survey 2001/2002* (Johannesburg: South African Institute of Race Relations, 2001), p. 128; and John Kane-Berman (ed.), *South Africa Survey 2002/2003* (Johannesburg: South African Institute of Race Relations, 2003), p. 10.

19. Merle Lipton, *Capitalism and Apartheid: South Africa, 1910–1986* (Aldershot, UK: Wildwood House, 1986). This is the second edition with an appendix on the country's crisis of the mid-1980s; the first edition in hardback was published in 1985 by Gower.

20. Harrison M. Wright, *The Burden of the Present: Liberal-Radical Controversy over Southern African History* (Cape Town: David Philip, 1977).

21. For a robust discussion of this conflict and of views from a liberal perspective, see Merle Lipton, *Liberals, Marxists, and Nationalists: Competing Interpretations of South African History* (New York: Palgrave Macmillan, 2007).

22. Sampie Terreblanche, *A History of Inequality in South Africa: 1652–2002* (Pietermaritzburg, South Africa: University of Natal Press, 2002), p. 375.

23. See, for example, Roelf Meyer, *Paradigm Shift: The Essence of Successful Change* (Derry, UK: INCORE, 2003).

24. See, for example, Jannie Gagiano's analysis of the results of an opinion survey of White university students in 1989. Over 60% of those surveyed replied that they would emigrate or resist physically if the ANC came to power in the country; Jannie Gagiano, "Ruling Group Cohesion," in Gagiano and Giliomee, *Elusive Search*, p. 196.

25. Kane-Berman, p. 374; Marco Macfarlane (ed.), *South Africa Survey 2007/2008* (Johannesburg: South African Institute of Race Relations, 2008).

26. Macfarlane, *South Africa Survey*, pp. 236–7.

27. Mahmood Mamdani, "Lessons of Zimbabwe," *London Review of Books*, Vol. 30, No. 23 (2008), pp. 17–21.

28. See, for example, Richard Lapper, "Deft amid Difficulties," *Financial Times*, 14 Aug. 2009.

29. See, for example, Richard Lapper, "The Poor of South Africa Rebel," *Financial Times*, 29 July 2009.

30. See "Profiles," 2009, pp. 2–11.

31. See editorial, "Cope Must Deal Quickly with its Ethnic Rivalries," *The Times Online* (South Africa), 23 Feb. 2009; available www.thetimes.co.za.

9

Sri Lanka: The Challenge of Postwar Peace Building, State Building, and Nation Building

S. W. R. de A. SAMARASINGHE

Tulane University

Sri Lanka's ethnic war that lasted over 25 years produced a militarized country, political fragmentation, deep ethnic division, poor governance, and a weak economy. Reconciliation, peace building, and transformation of the politics and economy are essential for Sri Lanka to recover. However, prospects are not as good as they could be. Its major Western trading partners and donors are unhappy with the country's human rights record. The government is further strengthening the military. The current leadership is using the undemocratic institutions and practices of governance that the war created. Two-thirds of the people who have known little other than war, poor governance, and patronage politics may take a long time to realize their responsibility to pressure the rulers to mend their ways.

INTRODUCTION

As recently as five years ago, in 2004, any article dealing with the process of political reconstruction in Sri Lanka would have had as its starting point the reality of a profound conflict between a Tamil nationalist movement demanding separate statehood (creation of Thamil Eelam) and the forces of the central government seeking to assert the unity of Sri Lanka.[1] But the relationship between the two sides was changed fundamentally by the May 2009 defeat of the Liberation Tigers of Tamil Eelam (LTTE) by the armed forces of Sri Lanka, bringing to an end a war that had lasted over 25 years. The focus of this article is on the challenges that Sri Lanka faces following what appears to be a comprehensive military defeat of the LTTE, whose entire top leadership, including its ruthless leader Velupillai Prabhakaran, has been killed.[2] It is reported that the LTTE lost 22,000 fighters in the so-called Eelam War IV over the three years 2006–09.[3] As of early October 2009 the government is holding an estimated 275,000 internally displaced Tamil persons in the northern city of Vavunia under military control and without freedom of movement. They had been living in an ever-shrinking LTTE-controlled area in the northeast section of the country in the first half of 2009. The government's declared main justification for holding them in camps is that it was not safe for them to return to their villages until demining was completed. However, it is well known that the government is determined to thoroughly screen these people to weed out LTTE cadres.

Now that the war is over, one would expect the government to downsize the military, which in July 2009 had over 200,000 personnel in a relatively poor country with a GDP per capita of $2,014 (2008), a population of 20 million, and no known external enemies. In 2007 the country had 1,065 active duty military personnel for every 100,000 in the population; the comparable ratio for India, Pakistan, Bangladesh, and Nepal was 229, 569, 139, and 368 respectively, making Sri Lanka the most militarized country in South Asia.[4] But the government, instead of downsizing the military, is recruiting 100,000 more. The goal, the government says, is never again to allow the reconstitution of the LTTE or any other armed movement to challenge the state.

The government has taken a few steps to recruit ethnic Tamils to the military. These are men who belonged to certain Tamil paramilitary groups, especially in the east, that fought on the side of the government against the LTTE in the last two to five years of the war. However, there are no plans, as yet, to integrate former LTTE combatants into the Sri Lankan military.

This postwar military strategy has important implications for Sri Lanka's postwar ambition to build a united Sri Lanka from its multiethnic population. If this massive and mainly ethnically Sinhalese army is deployed in the north and east it is likely to be seen as an occupation army. Even during the war there was a great deal of pressure from the population in the north, possibly encouraged by the LTTE, to remove the so-called "security zones" that were a euphemism for military camps. At that time the government resisted such demands on grounds of security. It will be harder to make the same argument when the government proclaims that the LTTE has been liquidated and peace reestablished. If the military force that it plans to deploy in Tamil areas is used for physical infrastructure development work there will be three drawbacks. First, the locals will be deprived of jobs. Second, using relatively well-paid military men for unskilled labor is inefficient. Third, donors may be reluctant to fund civilian projects that employ military personnel.

The Sri Lankan case thus represents a particular challenge in the study of the process of ethnic conflict management. If one side has won a decisive military victory, what options are open to it in ensuring a successful transition to peace and stability via postconflict reconciliation, peace building, and reconstruction? We may discuss this question by considering in turn three related issues: the political background to the conflict as expressed in particular in the tension between peace building and nation building, the conduct and outcome of the war itself, and the set of postwar realities that constrain the positions of the contending actors.

RECONCILIATION AND TRANSFORMATION: A CONCEPTUAL FRAMEWORK

In this article we define postconflict peace building broadly as a process that falls under the concepts of *reconciliation* and *transformation* that are widely used in the conflict resolution and political science literature.[5] Paul Lederach identifies truth, justice, mercy, and peace as four components on which reconciliation can be built.[6] But there is a psychological dimension to this as well.

Reconciliation will play out in different societies in different ways depending on, among other things, culture, religion, social norms, and history. Reconciliation itself may be a long-term process. However, it carries immediacy in the sense that some degree of reconciliation has to take place as the initial short-term step of peace building. The main requirement for this is mercy and forgiveness on the part of the protagonists for the wrongs that they have done during the conflict. The actual dynamic, especially the way in which justice is meted out, will depend very much on who won and who lost, and who wronged whom; and perceptions that the parties to the conflict have of what happened will matter as much as what actually happened. In particular in a conflict where there is a clear-cut victor and a clear cut-loser, a greater responsibility lies with the former to bring about lasting reconciliation. The 1995 South African Truth and Reconciliation Commission (TRC), for example, was quite successful in reaching out to the White community at large to make them feel that they were wanted in a postapartheid South Africa and also to convince the Blacks that reconciliation was essential for the success of the new South Africa. Since then a large number of other countries emerging from conflict have created their own versions of the TRC.

Successful reconciliation is essential to lay the groundwork for long-term postconflict transformation that will bring about long-term peace. This is a challenging long-term process that requires transformation of a society in almost all its dimensions, political, economic, social, cultural, and psychological. It requires a voluntary coming together of protagonist groups that were bitter enemies not so long ago to work for the common good and for a higher purpose. This requires agreement on sharing resources that are often in short supply in an equitable manner, and an agreement that, despite their apparent differences, be they racial, ethnic, religious or any other, there are higher common goals and purposes in their shared country.

This brings us to the complex issue of state building and nation building. Nineteenth-century Europe saw the birth of the "nation" state. The Germanic model of the nation state brought together people who spoke one language and shared a common culture and history, living in a clearly demarcated territory under one sovereign state.[7] But there was an alternative multiethnic or multiracial model of the state. The United States and some European countries such as France and Britain that had multiracial societies owing to their colonial pasts and migration of peoples from other parts of the world represented this second model. Most of the colonies of European countries in Asia, Africa, and elsewhere that became independent after the Second World War also fell into the same category. When we look back at the period since then we see varying degrees of success in the construction of the postcolonial multiethnic state. At one end stand countries such as India, which have succeeded in holding together despite incredible diversity.[8] At the other extreme are failed states such as Somalia and Liberia. In between are a range of states that have had varying degrees of success and failure.[9]

Ethnic conflict and the protracted civil war in Sri Lanka are symptomatic of the failure of multiethnic Sri Lanka to build a state that commanded the allegiance of all its citizens irrespective of ethnicity. In that sense the country has failed to integrate the different ethnic groups for a common national purpose after independence from Britain in 1948. As the examples that have been cited above demonstrate, successful nation building does not negate ethnic and cultural differences. On the contrary, in progressive multiethnic societies these are celebrated as strengths.

GENESIS OF THE CONFLICT

In the early twentieth century political leaders of all communities in Sri Lanka joined together to form the Ceylon National Congress (CNC;1919–46) and to demand independence from British rule. Some of the most prominent leaders of the CNC, were Tamils. However, this show of unity gradually broke down in the 1930s and 1940s. In 1936 a Pan-Sinhalese Board of Ministers was formed by the State Council, a body that was elected by popular vote the same year. In that year the Sinhalese constituted about two-thirds of the population, Tamils 25% and the Muslims 5%.[10] The Tamil leadership saw this as an unfair, manipulative move on the part of the Sinhalese leadership and a precursor of things to come. Tamil mistrust of Sinhalese political motives increased as a result. The solution of the Tamil leaders was to demand a "fifty-fifty" split in seats in the legislature, meaning 50% for the majority Sinhalese and 50% for the minorities. The British did not concede this demand. However, the independence constitution of 1948 provided for a secular state. Section 29 (2) of the constitution also provided for safeguards against legislation that would discriminate against minorities.

In 1948–49 the government passed legislation that effectively disenfranchised the vast majority of plantation Tamils, 11.7% of the total population in 1946.[11] They had the right to vote in the 1931, 1936, and 1947 general elections, and in 1947 seven plantation Tamils were elected to parliament. But in the six parliamentary elections that followed (1952–70) not one was elected, and in 1977 just one was returned.[12] These events caused a radical section of the Tamil political leadership to form the Federal Party in 1948; this had as its goal a federal if not a secessionist solution to the political grievances that Tamils experienced.

Three more issues further aggravated relations between the Sinhalese and Tamils in the period 1950–70. One was the language policy of the administration of S. W. R. D. Bandaranaike of the left-of-center Sri Lanka Freedom Party (SLFP), elected to office in 1956.[13] The Official Language Act of 1956 provided that "the Sinhala language be the one official language of Sri Lanka." Prime Minister S. W. R. D. Bandaranaike and the leader of the Federal Party S. J. V. Chelvanayakam signed a pact in July 1956 to recognize Tamil as the "language of the minority." But the pact was abrogated under pressure from Sinhalese nationalists. The government, however, passed the Tamil Language (Special Provisions) Act of 1958, which made provision for the use of Tamil in government for prescribed purposes. Nevertheless actual policy moved in the direction of enforcement of the 1956 Official Language Act. New recruits to government service were required to be proficient in Sinhala, putting Tamils at a disadvantage. The Language of Courts Act of 1961 made way for the courts to switch from English to Sinhala. The United National Party (UNP) government of 1965–70 enacted regulations under the 1958 Tamil Language Act to meet Tamil demands.[14] However, the new constitution of 1972, the "First Republican" constitution marking Sri Lanka's change of status to a republic, declared that Sinhala would be the official language and also made regulations under the 1958 Tamil Language Act as subordinate legislation.

For Tamils, the language dispute was more than an identity and cultural dignity issue. In a country where secure jobs with pensions and other perks were in short supply, government positions were at a premium. The fact that Sinhala was made the only official language was seen by many Tamils as a ploy to secure government jobs for the Sinhalese. Having said that, it must also be noted that throughout this period both Sinhala and Tamil remained the medium of instruction in state schools. In state universities too, the humanities and social sciences were taught in both languages and the sciences typically in English only. In the predominantly Tamil areas, state institutions including the law courts generally transacted business in Tamil. However, there were exceptions, especially in regard to the police and security forces.[15]

The 1972 Constitution removed section 29 (2) of the independence constitution (1948) that protected the minorities. It also gave Buddhism the "foremost" place and declared that "it shall be the duty of the State to protect and foster Buddhism,"[16] steps that further alienated the Tamils from the Sri Lankan state. In 1978, a new "Second Republican" constitution took a major step to resolve the language dispute when it made Tamil a "national language." In 1988, following the Indo-Lanka Peace Accord, Tamil was made an official language, giving it legal parity with Sinhala. However, it still remains a fact that in many parts of the country in the south even today, government agencies do not have adequate facilities to transact business in Tamil with Tamil-speaking people.

There were two other contentious areas that deepened the chasm between the Sinhalese and Tamils. One was the state-sponsored settlement of landless Sinhalese from the south in the north, and especially in the east, in what were called land colonization schemes. These schemes were developed with state funds for cultivation of rice and other crops. The program started in the 1930s and continued after independence. The Tamils objected on the grounds that it was state-sponsored intrusion in the "traditional Tamil homeland." There were two main reasons for the objection. First, land was a scarce resource. Second, Sinhalese settlements altered the ethnic composition of the region. In reality such settlements did not alter the ethnic balance in the Northern Province. However, in two of the three districts in the Eastern Province it did. In the Trincomalee District the Tamil population dropped from 53.2% in 1921 to 33.8% in 1981 and in Ampara District from 30.5% to 20.1%. The Sinhalese percentages in the two districts increased from 4.5% to 33.6% and from 8.2% to 37.6%, respectively.[17] In a country where people voted along ethnic lines this also had an appreciable impact on parliamentary representation from these districts.

Finally, the affirmative action program that the government initiated in 1970 for admissions to state universities riled the Tamil youth in particular. The admission figures for 1969 show that the northern Tamils who were 12% of the population took about half of the places available for medicine and engineering, the most popular courses of study. The system of admission was based on "merit," meaning that those who scored the highest aggregate in competitive admissions examinations were admitted according to the availability of places. The government introduced a scheme of standardization in 1970, and two years later replaced it with a district quota system that reduced the Tamil share to less than 20% and increased the Sinhalese share to 70% or more. As would be expected, Tamils saw this as discrimination, while the Sinhalese saw it as fair distribution of the limited number of places that were available.[18]

EVOLUTION OF THE CONFLICT

Given the above events, the fact that Tamils questioned the legitimacy of the Sri Lankan state was not surprising. Until about 1975 the Tamils challenged the government within the confines of the political mainstream. There were nonviolent protests from time to time. Unfortunately some of these, such as the *Satyagraha* (peaceful protests) of January 1961 in the north and east, were mishandled by the government, which deployed the police and the army to disperse protesters, resulting in violence.

The rising tension between the two communities also led to several episodes of communal violence, notably in 1956, 1958, 1977, and 1983. In all these most of the victims were Tamils at the hands of Sinhalese mobs. The worst episode was in July 1983 and resulted in at least several hundred deaths of Tamils in Colombo and elsewhere in the south, extensive destruction of Tamil-owned property, the flight of internally displaced Tamils from the south to the north and east, and an outflow of over 100,000 Tamil refugees to India, and another 200,000–300,000 to Western countries. "Black July," as it later came to be called, undermined the economic boom that economic liberalization in the late 1970s had initiated, reversed the growth of a booming tourist industry and tarnished the image of the country.

From the early 1970s incidents of violence, mainly against the police, were reported from the Jaffna peninsula. In 1975 the elected Tamil mayor of Jaffna, who represented the SLFP, was assassinated. But these incidents of violence grew into a full-fledged guerrilla war only in the early 1980s. The immediate cause of the outburst of anti-Tamil violence in July 1983 was the killing of 13 Sinhalese soldiers in Jaffna by the Tamil Tigers (LTTE). Starting from that date, the Sri Lankan ethnic war had the following phases.

Eelam War I, July 1983 to July 1987

This phase included fighting between the Sri Lankan army and Tamil guerrilla forces led by the LTTE that lasted until July 1987, when India intervened and stopped the Sri Lankan army from possibly destroying the Tamil guerrillas. India sent a peace-keeping force to implement the Indo-Lanka Peace Accord (1987) that Sri Lanka accepted under considerable pressure from India. But the LTTE did not wish to lay down arms and to accept the creation of provincial councils with devolved powers that the peace accord proposed as a solution to the conflict. The LTTE defied the Indians, battled against the Indian peace-keeping force and eventually used the opportunity to emerge as the dominant Tamil rebel group. The presence of the Indians was wanted neither by the LTTE nor by the Sri Lanka government, and the peace-keeping force withdrew from the country in early 1990. The government and the LTTE engaged in peace negotiations, but these collapsed in a few months.

Eelam War II, July 1990 to July 1994

This phase of the war lasted for four years. The fighting stopped when the government in Colombo changed in 1994. The new People's Alliance government headed by Chandrika Kumaratunga, who attracted a significant Tamil vote, negotiated with the LTTE from August 1994 to April 1995 but the talks proved to be abortive.

Eelam War III, May 1995 to December 2001

War broke out soon after the talks collapsed and lasted for seven years until December 2001. In late 1995, the government captured the Jaffna peninsula from the LTTE, who moved to the Vanni district. These seven years were probably the most destructive phase of the entire war, with large numbers of deaths in battle on both sides and a series of major terrorist attacks in Colombo and elsewhere in the south mounted by the LTTE. This phase ended in December 2001 with a ceasefire agreement signed between the LTTE and the new Sri Lankan government elected in 2001. The agreement was brokered by Norway and monitored by a monitoring mission consisting of members drawn from Scandinavian countries. The ceasefire agreement has been criticized from all sides. Some saw it as an opportunity that the government exploited to build international support against the LTTE and to procure weapons. Others have criticized it as an opportunity that wholly favored the LTTE, allowing it to strengthen its forces to prepare for a final battle to establish a Tamil Eelam state in the north and east.[19] Yet others saw it as a missed opportunity to broker a permanent peaceful political settlement.

Eelam War IV, July 2006 to May 2009

A new president, Mahinda Rajapakse, was elected in November 2005. He was also from the ruling United Peoples Freedom Alliance (UPFA), an interparty coalition headed by the SLFP. Rajapakse in his election manifesto promised an "undivided country, a national consensus and an honourable peace."[20] However, his platform rhetoric clearly suggested a more militant response to the LTTE and some of his prominent backers openly talked of a military solution. He was elected with the overwhelming support of the Sinhalese but with very few Tamil or Muslim votes. He held one round of talks in Geneva with the LTTE but it did not yield positive results. In an atmosphere of mutual recrimination, Eelam War IV commenced in July 2006. There was considerable Western pressure to stop the war in its closing stages but the government rejected all such pleas.[21] It finally ended in May 2009 with the complete liquidation of the LTTE.

Shorty after Eelam War IV commenced it became evident that the Rajapakse administration was determined to pursue the war to its end. This was a calculated strategy, because the government believed that the LTTE was not interested in a political settlement short of dividing the country and establishing a separate state in the north and east. Western nations brought considerable pressure on the government to halt the war and to return to peace talks with the LTTE. The government rejected all such pleas on the grounds that the LTTE could not be trusted. It pointed out that the LTTE had used previous ceasefires and peace talks to replenish and build up its military strength. Thus the government was not prepared to fall into the same trap again. After the LTTE abandoned its base in the town of Kilinochchi in January 2009, it moved to the northeast with its civilian population to an ever-shrinking area of land. By May 2009 it occupied only a sliver of land in the north east by the sea.

One notable feature that emerged in the last few months of the war was the plight of the 300,000 civilians who were trapped in the diminishing area that was under LTTE control. Without a doubt the conditions were atrocious for the trapped civilians. The government asserted that they were used as a human shield by the LTTE. The LTTE portrayed them as innocent civilians who were under attack from a ruthless military. The government called its final military push not an attack on the LTTE but a humanitarian rescue operation to bring the trapped civilians to safety. The international community expressed concern for their safety to both sides. The LTTE disregarded pleas to allow the civilians to leave the war zone. The government did not allow journalists or other independent observers to visit the area. In February 2009 the government turned down a request from Britain to send a special envoy to assess the plight of these civilians. However, following an expression of concern from the UN, the government invited John Holmes, the UN's Under-Secretary-General for Humanitarian Affairs, to visit Sri Lanka.[22] As noted earlier, this phase ended with the annihilation of the LTTE.

In this rather dismal picture of interethnic relations in postindependence Sri Lanka there is one relationship that evolved in a more peaceful and constructive direction: the relations between the leadership of the plantation ("Indian") Tamil community and the Sinhalese political leadership of both major parties. The plantation Tamils acquired Sri Lankan citizenship, and with that the right to vote, thanks to an agreement that Sri Lanka's Prime Minister, Mrs. Sirima Bandaranaike, reached with her Indian counterpart, Lal Bahadur Shastri, in 1964. India granted citizenship to about 500,000 people who returned to that country; Sri Lanka granted citizenship to the remainder, including their children. In the 1981 census they numbered 757,000 (5.5% of the population) and in the 2001 census 855,000 (5.1%).

The overwhelming majority of the plantation Tamils showed their allegiance to the Ceylon Workers Congress, which has doubled up as a trade union and political party. The Congress leadership kept the plantation Tamil community out of the conflict and used its electoral clout to win concessions from the government on improving conditions for their community. The plantation Tamils are still among the more backward segments of Sri Lankan society. However, they have made significant strides in social development. When the LTTE tried to penetrate the plantation areas to entice the plantation Tamil youth to join their ranks, they had very little success.

The above account provides adequate evidence to show that the Sinhalese and Tamil communities had sufficient reason, real or imaginary, to drift apart. The Sri Lankan Tamils increasingly nursed the grievance of discrimination against them by Sinhalese-dominated governments. From their perspective there were compelling reasons to challenge the legitimacy of the Sri Lankan state, first politically and later militarily. The fact that the country had to endure a bloody civil war lasting one generation that claimed around 100,000 lives, that retarded economic and social progress, and that undermined its democratic governance and credentials suggests that there was something fundamentally at fault in the polity that prevented Sri Lanka from emerging as one united country with a multiethnic population. That is the fundamental challenge that Sri Lanka needs to address in the postconflict environment if it is to build a viable state from the rubble of an ethnic war. Although reconciliation is an immediate need and transformation is a long-term process, the two are not mutually exclusive. They can run parallel to and mutually reinforce each other.

POLITICAL CONSEQUENCES OF THE CONFLICT

One obvious effect of the conflict and the war was to deepen ethnic cleavages, causing political fragmentation that affected almost every political party. In Sinhalese politics, the more Sinhalese nationalist SLFP-led coalitions have ruled the country since 1994 except for a brief two years in 2002–04 when the UNP, generally believed to be more sympathetic to the minorities, formed a government. But even during those two years Chandrika Kumaratunga of the UPFA remained the executive president. After the 2005 presidential election a large number of UNP members of parliament crossed over to Rajapakse's UPFA, suggesting that ideology and belief in principles no longer mattered very much in Sri Lankan politics.

Certain minor political parties, which have emerged largely owing to their ability to exploit the ethnic and religious sentiments of the voters and the proportional representation system of elections that replaced the first-past-the-post system beginning 1989, have helped to reinforce the political fragmentation, while fuelling the Sinhalese nationalist position. For example, the strongly nationalist and Marxist *Janatha Vimukthi Peramuna* (People's Liberation Front) strengthened its position in national politics after 1994. In 2004 the Front played a crucial role in bringing down the government of Ranil Wickremasinghe, who had signed the ceasefire agreement of 2002 with the LTTE. In the 2005 presidential election, it played a big part in mobilizing Sinhalese voters for the Sinhalese nationalist candidacy of Mahinda Rajapakse. In 2008 the Front itself split, with a dissident group that passionately stands for a unitary state and strongly opposes any form of devolution joining the ruling UPFA. The Jathika Hela Urumaya (National Legacy Party), consisting mainly of Buddhist monks, also represents Sinhalese-Buddhist interests and has considerable influence in the current ruling coalition.

In addition, the war had a major impact on the political leadership of what we could call Sri Lanka's "baby boomer" generation. In the case of the Sinhalese, LTTE suicide bombers killed one sitting president, R. Premadasa (UNP), in 1993, and maimed another, Mrs. Kumaratunga, in 1999. It also killed a large number of the top Sinhalese political leader, including the candidate of the UNP for the presidency in 1994, Gamini Dissanayaka, and many others who held cabinet portfolios in both major parties. It is possible to argue that the current weak leadership of the UNP opposition is largely attributable to the success of the LTTE suicide bombing campaign.

The traditional Tamil political leadership in the north and east, which believed in mainstream parliamentary democracy, has been virtually decimated in the last 30 years. Many of its members, including the leader of the opposition in the 1977 parliament and leader of the Tamil United Liberation Front, Appapillai Amirthalingam, were killed by the LTTE, which brooked no challenge to its leadership of the Tamil community. But the LTTE was not alone in using assassination as a tool in political power struggles. In the east, Tamil political leaders were killed by various rival factions that jockeyed for power. In more recent years, several Tamil political leaders were assassinated, some in Colombo, by "unidentified" killers whom the police have failed to track down. Consequently, with the demise of the LTTE the Tamil population is virtually leaderless and broken. Around 200,000–300,000 Tamils are estimated to have migrated abroad permanently in the past 25 years, creating a population deficit that will affect the availability of potential future leaders.[23]

Tamils who live in Sri Lanka have, then, been generally subdued since the end of the war. The few Tamil political leaders who are not on the side of the government and who have spoken in public have focused on the plight of the internally displaced persons. Those Tamil politicians who are on the government's side have noted that Prabhakaran's intransigence doomed the LTTE to failure and have called for national reconstruction and for the grievances of the Tamils to be addressed. The Tamil diaspora in Western countries, for long a major source of funds for the LTTE and strong campaigners on behalf of the Tamil cause (especially in the first half of 2009 when the war intensified), are confronted by a new set of realities with which they have to come reluctantly to terms.

The Muslims did not have a direct stake in the conflict before it escalated in the early 1980s. Politically, they followed a somewhat different track. They generally participated in parliamentary politics as members of the major parties and normally held cabinet portfolios in successive governments. But from the mid-1980s, as the ethnic war intensified, the Muslim community began to feel the need for their own ethnic political party. The result was the formation in 1981 of the Sri Lanka Muslim Congress, which claimed to represent Muslim interests and has even committed itself to the establishment of the Sharia Law.[24] In the peace talks between the government and the LTTE, the Muslim Congress became increasingly vocal about having their own seat at the table.[25] In the Eastern Province, where the Muslims accounted for 32% of the population in 1981 and 38% in 2007, the party scored several electoral successes. The UNP and the SLFP began to compete for the support of the Muslim Congress, which in turn asserted the right of Muslims in the east to a share of power in any devolved form of government.

Some of the new political alliances that have been forged are between Tamil political groups and the ruling Rajapakse administration and his UPFA. For example, the former deputy leader of the LTTE, which he left in March 2004, is now a vice president of the SLFP and Minister for National Integration and Reconciliation. He also heads a Tamil political party that joined with the governing UPFA and contested the Eastern Provincial Council elections successfully. The Chief Minister of the Eastern Province is an ex-LLTE child soldier; and the current Minister of Social Service and Social Welfare is also a former militant who gave up violence after the Indo-Lanka Peace Accord in 1987 and entered mainstream politics.[26]

It is too early to conclude whether these alliances are simple opportunistic political marriages of convenience or the beginning of an enduring new multiethnic political culture. The evidence points to the former. For example, in the Eastern Province, while the police and the military are present in significant numbers supposedly to enforce law and order, regular reports appear in the Sri Lanka press of informal paramilitary gangs owing allegiance to rival local leaders resorting to violence and terrorizing the community. The government appears to be acquiescing in this situation, presumably for its own political reasons. But the final outcome could well be the further militarization of Sri Lanka.

There is no doubt that Sri Lanka's democratic governance has been seriously weakened by the war. For example, for over 25 years the country has been ruled under emergency law that gives parliament the power to make regulations overriding any law of the country except for the constitution itself.[27] The Prevention of Terrorism (Temporary Provisions) Act of 1979, which gave extraordinary powers to the security forces, is the best example. In 1982 it was made a permanent law of the land. Many of the provisions of this act were copied from the South African Terrorism Act, which has been described as "a piece of legislation which must shock the conscience of a lawyer."[28] A culture of impunity also pervades society. The threat to media freedom is one telling example. Eleven journalists have been killed in the last three years (2006–09) and many more have been physically harmed. Several have left the country in fear of their lives. The Paris-based organization Reporters Without Borders ranked Sri Lanka 165th out of 173 countries on its 2008 Press Freedom Index, while in 2002 it had been ranked 51st among 139 countries on the same index—obvious evidence that the situation has deteriorated rapidly in the course of the present decade.

The ingredients for a renewal of conflict are, then, unfortunately present. A bitter Tamil population at home and an angry Tamil diaspora will be fertile ground for a revival of Tamil militancy. The military victory has produced a Sinhalese triumphalism that is evident in the celebrations that the government has sponsored and the propaganda surrounding them. This can give the government and the people, especially the Sinhalese, a false sense of security that would prevent them from addressing the need for a viable long-term political solution. This, in turn, would transform the political landscape to something that is more accommodating of the ethnic minorities, especially the Tamils, who need to feel secure and wanted in a postconflict Sri Lanka.

RECONCILIATION

Since the war ended only on 18 May 2009 after a protracted civil conflict and a brutal last few months, its wounds are still raw. The issue of the 275,000 internally displaced persons who are interned in camps in Vavunia is one of the major obstacles to the easing of tension. The government promised in mid-2009 to empty the camps within 18 months. However, progress on the release of occupants from the camps has been slow. This is more than a disappointment to Tamils in Sri Lanka as well as to the large diaspora community.

A second factor that stands against reconciliation is the tardy attitude of the Rajapakse administration in considering a lasting political solution. The president, who has declared on several occasions that he would implement the current provincial council system to the maximum to devolve power, is now talking of waiting for a fresh mandate in the next parliamentary and presidential elections. This does not inspire confidence in the Tamil community and also undermines potential donor support for rebuilding the economy.

Third, the ruling party naturally wants to profit politically from the popularity that it has gained in the Sinhalese community for defeating terrorism and secession. However, this has a downside that may undermine the long-term goal of building a united Sri Lanka that the president has promised.[29] This is the Sinhalese triumphalism that is evident in some of the more extremist Sinhalese nationalist segments of the political community.

Finally, we have to consider the implications for reconciliation (and for longer term peace building) of the fight that has developed between Sri Lanka and some Western countries in the aftermath of the war. There was a bitter and acrimonious debate in the UN Human Rights Council in Geneva in May 2009, over alleged violation of humanitarian law by the Sri Lankan military. Sri Lanka opposed a resolution in the council, backed mostly by Western nations, for the holding of a UN supervised war crimes inquiry. The view of the Sri Lanka government prevailed by a vote of 29 to 12, with six abstentions, thanks to the support of developing country members who are a majority in the council.[30]

The Office of War Crimes Issues of the US State Department is preparing a report on Sri Lanka at the request of the powerful Democratic Senator Patrick Leahy. Originally scheduled for release in the third week of September 2009, the date has been postponed, and there is concern in Sri Lanka as to what its content might be.

The government sees itself as a rare success story in the fight against terrorism. It also sees Western calls for war crime inquiries as nothing but double standards and hypocrisy. The government also believes that in some Western countries politicians who are lobbied by their Tamil diaspora constituencies take a biased position against Sri Lanka for their own domestic political reasons. The government has repeatedly urged the international community to look to the future and become "partners" and not "monitors" in building a postconflict Sri Lanka.[31]

It would be easier to persuade the international community to agree with the government if the latter were able to take a few vital steps, especially to improve the quality of governance in the country in order to help political transformation. Such a strategy would convince the international community that Sri Lanka is firmly on the way to building a united multiethnic society with a state that is acceptable to all communities. Unfortunately there are not many signs thus far that this is happening.

The position of the Western international community is also ambiguous. For example, the United States played a role in delaying an International Monetary Fund (IMF) loan to Sri Lanka in March 2009 but later made an official announcement that it had no objection to the loan being given. The EU could have withheld tariff concessions in 2009 when they came up for renewal but instead extended the facility for a further year subject to a review of Sri Lanka's human rights record. This ambiguity partly reflects the fluidity of current global international relations. In the post-Cold War world, there are no clear-cut criteria to identify friends and foes. Moreover, Sri Lanka's criticism of Western countries for having double standards appears convincing to other third-world countries, which rally to defend "one of their own." When civilians by the tens of thousands have been killed in Iraq since the United States and its allies invaded that country in March 2003, and large numbers of civilians are killed in drone attacks in Afghanistan and the Afghanistan-Pakistan border area, criticism of Sri Lanka for the civilian deaths in the last phase of the war sounds less convincing, especially to third-world ears. Moreover, Western nations lose credibility when official statements are made that cannot be supported with facts. The best example is US Secretary of State Hilary Clinton in one of her statements to the UN

Security Council including Sri Lanka as an example of a country whose military used rape as a weapon of war.[32] For sure, there were some rape incidents and some perpetrators were prosecuted during the 25-year war. However, at no time did credible evidence ever emerge of the military using rape as a weapon. Even the most bitter but knowledgeable critics of the Sri Lankan war have not made such an accusation. Mrs. Clinton's statement raised a tremendous outcry in Sri Lanka;[33] it provided further ammunition to the Sinhalese nationalist segments who argue that the West and the liberal policies it purports to stand for should be disregarded.

Be that as it may, acrimony of the type that has developed between Sri Lanka and Western countries does not help the reconciliation process for several reasons. First, it strengthens the Sri Lankan Sinhalese domestic constituency that sees the conflict purely in military terms as a fight against "terrorists" and opposes any political settlement that involves meaningful devolution of power to the north and east. Conversely, it has weakened civil society, which is supportive of political compromise and reconciliation. For example, journalists and nongovernmental organizations that have criticized the government for impunity and human rights violations have been berated as Western lackeys who "bark for dollars." Second, it also keeps alive the hopes of the Tamils in Sri Lanka and especially of the diaspora that the fight for a separate state could be revived. Third, Western countries that want to see reconciliation, transformation, and peace building in a democratic environment lose their leverage.

POLITICAL TRANSFORMATION

Sri Lanka proudly proclaims that it has one of the longest functioning democracies in the developing world. The first national election under universal franchise was held as far back as 1931. The country also has a history of changing governments peacefully using the ballot box. The two major political parties, UNP and SLFP, have tended to alternate in power. They have governed the country sometimes with coalition partners and sometimes without. From 1947 to 2009 the political party that controlled parliament has changed nine times. The executive presidency that was established in 1978 was held by the UNP for the first 16 years and by the SLFP for the last 14 years. This scenario may appear to suggest a mature democracy. In reality, the position is less straightforward because of the ethnically fragmented polity that Sri Lanka's democracy has produced.

The Sinhalese, who make up 75% of the population, are roughly equally divided politically between the UNP and the SLFP. Each has a base vote of about one-third of the Sinhalese electorate, with the balance acting as "independent" floating voters. In both major parties there are members and elected parliamentarians who belong to the minority Tamils (18% of the population) and the Muslims (7%). However, a significant majority of Tamils and a size-able proportion of the Muslims prefer to support their own ethnic political parties, resulting in political divisions with a deep ethnic basis. The most neg-ative consequence of this development is that politicians are always prepared to exploit the ethnic sensibilities of the voters. Under the Second Republican Constitution of 1978, the 225-member parliament is elected by proportional representation (PR). While this has fuelled political fragmentation, it has also helped minority viewpoints gain representation in parliament and enter the political mainstream. This has compelled the two major parties to seek the support of smaller parties to form coalitions in a manner that is positive for democracy. The best example is the Marxist People's Liberation Front already discussed, with a Sinhalese support base in the south. It rebelled twice, once in 1971 and again in 1989–90, creating mayhem and bloodshed. In the parliamentary elections of 2004, as a coalition partner of UPFA, they gained as many as 40 seats and became a powerful voice in government.

Sri Lanka's presidential elections have a preferential voting system. If there are three candidates, the voter may, if he or she so wishes, mark a second preference. If there are more than three candidates the voter may mark a third preference as well. However, in the five presidential elections held to date the preferential vote has been of no consequence because the winner has obtained more than 50% of the vote in the first count. Neverthe-less, the country's electoral arithmetic gives the minorities an important say in the presidential election in a very different way. To date, all credible can-didates with a chance of winning have been Sinhalese candidates nominated by the two major political parties, UNP and SLFP, or by their coalition allies. Since the Sinhalese electorate divides fairly evenly in presidential elections between the UNP and SLFP with a slight tilt towards the latter, the votes of the Tamil and Muslim minorities are decisive. This was clearly evident in the 1982 and 1988 presidential polls. It was less obvious in the 1994, 1999, and 2005 presidential polls, each of which was affected by exceptional factors.[34] In future presidential polls held under more normal conditions the minority vote is certain to play a decisive role.

It could be argued that the Sinhalese majority suffer from a "minority complex" on account of the 60 million ethnic Tamils who live in Tamil Nadu, just 53 kilometers at its narrowest point across the Palk Strait. The Sinhalese fear that the small island nation of 25,000 square miles could be split in two, as envisaged by the LTTE. On the other side, the Tamils have their own psychological fear that the Sinhalese will use their numerical superiority to deny them their rights and to make them second-class citizens. Sri Lanka's competitive electoral politics has thus created ample scope for politicians to exploit these fears, which are embedded in the psyche of both communities.

The president of Sri Lanka, in his address to parliament in May 2009 after the war ended, asserted that "we have abolished the word minority from our vocabulary."[35] What he probably meant was that the people of

Sri Lanka should think and act as Sri Lankans rather than as Sinhalese, Tamils, or Muslims. One could argue that if that happened minorities would risk the right they have to articulate their grievances based on their minority status. However, it is possible to invert the argument and to consider such a situation to be highly desirable provided postconflict Sri Lanka abandons 60 years of ethnic politics and public policy based in part on group rights, and adopts classical liberal democracy based on individual rights. The prospects of such a radical change happening are quite remote. All the signs are that, presidential pronouncements cited above notwithstanding, ethnic politics will continue and thrive in postconflict Sri Lanka. The 1948 constitution prohibited parliament from enacting laws that were discriminatory towards any particular group. The 1972 and 1978 republican constitutions enshrined fundamental rights. But public policy continued to recognize ethnicity as a factor in diverse fields, ranging from university admissions to jobs in government and appointments to high-level positions.

A number of instruments lie at the disposal of the government in trying to consolidate peace and to reconcile Tamils to life within the Sri Lankan state. The first is the long-planned devolution of power to the provinces, a gesture that would allow a significant measure of Tamil self-rule in Tamil-dominated provinces. The second is the principle of power sharing at the center. The third is the simple practice of good, equitable, and just government. Of these three the first, devolution, is formulated in Sri Lanka in explicit ethnic terms. The second also has a strong ethnic component, but the third can be developed in a manner that is ethnicity blind.

Tamil hopes of devolution beyond the current provincial council system are unlikely to be realized in the foreseeable future. As noted earlier, the Rajapakse administration has promised to implement the thirteenth amendment to the constitution, enacted in 1987, which created the provincial councils to which power would be devolved. The provincial council for the Eastern Province was elected in 2008 when the LTTE was expelled from the province. The council for the Northern Province is yet to be elected. It appears that the full implementation of the provincial council system will achieve a large measure of devolution and would probably satisfy those Tamils who wish to work within a united Sri Lanka. Given resistance to even the thirteenth amendment in some important sections of the Sinhalese community, this appears to be the only form of devolution that is politically feasible at the moment. But the evidence that is available indicates that even the thirteenth amendment is unlikely to be implemented fully in the manner the current statutes permit.

One reason is that the ruling coalition is sharply divided on devolution of power and on the role of the provincial councils. The Sinhalese nationalists within its ranks believe in the inviolability of the "unitary" state. Media reports in mid-2009 suggest that the government will not devolve power over state land and over the police, as provided for in the law. The government also does not wish to concede anything more than weak and ineffectual local government institutions of the kind that already exist. Unless president Rajapakse takes the lead—and the opposition, including most Tamil members in parliament, probably can be persuaded to back him on this issue—meaningful devolution will not happen. However, his personal track record leaves room for doubt: as a parliamentarian and as a minister under the Chandika Kumaratunga administration, he showed little enthusiasm for provincial councils. In September 2009 he hinted that he would seek a fresh public mandate by way of a presidential election or parliamentary election before considering the full implementation of the thirteenth amendment.

The experience with provincial councils in the last 20 years is also discouraging. The current taxation powers for provincial councils are so inadequate that, perhaps with the exception of the Western Provincial Council, they are effectively wards of the Colombo government. Their budgets are overwhelmingly funded by annual grants from the center. There is no reason to believe that the central government will let go of its tight grip on taxation. The Eastern Provincial Council, established in 2008, is not in effective control of reconstruction activities in the province. The council is overshadowed by a presidential task force headed by the president's brother, who himself is a senior advisor to the president and a member of parliament. An open row between the Eastern Provincial Council and Colombo has been averted so far, but it is difficult to forecast how long this will last.

A further device, power sharing, can also be installed at the center in a unitary state. For example, a vice presidency that is always occupied by a member of the minority community, a powerful second chamber in a bicameral parliament with strong representation for minority groups, and constitutional provisions emulating the 1947 Sri Lanka constitution to protect minority rights are possibilities. Just now these options are not a part of the public discourse in the country. However, it is possible that they may come into play in the longer term as the postwar euphoria subsides among the Sinhalese, and a longer time horizon comes into view. In particular, opposition political parties that are currently groping for a program that offers a credible alternative to that offered by the current regime may take up some of these ideas.

Finally, long-term reconstruction of course requires good governance. In principle, good governance can underpin a liberal individual rights framework that will make group rights and even devolution of power less important. But here again the evidence suggests the opposite. To promote good governance the first essential step to take is the implementation of the seventeenth amendment to the constitution that was passed unanimously in parliament in 2001 with the strong backing of civil society.[36] This amendment establishes a National Constitutional Council, which is vested with the sole authority to recommend suitable individuals to the president of the country to be appointed to the Elections Commission, Public Service

Commission, Police Commission, Human Rights Commission, Bribery and Corruption Commission, Finance Commission (which allocates funds to the provincial councils), and the Delimitation Commission of parliamentary electorates. The council is also vested with authority to recommend suitable appointees for major offices of state, including that of Chief Justice, Supreme Court Justices, Attorney General, Inspector General of Police, and several others. The president can refuse to accept the recommendations of the council but the seventeenth amendment makes no provision for him or her to make alternative appointments. The first National Constitutional Council itself finished its term in October 2005. President Rajapakse has avoided appointing a fresh commission, instead arrogating to himself the task of choosing appointees to commissions and senior official positions in government in violation of the constitution.

ECONOMIC TRANSFORMATION

Undoubtedly, Sri Lanka's economy will benefit from the end of the war. The Colombo stock market index rose by 58% between 1 May and 23 September 2009. The end of the war will also help the tourist industry and foreign direct investment. For example, just a month after the end of the war tourist arrivals in June 2009 numbered 30,300, up 9% from the June 2008 figure.[37] On the other hand, a peace dividend from fiscal savings is unlikely if the government increases the size of the military as planned. The government announced that Sri Lanka's military spending for 2009 would be 144 billion rupees compared to a total budgetary allocation of 178 billion rupees at the start of the fiscal year.[38] More seriously, the global recession will continue to have a negative impact on the economy, and especially on exports.

In the economic domain, however, Sri Lanka is particularly vulnerable to international pressure, and this has been strongly conditioned by Western perceptions of domestic developments. The government needs the assistance of the international community mainly to sustain economic growth and to rebuild the country. In the last quarter of 2008 and the first quarter of 2009 Sri Lanka faced a major external payments crisis, with foreign reserves falling to the equivalent of seven weeks of imports. The government applied to the International Monetary Fund (IMF) for assistance in March 2009, as we have seen, opening the door to potential US pressure. While the loan was eventually forthcoming, pressure has continued: Congress is about to get a report from the State Department on what it calls "war crimes" in Sri Lanka, a report with potentially serious adverse repercussions for the country.

There are signs that some donors who are displeased with Sri Lanka may retaliate by using donor assistance as leverage. For example, soon after the British Foreign Secretary and his French counterpart returned from a visit to Sri Lanka in late April 2009, where they failed to persuade the government to suspend military activity, there were reports in the international press that a loan from the IMF that Sri Lanka had requested was being delayed to put pressure on the government.[39]

The more serious threat concerns exports to the EU. After the tsunami in December 2004 the EU granted Sri Lanka special ("GSP+") tariff concessions for exports to the EU that covered around 6,400 separate tariff lines. The most critical items for Sri Lanka are garments and textiles, which accounted for 43% of total exports of the country in 2008. That year Sri Lanka exported about three billion dollars worth of goods to the EU, accounting for 37% of total exports. The concessions allow the exporting country to send goods to the EU at low or zero duty. To qualify, the beneficiary country must ratify and effectively implement the "16 core conventions on human and labour rights and 7 [out of 11] of the conventions related to good governance and the protection of the environment."[40] The concessions are currently under review for renewal in respect to Sri Lanka. The Sri Lanka government refused to cooperate with an EU-appointed investigation team on Sri Lanka's adherence to the requirements on human rights, labor rights, and good governance. However, the government is strongly lobbying for an extension of the concessions on the grounds that Sri Lanka deserves this on economic considerations. There is a strong fear in Sri Lanka government circles that the country may lose the concession when the EU makes its decision in October 2009. If that happens, Sri Lankan exports will go back to a less generous lower tariff regime of the EU. Sri Lankan suppliers will have to cut costs and accept lower margins to remain competitive. However, it is more likely that the EU will extend the concession with conditions attached. This also has a downside because buyers who like stable trade relations may not deal with suppliers who face uncertainty.

India and China have been more helpful to Sri Lanka in recent times. India has announced that it would assist reconstruction in the north and east with loan funds. China has emerged as a major bilateral lender to Sri Lanka. In 2007 China's net lending to Sri Lanka totalled $152 million, double the amount of the Asian Development Bank, the next highest lender.[41] However, Indian and Chinese funds are loans that have to be repaid with interest, and not grants. Moreover, neither has the capacity to replace the Western markets for Sri Lanka's exports, which account for 30% of GDP.

In principle, the end of the war should help to revive the economy. The removal of the threat of violence will increase investor confidence. Peace will also encourage tourists to return. Between 1978 and 1982 Sri Lanka's tourist arrivals grew at an annual rate of about 20% and reached 410,000 in 1982. The highest figure reached since then was 566,000 in 2004 when the ceasefire was in effect. The government expects a 20% growth in arrivals to over 600,000 in the next 12 months.

However, there are several factors that may stand against a rapid growth in the economy. One is the global financial crisis. If Sri Lanka fails to mobilize substantial donor aid for reconstruction, the hoped-for recovery of the post-war economy, especially in the north and east, will suffer a serious setback. This means that the present confrontational posturing vis-à-vis the West emanating from some sections of the ruling coalition and sections of the Sri Lankan media will have to give way to more moderate counsel. Radical reforms in economic policy will also be needed to resurrect the economy. Such reforms include reducing the budget deficit, which is in the region of 7.7% of GDP in 2007 and 2008, cutting back on wasteful spending such as the government-owned loss-making budget airline Mihin Lanka that is sucking in billions of tax rupees, and streamlining loss-making government utilities such as the Ceylon Electricity Board. However, political constraints are a serious impediment to reform.

CONCLUSION

Recent international experience is replete with failed UN-led attempts at establishing democracy in postconflict societies such as Cambodia, Liberia, Rwanda, Zimbabwe, and many more. Arguably Sri Lanka appears to be in a better position because it is supposed to have a reasonably functioning democracy. What lessons may we draw from Sri Lanka for postconflict reconciliation and transformation?

The most evident lesson is that it is not easy to heal the polarization of ethnic groups that has developed during a war that lasted one whole generation. The end of the war has stopped the killings in the battle field; there are no more body bags coming into Sinhalese villages and no serious threats from LTTE suicide bombers. For that the government and especially President Rajapakse can claim credit. The recent Provincial Council election results show that the rural Sinhalese voters in particular are thankful to the government for that. The ruling UPFA won between 60% and 70% of the vote in three provincial council elections in predominantly Sinhalese provinces held between February and April 2009 before the war ended, and 72% of the vote in the Uva Provincial Council election held in August after the war ended.[42] A glimpse of the northern Tamil disaffection for the government after the war ended was revealed in the urban council election on 8 August 2009 in Vavunia, where 275,000 internally displaced Tamils are held in camps. In a poll where about half of the registered voters cast their ballot, the governing UPFA came third with about 25% of the total poll. Two Tamil parties that opposed the government each polled about one-third of the total poll.[43]

The second important lesson of the Sri Lankan experience is how a country can get militarized in a protracted civil war, and how such militarization gets institutionally entrenched. Three powerful examples should suffice to establish this point. The first is the proposed increase in military expenditure, already discussed. The second example is the militarization of the police, who were co-opted into battle over the years. A police Special Task Force (STF) with military-type training was created to be deployed in the east. More importantly, the ordinary police intended for civilian work was increasingly armed for paramilitary and antiterrorist security duties. The third example is the Prevention of Terrorism (Temporary Provisions) Act of 1979, which was made permanent in 1982 and allowed the government and security forces to trample on basic democratic norms. Sri Lanka will need to dismantle these institutions of war if it wishes to regain its democratic credentials.

The third important lesson that Sri Lanka teaches is the challenge that a postconflict society faces in establishing democracy after a country's democratic values have been severely undermined by a protracted war that brutalizes society. It is true that the country maintained a veneer of democracy for over 25 years while a war raged on parts of its territory. Since elections were held and governments were changed, the world was led to believe that Sri Lanka's democracy was more or less intact. However, it is clear in retrospect that what survived of Sri Lanka's democracy was increasingly flawed. K. M. de Silva, responding to widespread electoral malpractices that have become almost the norm, describes the period 1994–2001 as an "electoral process in crisis."[44]

We documented earlier the restrictions on media freedom in the country and the difficulties that journalists have faced. In the last few years of the war in particular the government imposed severe limits on reporting of the war and on military-related news. After a number of journalists were killed—most of these cases still remain unresolved—several leading journalists left the country for reasons of personal security. The end of the war has not resulted in a significant change in this culture of impunity. Some journalists and civil society activists still feel deeply insecure. The government, instead of relaxing its grip on the press, is resurrecting the Press Council, which has been defunct since 2002, giving it authoritarian powers to control the media.[45]

In conclusion, it is useful to draw attention to two important factors that often do not get the attention that they merit in discussion of postconflict peace building: the human environment that is required and the kind of political leadership that is needed. As regards the former it is useful to note that those who are 40 years of age today in Sri Lanka were 15 years old when the war started in 1983. None of the under-25 age group today (46% of the population) has ever known a peaceful Sri Lanka even as children; and another 23% were children under the age of 15 when the war started in 1983. In effect, two-thirds of the people have experienced a Sri Lanka exposed to violence and ethnic division, without elections free of violence and fraud. They have lived their lives under emergency rule in an increasingly militarized state and need to be convinced that democracy offers prospects for a better life than the kind of patronage politics that they see in Sri Lanka today.

The second factor concerns leadership. Strong institutions are undoubtedly important for postconflict peace building. However, the institutions are only as good as those who are entrusted with their management. In our analysis we showed how Sri Lankan political leaders have deliberately undermined with impunity viable and desirable democratic institutions of good governance such as the Constitutional Council and even the constitution itself, which is supposedly the "supreme law" of the land. In a normal established democracy such leaders would be challenged by ordinary voters who cherish democracy. However, in postconflict Sri Lanka about two-thirds of the population are most familiar with war, impunity, flawed elections, poor governance, and the personal gains that patronage politics bring. This mix of voters and leaders creates a vicious circle from which it is not easy to break out.

ACKNOWLEDGMENTS

The author wishes to thank the editor of this volume, Professor John Coakley, for his assistance, and the two anonymous referees for their comments and suggestions that helped produce the final draft.

NOTES

1. See, for example, Kenneth D. Bush, *The Intra-Group Dimensions of Ethnic Conflict in Sri Lanka: Learning to Read Between the Lines* (New York: Palgrave Macmillan, 2003); K. M. de Silva, *Reaping the Whirlwind: Ethnic Conflict, Ethnic Politics in Sri Lanka* (New Delhi: Penguin India, 1999); Jayadeva Uyangoda, *Ethnic Conflict in Sri Lanka: Changing Dynamics* (Washington, DC: East-West Center, 2007); S. W. R. de A. Samarasinghe, *Political Economy of Internal Conflict in Sri Lanka*, Working paper 16 (The Hague, The Netherlands: Clingendael Institute, 2003). http://www.clingendael.nl/publications/2003/20030700_cru_working_paper_16.pdf [accessed 22 Sept. 2009].

2. For a profile of Prabhakaran, see M. R. Narayan Swamy, *Inside an Elusive Mind: Prabhakaran* (Colombo: Vijitha Yapa Publications, 2003).

3. The Lanka Academic Forum, Lankan Army Killed 22,000 LTTE Cadres, *The Lankan Academic Forum*, October 11, 2005. http://www.expressbuzz.com/edition/story.aspx?Title=Lankan+army+killed+22,000+LTTE+cadres&sectionID=oHSKVfNWYm0=&MainSectionID=oHSKVfNWYm0=&SEO=Sri+Lankan+Chief+of+Defence+Staff+(CDS)+Gen+Sarath&SectionName=VfE7I/VI80s= [accessed 22 Oct. 2009].

4. World Bank, *World Development Indicators 2009* (Washington, DC: World Bank, 2009).

5. John Paul Lederach and Michelle Maisse, *Conflict Transformation*. http://www.beyondintractability.org/essay/transformation/ [accessed 22 Sept. 2009].

6. Ibid., cited by Charles (Chipp) Hauss, *Reconciliation* (Beyondintractability.org, September 2003). http://www.beyondintractability.org/essay/reconciliation/ [accessed 22 Sept. 2009].

7. John Breuilly, *The Formation of the First German Nation-State, 1800–1871* (New York: St. Martin's Press, 1996). Mainly due to post-Second World War migration, today's Germany is as multiethnic as almost all of the other European nations.

8. See Edward Luce, *In Spite of the Gods: The Rise of Modern India* (New York: Doubleday, 2007); Nandan Nilekani, *Imagining India: The Idea of a Renewed Nation* (New Delhi: Allen Lane—Penguin, 2009).

9. See I. William Zartman, *Collapsed States: The Disintegration and Restoration of Legitimate Authority* (Boulder, CO: Lynne Rienner, 1995).

10. The ethnic ratios are based on the 1921 population census (see Government of Sri Lanka, *Report on the Census of Ceylon, 1921 (Colombo, 1923–1926)*).

11. Department of Census and Statistics, *Census of Population 1946* (Colombo: Department of Census and Statistics, 1952). The Plantation Tamils are the descendents of South Indian indentured laborers who came to Sri Lanka from the early 1830s to the late 1930s to work on the plantations. They live mainly in the central part of the island in the tea and rubber plantation districts amongst the Sinhalese. The Sri Lankan Tamil community in Sri Lanka has been in the country probably as long as the Sinhalese have been. About two-thirds of them live in the north and east and the rest elsewhere, mainly in the Colombo District. Both Tamil communities speak the same language and the majority is Hindu. However, the plantation Tamils are less prosperous, less educated, and more socially disadvantaged that the Sri Lankan Tamils. There is also a social divide between the two groups based on caste.

12. See A. Jeyaratnam Wilson, "General Elections in Sri Lanka 1947–1977," in K. M. de Silva, *Universal Franchise 1931–1981: The Sri Lankan Experience* (Colombo: Department of Information, Democratic Republic of Sri Lanka, 1981), pp. 93–107.

13. The SLDP (founded 1951) is one of the two major Sinhalese-dominated political parties in the country. It has had a more Sinhalese-Buddhist orientation that made it more attractive to the Sinhalese voters.

14. The right-of-center United National Party (founded 1946) is the second of the two major Sinhalese-dominated political parties in the country. Traditionally it has been able to attract more minority support than its chief rival, the SLFP.

15. See N. Selvakkumaran, "Reality Check and Recommendations on Language Rights," in B. Shanthakumar (ed.), *Language Rights in Sri Lanka: Enforcing Tamil as an Official Language* (Colombo: Law & Society Trust, 2008), pp. 5–36.

16. Government of Sri Lanka, *The Constitution of Sri Lanka (Ceylon)* (Colombo, Sri Lanka: Department of Government Printing, 1972), p. 4.

17. Government of Sri Lanka, *Report on the Census of Ceylon*; Department of Census and Statistics, *Report on the Census of Ceylon, 1946*, Department of Census and Statistics, *Statistical Abstract 1995* (Colombo, Sri Lanka: Author, 1996).

18. K. M. de Silva, "Affirmative Action Policies: The Sri Lankan Experience," in K. M. de Silva (ed.), *Sri Lanka's Troubled Inheritance* (Kandy: International Centre for Ethnic Studies, 2007), pp. 269–308.

19. See G. H. Peiris, *Twilight of the Tigers: Peace Efforts and Power Struggles in Sri Lanka* (New Delhi: Oxford University Press, 2009).

20. Mahinda Rajapaksa, *Mahinda Chinthana: Victory for Sri Lanka Presidential Election 2005* (2005, p. 31) http://www.president.gov.lk/pdfs/MahindaChinthanaEnglish.pdf [accessed 22 Sept. 2009].

21. The British Foreign Secretary David Miliband and his French counterpart Bernard Kouchner visited Sri Lanka at the end of April 2009 to press for a ceasefire. At a meeting that was reported to be tense, President Rajapakse rejected the request as a ploy to save the Tigers. Peter Beaumont, IMF Under Pressure to Delay Sri Lanka's \$1.9 Billian Aid Loan, *Guardian.co.uk*, May 1, 2009 http://www.guardian.co.uk/world/2009/may/01/imf-aid-sri-lanka-tamil-tigers [accessed 22 Sept. 2009].

22. See *AFP* "Sri Lanka stands firm in row over British envoy." February 18, 2009 http://www.google.com/hostednews/afp/article/ALeqM5gJCDpZqV5T1Wjk0bPQRgPF3OCVvQ [accessed 20 Feb. 2009].

23. Accurate migration figures are not available. Jaffna district, which probably was the source of the bulk of migration, had a Sri Lankan Tamil population of 716,000 in the 1981 Census. In the 2007 Special Census the figure reported was 559,000, a loss of 157,000 (22%). It is likely that some moved to other parts of the country, especially Colombo district where the Sri Lankan Tamil population increased from 171,000 (10% of the total population) to 250,000 (11%). The LTTE also forced an unknown number of Jaffna residents to move with it to the Vanni when it abandoned Jaffna in 1995. Allowing for such internal population movement, it is likely that there would have been around 200,000–300,000 Sri Lankan Tamil migrants during the war period (see http://www.statistics.gov.lk/home.asp; For 1981 Census, see Department of Census and Statistics, *Statistical Abstract 1995*, (Colombo, Sri Lanka: Department of Census and Statistics, 1996); For 2007 special census data see Department of Census and Statistics, *Basic Population Information on Jaffna District—2007 Preliminary Report* (Department of Census and Statistics—Sri Lanka July 31, 2009) http://www.statistics.gov.lk/PopHouSat/

Preliminary%20Reports%20Special%20Enumeration%202007/Basic%20Population%20Information%20on%20Jaffna%20District%202007.pdf) [accessed 22 Sept. 2009]

24. Sri Lanka Muslim Congress, *Objectives of the SLMC* (Sri Lanka Muslim Congress, September 2009), http://www.slmc.org.uk/objectives.htm [accessed 22 Sept. 2009].

25. M. H. M. Salman, *Only Muslims can Speak for Themselves at Talks* (Sri Lanka Muslim Congress, September 2009) http://www.slmc.org.uk/omcan1.htm [accessed 22 Sept. 2009].

26. EPDP News, *Profile of Kathiravelu Nithyananda Douglas Devananda—Leader of the EPDP* (Colombo, Sri Lanka: EPDP News, 2008) http://en.wikipedia.org/wiki/Douglas_Devananda [accessed 22 Sept. 2009].

27. Government of Sri Lanka, "Chapter XVIII Public Security," in *The Constitution of the Democratic Socialist Republic of Sri Lanka* (Colombo, Sri Lanka: Author, 1978), pp. 101–4.

28. See Virginia Leary, *Ethnic Conflict and Violence in Sri Lanka—Report of a Mission to Sri Lanka on behalf of the International Commission of Jurists* (Geneva: International Commission of Jurists, July/August 1981); Paul Sieghar, *Sri Lanka: A Mounting Tragedy of Errors—Report of International Commission of Jurists* (Geneva: International Commission of Jurists, 1984).

29. Government of Sri Lanka, *Address by HE President Mahinda Rajapaksa at the ceremonial opening of Parliament, Sri Jayawardhanapura—Kotte, May 19, 2009.* (Colombo: Government of Sri Lanka, May 19, 2009) http://www.president.gov.lk/speech_New.asp?Id=74 [accessed 22 Sept. 2009].

30. United Nations Human Right Council—11th special session of the Human Rights Council: *The Human Rights Situation in Sri Lanka* (Geneva: UNHRC, 26 and 27 May 2009). http://www2.ohchr.org/english/bodies/hrcouncil/specialsession/11/index.htm [accessed 3 June 2009].

31. Paul Tighe and Jay Shankar, "Sri Lanka Wants Partners Not Monitors of Post-War Aid" (*Bloomberg.com*, May 25, 2009), http://www.bloomberg.com/apps/news?pid=20601091&sid=aSr8RMitYI2Y&refer=india [accessed 22 Sept. 2009].

32. Hillary Rodham Clinton, *Remarks on the Adoption of a United Nations Security Council Resolution to Combat Sexual Violence in Armed Conflict* (Washington, DC: US Department of State, September 30, 2009). http://www.state.gov/secretary/rm/2009a/09/130041.htm [accessed 3 Oct. 2009].

33. Mawbima Sri Lanka, "Clinton says Rape used as Weapon of War in Sri Lanka. Government says 'Far from Truth,'" *Mawbima Sri Lanka*, October 2, 2009, http://www.mawbimasrilanka.com/2009/10/clinton-says-rape-used-as-weapon-of-war.html [accessed 3 Oct. 2009].

34. In 1982, J. R. Jayewardene (UNP) won with 52.9% of the vote with substantial support from Tamils and Muslims. In 1988, R. Premadasa (UNP) won 50.4% of the vote and again drew substantial minority support. In 1994, Chandrika Kumaratunga (People's Alliance) won a decisive 62.3% with overwhelming support from the minorities. In 1999, the sitting president, Kumaratunga (People's Alliance), was returned with 51.1% of the vote. The election was not that close because her nearest rival Ranil Wickremasinghe polled only 42.7% of the vote. An LTTE suicide bomber made an attempt on Kumaratunga's life three days prior to the poll. This attracted a significant sympathy vote for her, especially from Sinhalese voters. The LTTE imposed a poll boycott in the areas that they controlled. Wickremasinghe, who polled better than Kumaratunga in the northern and eastern districts with the exception of Jaffna, would have done better had there been a free poll in the north and east. In 2005, Mahinda Rajapakse (UPFA) polled 50.3% and Ranil Wickremasinghe (UNP) 48.3%. On this occasion Rajapakse polled heavily among the Sinhalese but Wickremasinghe, who polled well among the minorities, would have almost certainly won the election were it not for the poll boycott that the LTTE imposed in the areas that it controlled. Department of Elections, *Past Elections* (Colombo, Sri Lanka: Department of Elections, Sri Lanka, September 2009) http://www.slelections.gov.lk/pastElection.html) [accessed 22 Sept. 2009].

35. Government of Sri Lanka, *Address by HE President Mahinda Rajapaksa at the Ceremonial Opening of Parliament, Sri Jayawardhanapura—Kotte, May 19, 2009* (Colombo, Sri Lanka: Government of Sri Lanka, 2009) http://www.president.gov.lk/speech_New.asp?Id=74 [accessed 22 Sept. 2009].

36. Government of Sri Lanka, *Seventeenth Amendment to the Constitution of the Democratic Socialist Republic of Sri Lanka* (Colombo, Sri Lanka: Author, November 20, 2003) http://www.priu.gov.lk/Cons/1978Constitution/SeventeenthAmendment.html [accessed 22 Sept. 2009].

37. Lanka Business on Line, *Sri Lanka Tourist Arrivals up in June, 09* (Colombo, Sri Lanka: Lanka Business on Line, 2009) http://www.lankabusinessonline.com/fullstory.php?nid=729859300 [accessed 22 Sept. 2009].

38. Central Bank of Sri Lanka, *Annual Report 2008* (Colombo, Sri Lanka: Central Bank of Sri Lanka, 2009), p. 136.

39. *Guardian.co.uk*, "IMF Under Pressure to Delay Sri Lanka's $1.9bn Aid Loan" (May 1, 2009) http://www.guardian.co.uk/world/2009/may/01/imf-aid-sri-lanka-tamil-tigers [accessed 22 Sept. 2009].

40. European Union, The EU Generalised System of Preferences–GSP–The New EU Preferential Terms of Trade for Developing Countries (European Union, United Nations, February 10, 2005). http://www.euro.pa-eu-un.org/articles/en/article_4337_en.htm [accessed 22 Sept. 2009].

41. Central Bank of Sri Lanka, *Annual Report 2008* (Colombo: Central Bank of Sri Lanka, 2009), Statistical Appendix, Table 109.

42. Department of Elections, *Past Elections* (Colombo, Sri Lanka: Department of Elections, 2009) http://www.slelections.gov.lk/pastElection2.html [accessed 22 Sept. 2009].

43. Department of Elections, *Local Authorities Elections 2009 Final Results Vavuniya Urban Council* (Colombo, Sri Lanka: Department of Elections, September 2009), http://www.slelections. gov.lk/localAuthorities/2009/Sub%20Pages/vanni_VAVUNIYA_URBAN_COUNCIL.htm [accessed 22 Sept. 2009].

44. K. M. de Silva, "Sri Lanka," in Dushyantha Mendis (ed.), *Electoral Processes and Governance in South Asia* (New Delhi: Sage, 2008), pp.143–156.

45. Bob Dietz, "With Press Council, Sri Lanka Revives a Repressive Tool," *CPJ Blog* (June 26, 2009) http://www.cpj.org/blog/2009/06/with-press-council-sri-lanka-revives-a-repressive.php [accessed 22 Sept. 2009].

10

Ethnic Conflict Resolution:
Routes Towards Settlement

JOHN COAKLEY
University College Dublin

This chapter generalizes on the basis of a set of case studies of ethnic conflicts that have followed different routes towards the goal of a long-term settlement: Belgium, Spain, Northern Ireland, Bosnia and Herzegovina, Cyprus, Lebanon, South Africa, and Sri Lanka. It begins by reviewing the significance of ethnicity in the modern state, exploring the political implications of different terminologies in this area. Having examined the patterns of political mobilization of ethnic groups (whether in the form of the party system or in the shape of military-type formations), it looks at the kinds of political outcome that have been associated with settlement processes. In addition to "solutions" that would be regarded as politically unacceptable, it identifies three common features which, depending on specific local circumstances, commonly occur: federal or other territorial arrangements, consociational government, and the political integration of minorities.

INTRODUCTION

As is well known, ethnic conflicts are not just a ubiquitous feature of modern life; they are also commonly characterized by an intensity that makes their resolution not just of exceptional importance but also of extraordinary difficulty. The introduction to this set of case studies identified its primary objective as an attempt to advance further our understanding of efforts to respond to this big challenge posed by ethnically based unrest. This entails exploring the character of ethnic coexistence, the form taken by ethnic mobilization, and the manner in which state structures respond to this. Such responses range from the most adaptive, based on fundamental institutional redesign that offers a stake in the future of the state to ethnic minority leaders, to the most repressive, where the dominant group seeks to neutralize or eliminate the capacity of dissident minorities to disrupt conventional decision-making structures in pursuit of their goals.

It is appropriate now to see what can be learned from these case studies. It is useful, in doing so, to begin with the same framework as that outlined in the introduction, and as followed in the various case studies. The first issue is the nature of ethnic difference: the manner in which a particular society has emerged as a deeply divided one, and the extent to which divisions may have been deepened or alleviated by such factors as historical experience, geographical settlement patterns, and uneven rates of demographic and socioeconomic development. The second issue is the trajectory of mobilization of ethnic identity: sociocultural differences may remain relatively passive, or they may be channelled into distinctive patterns of political organization, with or without the involvement of militant groups or external interests. The third issue is the route to a settlement: the mechanisms by which a far-reaching agreement is arrived at, and the interplay between the content of such an agreement and the short- and long-term perspectives of the competing groups. These three matters are considered in the three following sections of this chapter.

DYNAMICS OF CONFLICT

Several themes relating to the character of ethnic identity emerge from the case studies undertaken in this volume, and they may be grouped into three categories. First, we need to consider the complex character of identity, as reflected in shifting terminology and changing boundaries. Second, in all cases the contemporary conflict has evolved in response to complex historical factors, and in varying degrees these may incorporate significant economic inequalities, whether because ethnic distribution coincides with big regional differences or because there are elements of an ethnic division of labor. Third, there are particular, traditional relationships between ethnic groups and state structures that have implications for future institution building.

Measuring Ethnic Identity

The question of terminology commonly arises at the beginning of studies of this kind and may be a pointer to certain significant social realities. The term "ethnic" has been used in the chapters in this volume as a generic way of referring to the primary social boundary in which we are interested. It would be pointless to get involved here in defining what precisely "ethnic" means.[1] But it is important to note that, reflecting local usage, an alternative terminology tends to be used by the authors of the case studies. Thus, in discussing Belgium Lieven De Winter and Pierre Baudewyns generally use the term "community" in referring to the main contending groups, and this is the general terminology that is used by Jennifer Todd in relation to Northern Ireland, by Francisco Llera in describing Spain, by Joseph S. Joseph in the case of Cyprus, and by Simon Haddad in relation to Lebanon. In these cases, the term "ethnic" is sparingly used (most frequently by Joseph, least frequently by Haddad); authors tend to prefer related compounds, such as "ethnoregional" (De Winter and Baudewyns), "ethnocultural" (Llera), "ethnonational" (Todd), or "ethnoreligious" (Todd, Haddad). In dealing with Sri Lanka, Stanley Samarasinghe makes much more extensive use of the adjective "ethnic" to refer to domestic divisions (though he also uses the term "community" widely), and "ethnic" is the main term Roberto Belloni uses in relation to Bosnia's internal divisions (with "national group" as an alternative). In the South African case, Adrian Guelke generally uses the term "race."

In this, authors are deferring to norms of social science linguistic usage in English, but they are likely also to be influenced by prevailing official and colloquial usage in the countries in question. Thus, in Belgium three linguistic "communities" are constitutionally recognized, and the official statistics offices in Northern Ireland and Cyprus use the term "community." In the South African census, the vague term "population group" is officially used to refer to the four racial groupings; in Sri Lanka the term "ethnic group" is used and in Bosnia the population is broken down in official statistics by "ethnicity." In Lebanon, the Ta'if Accord of 1989 refers to "sects," "denominations," and "spiritual families." Finally, the case of Spain is particularly interesting: the constitution proclaims "the indissoluble unity of the Spanish nation" but recognizes the right to autonomy of "the nationalities and regions which make it up"; this has taken the form of the creation of "autonomous communities" (Constitution, arts. 2, 137). As Llera shows, this may result in relatively assertive terminology, with certain areas and local populations describing themselves as "national" rather than merely "regional" entities. But a warning is necessary: these terms are almost all English translations of words whose meaning in their original language may have quite different connotations. To give just one example, the Bosnian Federal Office of Statistics uses the term "ethnicity" in English to refer to the manner in which the population is divided, but the corresponding Serbo-Croatian expression is *nacionalna pripadnost*, with implications of "national affiliation" rather than ethnicity.[2]

This discussion of terminological issues is not just an esoteric technical digression. Decisions to measure a population in terms of some variable, and about the categorization of people in respect of this variable, are likely not just to reflect underlying realities but also to influence them. Words do not just emanate from social phenomena; they also help to shape them. Thus, we need to be aware of the symbiotic relationship between statistical reporting and patterns of identity. The introduction of an ethnic Muslim category in the Yugoslav census had an impact on the reported ethnic composition of Bosnia, and the existence or otherwise of a "Yugoslav" category has a similar effect. In Sri Lanka between 1901 and 1971 the Sinhalese population was divided in official statistics between "Low Country Sinhalese" and "Kandyan Sinhalese," and the Moors were similarly divided (1911–71) between "Sri Lanka Moors" and "Indian Moors." A distinction has continued to be made since 1911 between "Sri Lanka Tamils" and "Indian Tamils." In these cases, while such linguistic distinctions would be possible only if they reflected underlying social realities, it is reasonable to assume that intervention by census takers is not a neutral, information-gathering exercise but itself has some influence on individuals' sense of identity. As two Hungarian scholars suggested more than 70 years ago:

> The censuses forced declarations and decided attitudes out of persons who might otherwise have served as connecting links between divergent groups of human beings—in particular between different nationalities to which they were bound by family ties. Had European science and politics not classified, defined and analysed so much during the nineteenth century—a process by which the rich and valuable syntheses of life were so often torn asunder—the persons referred to, together with the transitional groups of human beings, might well have been employed for the purpose of eliminating antagonism.[3]

It should be stressed that while some of the authors of the chapters above have sought to measure patterns of identity, the capacity to produce simple summary tables does not imply that in reality national or communal identity is a simple categorical variable, with clearly defined boundaries between groups. In his discussion of the Spanish case, Llera shows clearly just how subtle and complex ethnic-type identities are: state-wide identities can coexist with regional ones, with the balance between the two shifting over time and sometimes even within the same individual. It is to be assumed that similar patterns of complex, overlapping identities will be found elsewhere; there is abundant evidence of this in Northern Ireland.[4]

The Impact of Social and Economic Asymmetry

The various ethnic groups whose interrelations are the subject of the chapters in this volume are not just communities that happen to coexist with each other; each has a dynamic history, and each tends to be a product not just of the historical forces that account for its social and political status today but also of the manner in which this is recalled by the community—its distinctive historical myth. The contemporary position may have arisen as a consequence of long-term developments, such as the gradual stabilization of the Germanic-Romance fault line running from East to West through Belgium separating Dutch speakers from French speakers. As De Winter and Baudewyns point out, while the border continues to have slightly unstable edges, it has been located in substantially the same position for over a thousand years. Todd, similarly, vividly describes the heavy hand of history that lies over Northern Ireland, where the seventeenth-century "plantation" of a community of English and Scottish settlers left a legacy that led later to separatist Catholic mobilization in the nineteenth century, partition of Ireland in 1921 and profound communal unrest after 1968. But the impact of the legacy of the past is to be seen in each of the other cases too, as the significance of pre-medieval settlement patterns was altered by later population movement and by shifting state frontiers.

For the winners and losers of history there was more at stake than just political power: of the spoils of victory, economic advantage was one of the most important. In all cases, then, communities that coexisted within the state tended to follow separate patterns of economic development. The huge economic disparities that separated the main groups in South Africa are well known. In 1946, for instance, per capita income of Asians and Coloureds was approximately double that of Africans, but that of Whites was five times greater than that of Asians and Coloureds, or 10 times greater than that of Africans; and 20 years later the position had barely changed.[5] Certain minority groups elsewhere enjoyed similar status: Protestants in Ireland (later to become a Protestant majority in Northern Ireland), for instance, and French speakers in Belgium. Furthermore, just as the British had enjoyed a close relationship with Protestants in Ireland during their centuries of rule there, one that gave Protestants exceptional privileges, so too did they cultivate alliances with minorities in Cyprus and Ceylon during their period of rule in these territories. So it was that the Ceylon Tamils (later to become the Sri Lanka Tamils) and the Turkish Cypriots saw themselves, and were seen by their rivals, as gaining a range of advantages from their political relationship with their colonial overlord.

Differences in socioeconomic status, then, tended to aggravate interethnic tensions, and it became difficult to disentangle conflict over symbols (and political issues) from conflict over resources (and economic issues). Sometimes this took the form of interregional conflict: relatively poor peripheries (such as Ireland within the United Kingdom in the nineteenth century) could attribute poverty to exploitation; but relatively wealthy peripheries (such as the Basque Country within contemporary Spain) could complain of the siphoning off of resources by the center. The salience of the economic dimension was at its highest point in circumstances where the relative position of the communities began to shift. De Winter and Baudewyns describe the phenomenon of center and periphery exchanging positions in Belgium, as the old industrial structure in Wallonia came under strain in the mid-twentieth century, and formerly less-developed Flanders overtook it as the powerhouse of the Belgian economy. In Northern Ireland, similarly, as traditional heavy industry declined so too did the fortunes of the Protestant community, with Catholics playing an effective game of "catch-up." These changes contributed further to the insecurity of the formerly dominant community (the Walloons and the Northern Irish Protestants) and to growing confidence on the part of their rivals (the Flemish and the Northern Irish Catholics).

Ethnic Groups and State Structures

A long period of shared history has not just defined the framework for intergroup conflict; it has also provided durable institutions that help to shape the character of such conflict. Life in the same state may promote elements of a common perspective on particular matters: collective experience in war, for example, or a perception of elements of a shared past. But this will depend on the existence of institutions that can reinforce or at least propagate these attitudes, notably an educational system. Commonly, though, the educational system and other public institutions, far from promoting integration, help to encourage difference. This was clearly the case in Belgium, Lebanon, and Cyprus, where powerful internal social barriers impeded contact between the communities.

Nevertheless, the central state may still have an important role to play in maintaining cohesion. It may possess sufficient material resources to buy off dissent, as was the case in the past in Belgium and Northern Ireland. But particular institutions may also have a contribution to make. Traditionally, the army has played a major "nation-building" role in many societies, as conscription has brought together people from a range of cultural backgrounds and helped cultivate a sense of membership in a broader community. But military service may also highlight cultural differences, as De Winter and Baudewyns show in the Belgian case, citing wartime instances of a breakdown in communication between French-speaking officers and Dutch-speaking soldiers. Furthermore, the army and the security services may be particularly associated with the dominant community. This is the case in Sri Lanka, and resolving the issue of predominantly Protestant security forces was an important challenge during the Northern Ireland peace process. In Lebanon, however, as Haddad points out, the army acts as an important national institution, with all major groups represented in its ranks.

Other central institutions may act as a rallying point that promotes state unity. In Belgium, the monarchy is one of the few unitary institutions that has an integrative effect. More commonly, though, state symbols, such as flags and anthems, tend to be associated with the dominant community and, far from assisting the process of integration, they may provoke a sense of alienation among minorities. Thus, as Joseph points out, independent Cyprus survived without any such symbols, with the two communities using the

Greek and Turkish flags. There is no flag that is acceptable to both communities in Northern Ireland, and the Union Jack and Irish tricolor continue to be the favored symbols of the two communities. In South Africa, White acceptance of the flag and national anthem favored by the African majority suggests not so much that symbols may help to reconcile as that they signal reconciliation when it has already taken place for other reasons.

PARTIES, PARAMILITARIES, AND THE EXTERNAL DIMENSION

The ethnic composition of a society need not of itself be problematic from a political perspective; the critical issue is the extent to which ethnic differences are translated into political divisions and the ease with which these divisions may be accommodated by existing political structures. It is important therefore to look at the pattern of political mobilization in the eight cases considered here. Following that, we turn to two related issues. One is the extent to which the party system is capable of containing ethnic divisions; there are obviously circumstances in which these overspill the world of conventional politics and find expression instead in the form of armed conflict. The other is the involvement of external interests in the process of ethnic mobilization.

Party Politics

The eight cases considered here seem to fall into three categories as regards party development. There were four cases (Lebanon, Northern Ireland, Sri Lanka, and Cyprus) where the party system emerged as part of a colonial withdrawal process. Although South Africa shares some similarities with this group, it may more appropriately be classed with Spain and Bosnia in a second category, where a new party system emerged in the wake of the disappearance of an authoritarian state. Belgium alone represents a case of the organic evolution of the party system over a period of more than a century.

In Lebanon, the shape of the party system has been constrained by the content of the National Pact that marked independence in 1943, under which a fixed number of seats was allocated to each confessional group. Based on the results of the 1932 census, 54 seats in the 99-member parliament were allocated to Christians (with 30 Maronite, 11 Greek Orthodox, six Greek Catholic, and four Armenian Orthodox seats, and one each for Armenian Catholics, Protestants, and other Christians) and 45 to Muslims (20 Sunni, 19 Shia, and six Druze).[6] The Ta'if accord of 1989 revised these proportions, allocating 64 seats each to Christians and Muslims and making small adjustments to the allocations within these groups. Loosely organized confessional parties emerged in independent Lebanon, with a few weak secular parties cutting across them.[7] Nevertheless, parliamentary coalitions spanning confessions have appeared, most notably the current March 8 Alliance and March 14 Bloc, as described by Haddad.

In Sri Lanka, the party system has not been particularly effective in reflecting the country's deepest political division. It is true that the initial, postindependence configuration quickly came to reflect the Sinhalese-Tamil cleavage. The cross-ethnic Ceylon National Congress of the preindependence period gave way to the United National Party after independence in 1948, and this became increasingly Sinhalese dominated; its main electoral rivals were the Sri Lanka Freedom Party (a Sinhalese nationalist party founded in 1951), and the Sinhalese-oriented left. Sri Lanka Tamil politics quickly went its separate path, initially under the umbrella of the Tamil Congress, later with the Federal Party playing a leading role, and then with alliances centered on the Tamil United Liberation Front.[8] But this separate path ultimately became a separatist one, and mainstream Tamil politics has tended to be marginalized within the Sri Lankan party system. Nevertheless, smaller Tamil parties are to be found as part of the governing bloc, as Samarasinghe shows.

In Cyprus, the position has been simpler: the 1960 constitution allocated seats in the House of Representatives to the two communities, with 30% going to the Turkish minority.[9] Although the first election showed near-complete dominance by communal parties, the Communist party, with an ideology that advocated the pursuit of common ground with Turkish Cypriot workers, won a small share of the Greek Cypriot seats. This was insufficient to put a dent in the intercommunal barrier; the later breakdown of the system and the partition of the island in 1974 confirmed a division between the two sides that was so stark that there was virtually no shared or middle ground.

After the creation of Northern Ireland in 1921, the old two-party system of nineteenth-century Ireland survived, with a Unionist Party (representing Protestant opinion and standing for protection of the link with Great Britain) becoming the ruling party of the new state and a Nationalist Party representing the Catholic minority supporting Irish unity. This bipolar arrangement lasted for 50 years, until the period 1969–73, which saw a major reconfiguration of the system. In addition to a small center represented by the cross-confessional Alliance Party, the two communal poles are each internally divided: Protestants between the old Ulster Unionist Party and its militant rival, the Democratic Unionist Party (DUP), Catholics between a party that has taken up the mantle of the old Nationalist Party, the Social Democratic and Labour Party (SDLP), and the more radical Sinn Féin, for long the public voice of the Irish Republican Army (IRA).[10]

In South Africa, Spain, and Bosnia revolutionary change resulted in the appearance of new party systems. The first elections under universal suffrage at the end of the apartheid regime in South Africa in 1994 of course led to the replacement of the old Afrikaaner-dominated ruling party, the

National Party, by the African-dominated African National Congress (ANC). The subsequent evolution of the party system saw the emergence of some new parties that were substantially ethnically based (such as the Zulu-dominated Inkatha Freedom Party), but patterns of electoral behavior have shown a substantial measure of cross-communal voting. In Spain, as Llera shows, the first democratic elections in 1977 resulted in the emergence of a pattern that was to last, with parliament dominated by two strong parties, the right (now represented by the People's Party) and the Socialists, with a small communist or postcommunist party; but there has also been a significant presence of powerful regional parties, notably the (Catalan) Convergence and Unity party and the Basque Nationalist Party. In Bosnia, party politics developed in the absence of prior ideological roots, in the manner of other postcommunist societies; not surprisingly, despite efforts to define alternative fault lines, the system has been characterized by parties with an ethnic support base, with three big parties dominating the respective blocs: the (Bosniak) Party of Democratic Action, the Serb Democratic Party, and the Croatian Democratic Union.[11]

The evolution of the Belgian party system represents quite a different pattern. As De Winter and Baudewyns show, the old parties that had dominated Belgian political life since the early twentieth century (the Socialist, Christian Social, and Liberal parties) all split in two along communal lines in the 1970s and were joined by a range of smaller parties with a strong communal orientation.

The extent to which ethnic divisions have been translated into party political ones may be summarized relatively easily. In Sri Lanka and in Cyprus political events have, for very different reasons, left the majority community in almost exclusive control of the central institutions. In Lebanon, confessional politics has been associated with a system in which political parties are weak, and they are currently clustered in two main blocs. In Spain, the dominant parties of the center are not simply confined there: they have a significant presence in the regions, whose electorates (even in Catalonia and the Basque Country) do not confine their support to regional parties but also support parties of the center, or their local allies.

In the remaining four cases, though, it is possible to look in greater detail at the political mobilization of ethnic difference by considering a range of survey data. The results are reported in Tables 1–4, each of which initially divides respondents by community and then shows the manner in which each community distributes its political preferences between parties. Table 1 shows that in Belgium almost all Dutch-speaking respondents (98%) distributed their support in 2008 among the six main Flemish parties (the six to the left in Table 1); and 95% of French speakers supported the four main Francophone parties (the four to the right of this). Indeed, the level of polarization was even higher, since the "other" category consists mainly of small parties rooted in a single community.

210 J. Coakley

TABLE 1 Belgium: Party Support by Language Group, 2008

Language Group	SP	VLD	CD	Grn	VB	LD	PS	MR	CDH	Eco	Other	N
Dutch	18	20	38	6	13	4	1	0	0	0	1	760
French	0	2	0	0	0	0	37	27	17	14	3	469
Total	11	13	24	4	8	2	14	10	6	5	2	1,229

Notes. All figures except those in the last column (indicating number of cases) are percentages and total 100 horizontally. SP: Flemish Socialists; VLD: Flemish Liberals; CD: Flemish Christian Democrats; Grn: Flemish Greens; VB: Vlaams Belang; LD: Lijst Dedecker; PS: Francophone Socialists; MR: Francophone Liberals; CDH: Francophone Christian Democrats; Eco: Ecolo. Some parties were in coalition with smaller groups were not mentioned here.
Source: Computed from European Social Survey, 2008; available ess.nsd.uib.no.

The remaining tables are to be interpreted in the same way. As Table 2 shows, there is virtually no Protestant support in Northern Ireland for either of the two nationalist parties (though 3% in 2008 indicated that they would support the SDLP); and there is hardly any Catholic support for either of the unionist parties (though, surprisingly, 1% said that they supported the DUP). Only a small proportion of the two communities (9% of Protestants and 4% of Catholics) supported the Alliance Party, an explicitly cross-communal one. Table 3 shows the same kind of partition of electoral support along communal lines in Bosnia, where 2001 survey data suggest the existence of three separate party subsystems. However, one party, the Bosnian Social Democrats, did win substantial support from Bosniaks and Croats, and some even from Serbs (at least in 2001, the year of the survey). In South Africa, the pattern is rather different. Notwithstanding a strong relationship between parties and communal blocs (with some parties such as the Democratic Alliance and the Minority Front drawing their support overwhelmingly from a single group), as Table 4 shows, the capacity of the ANC to win support from all of the major blocs is impressive, though overshadowed by its massive support among Africans (95% of whom support it).

Notwithstanding the stark polarization that emerges from this discussion of the relationship between the party system and underlying patterns of ethnic division, there are three points of qualification that need to be made.

TABLE 2 Northern Ireland: Party Support by Religious Background, 2008

Religious Background	DUP	UUP	APNI	SDLP	SF	Other	N
Protestant	48	38	9	3	0	1	480
Catholic	1	0	4	54	40	1	356
Total	27	22	9	24	16	1	931

Notes. All figures except those in the last column (indicating number of cases) are percentages and total 100 horizontally. Persons with other religious backgrounds, or none, are omitted. DUP: Democratic Unionist Party; UUP: Ulster Unionist Party; APNI: Alliance Party; SDLP: Social Democratic and Labour Party; SF: Sinn Féin.
Source: Computed from Northern Ireland Life and Times Survey, 2008; available www.ark.ac.uk/nilt.

TABLE 3 Bosnia: Party Support by Ethnic Group, 2001

Group	BSDP	SDA	SBiH	BOSS	SDS	PDP	SNSD	SPRS	SRS	HDZ	NHI	Other	N
Bosniak/ Muslim	32	30	29	4	0	0	0	0	0	0	0	5	430
Serb	7	0	1	0	29	24	20	8	6	0	0	5	178
Croat	28	0	3	2	0	0	1	0	0	44	12	9	86
All	26	18	18	3	7	6	5	2	1	5	1	5	708

Notes. All figures except those in the last column (indicating number of cases) are percentages and total 100 horizontally. Persons with other ethnic backgrounds are omitted. BSDP: Bosnian Social Democrats; SDA: Party of Democratic Action; SBiH: Bosnia-Herzegovina Party; BOSS: Bosnian Party; SDS: Serbian Democratic Party; PDP: Party of Democratic Progress; SNSD: Party of Independent Social Democrats; SPRS: Socialist Party of the RS; SRS: Serbian Radical Party of the RS; HDZ: Croatian Democratic Union of BiH; NHI: New Croatian Initiative.
Source: Computed from World Values Survey, 2001; available www.worldvaluessurvey.org.

First, the fact that people vote for parties standing for sharply conflicting perspectives on interethnic relations does not always mean that supporters' views are as polarized as those of their leaders. De Winter and Baudewyns point out that among the Flemish population in Belgium there is a big gap between elites and masses: the latter tend to identify more strongly with Belgium than with Flanders and do not share their leaders' ambitions for radical autonomy. In Northern Ireland, too, public opinion polls over the years consistently showed a level of support for (or at least tolerance of) intercommunal power sharing among Protestants that was not reflected in the public positions of the leaders of the two main unionist parties, who expressed implacable opposition to such an outcome until the 1990s.

Second, even if the party system is made up of parties that are over-whelmingly monoethnic, solid interparty alliances may span ethnic fault lines and result in blocs whose support base is intercommunal. Thus, for many years after the breakup of Belgium's three main traditional parties in the 1970s, their Flemish and Francophone successors continued in effect to

TABLE 4 South Africa: Party Support by Population Group, 2004

Group	ANC	IFP	DA-DP	ID	NNP	ACDP	FF-VF	MF	Other	N
African	95	2	1	0	0	0	0	0	2	1,517
Coloured	58	0	16	13	10	2	0	0	0	277
White	9	1	64	5	3	9	8	0	3	196
Asian	44	2	23	1	6	2	2	19	1	108
Total	79	2	10	2	2	2	1	1	2	2,098

Notes. All figures except those in the last column (indicating number of cases) are percentages and total 100 horizontally. ANC: African National Congress; IFP: Inkatha Freedom Party; DA-DP: Democratic Alliance; ID: Independent Democrats; NNP: New National Party; ACDP: African Christian Democratic Party; FF-VF: Freedom Front; MF: Minority Front.
Source: Computed from International Social Survey Programme, 2004; available zacat.gesis.org/webview/index.jsp.

negotiate their position in government as a cross-communal alliance: if the Flemish Liberals were "in," so too were the Francophone Liberals, and if the Flemish Socialists were "out," so too were the Francophone Socialists. In Lebanon, similarly, as Haddad shows, the parties are clustered in two blocs that span confessional divisions, and these blocs function as coherent political actors.

Third, there are two specific technical issues. The data in Tables 1–4 include only those who indicated which party they would support, excluding those who would not vote for any of these (a possibly important group, especially in deeply divided societies). In addition, there are recognized problems in respondents' tendency to exaggerate their support for successful parties (such as the ANC), and, especially in deeply divided societies, to understate support for militant parties and overstate support for the centre (such as Sinn Féin and the Alliance Party respectively in Northern Ireland).[12]

Extraparliamentary Mobilization

When we look beyond the dimension of party politics to those circumstances where there is a spillover into intercommunal violence, Belgium is once again the exception. Flemish students may have rioted and even made occasional use of "Molotov cocktails" in Louvain in early 1968 but that represented the upper limit of the violence. In the other seven cases, though, armed violence became a continuous dimension of the conflict between the communities. It tended to follow two patterns: the development of ethnic militias as forces of communal defense to reinforce the positions of the parties, and the growth of illegal revolutionary armed forces seeking to overthrow the existing constitutional and territorial order.

The emergence of communal paramilitary forces followed quickly on the breakup of Yugoslavia and the emergence of an independent Bosnian state in 1992, though they were not always easily distinguishable from regular armies. One force with a claim to official status was the Territorial Defence Force of Bosnia and Herzegovina (TORBIH), based originally on reserve units of the Yugoslav army and ultimately Bosniak dominated; but it had its rivals in the Army of the Republika Srpska (VRS), drawn from regular units of the Yugoslav army, and the Croatian Defence Council (HVO), based in the predominantly Croat areas, among others. These were ultimately absorbed into the official Bosnian Army. In Cyprus, the army was originally to have been divided between Greeks and Turks in a 60–40 ratio, but the speedy collapse of the original power-sharing blueprint left the Cypriot National Guard as a predominantly Greek Cypriot force (but with the British, Greek, and Turkish armies also represented on the island). The vacuum on the Turkish side was filled in part by the Turkish Resistance Organisation (TMT), dating from the preindependence period, when it had been founded to counter the activities of the Greek Cypriot nationalist armed body, the National Organisation of Cypriot Fighters (EOKA), which had spearheaded the struggle against the British. In Lebanon, similarly, armed militias have for long stood for the interests of particular groups, with Hezbollah currently the most prominent example.

The second category is that of armed insurgent groups. Here the most successful ultimately was the military wing of the African National Congress, *Umkhonto we Sizwe* ("Spear of the Nation," [MK]), whose paramilitary campaign began on its foundation in 1961 and ended only in 1990. Next in importance was the Liberation Tigers of Tamil Elam (LTTE), founded in 1976 and, according to the US State Department, controlling 8,000–10,000 combatants in May 2008.[13] This was, of course, before its military defeat by the Sri Lankan armed forces in May 2009. One of the world's oldest paramilitary groups, the Irish Republican Army (IRA), descended from the Irish Republican Brotherhood founded in 1858 and organized as a guerrilla army since 1919, has been on ceasefire since 1997 (when it was estimated to have had "several hundred" activists), leaving only two small splinter groups, the Continuity IRA and the Real IRA (with an estimated 100 activists each in 2008).[14] Finally, the Basque nationalist paramilitary force, Basque Homeland and Liberty (ETA, founded in 1959), managed to sustain a long struggle against the security forces. This by no means exhausts the range of informal militias in these societies: nationalist insurgency on the part of one group tends to provoke reactive quasi-military organization on the part of the groups that feel threatened, especially if they believe that they cannot rely on the security forces.

The External Dimension

The external dimension has been of considerable significance in all eight of the cases considered here, though its importance has varied greatly. At one end of the spectrum is Belgium, where the conflict has been entirely domestically contained (though De Winter and Baudewyns draw attention to the role of EU structures in putting a damper on the prospects of a break-up of the state). There are similarities with Spain, but there the elements of an international dimension are more visible: ETA's efforts to draw support from the Basque diaspora, for instance, and the fact that Basque nationalist claims extend across the border into France, giving that country cause to align itself with the Spanish government in combating Basque violence.

In Sri Lanka, the fact that the Tamils share a culture with the population of the state of Tamil Nadu in India, and the arrival there of Tamil refugees, gave the Indian government a particular interest in the Sri Lanka conflict, and this was reflected in intervention, by agreement with the Sri Lanka government, by an Indian peace-keeping force in 1987–90. The international community played an important role in seeking to broker a settlement after 2000, a role that enjoyed considerable short-term success. Reliance by the Tamil insurgency on support from the Tamil diaspora, as described by Samarasinghe, gave an added international dimension here too.

In South Africa, the most obvious contribution of the international community lay in efforts to end the *apartheid* regime. This included support from certain neighboring states for the MK's armed struggle, and pressure from the United Nations, including an international boycott of the country (though, as Guelke points out, it is far from clear how important the impact of the boycott was, with external commentators attributing a much more influential role to it than internal observers).

In the remaining four cases the external factor was much more explicit. The IRA was able to rely on the Irish diaspora, and especially on Irish Americans; but the population for whom it claimed to act, Irish nationalists, had a more powerful ally. This was the Irish government, which managed to secure a place for itself alongside the British government in resolving what was not just a major intercommunal conflict but also a long-running dispute between Great Britain and Ireland. This significant contribution to the resolution of the conflict was assisted by proactive involvement of the United States during the Clinton presidency.

In Lebanon, as in Northern Ireland, the population looked in two directions—in this case, at the Arab world (on the part of Muslims) and at Europe, and particularly France (on the part of Christians). But adjacent states were able to intervene more directly; thus, as Haddad points out, Syrian influence and the Syrian military presence were of overriding importance in the period 1976–2005, and Israeli military intervention took place in 1978, 1982–2000, and 2006. The role of international intervention in promoting a settlement was, as Haddad stresses, critical: it is no accident that the major milestones in resolving the conflict took place in Ta'if (in Saudi Arabia) in 1989 and in Doha (in Qatar) in 2008.

The role of external agencies was even more crucial in Cyprus, divided between populations loyal to Greece and Turkey, respectively. At an early stage, the former imperial power, the United Kingdom, also played a role, and it continues to exercise sovereignty over those parts of the island where it maintains military bases. But it was the de facto military power of Turkey that recast the nature of the conflict and resulted in the partition of the island following the invasion of 1974. More recently, with impending EU membership, Brussels had considerable leverage in seeking to force an accommodation and, although this proved ineffective (when in 2004 Greek Cypriots voted against the plan drawn up under the auspices of UN Secretary General Kofi Annan), the EU continues to exercise a significant role.

It is, however, in Bosnia that the international community has intervened most vigorously. In a context where the Bosnian Serb and Bosnian Croat populations were generally loyal to their adjacent kin states (which had at one stage planned to partition Bosnia between them), it took decisive military intervention by NATO to bring the war of 1992–95 to an end. The international community continues to play a central role in the government of Bosnia through the Office of the High Representative, as Belloni shows.

So, while external intervention can be of great assistance in promoting a settlement (if, for example, the international community, or individual states, are prepared to play an "honest broker" role in promoting intercommunal accommodation), it may also have negative consequences. First, where internal divisions are accompanied by loyalties to external kin states, such external powers may use this as a cloak for covert or overt intervention, whose effects are not necessarily positive. Second, robust external intervention may result in the transfer of decision making to an external proconsular figure, who may exercise power without accountability to the local population, and whose role may simply allow local politicians off the hook when it comes to making difficult decisions. Belloni argues that this was the case in respect of the High Representative in Bosnia, and others argue that it has also been the case in Northern Ireland during periods of direct British rule.

SETTLING ETHNIC CONFLICTS?

The eight case studies that form the core of this collection devote a great deal of discussion to analysis of patterns of conflict resolution in each instance. We may now revisit these discussions and seek to generalize about the shape of the respective settlements. Three broad issues arise. The first is the route towards a settlement: the mechanics by which a political outcome is reached. The second is the form taken by this settlement: the kinds of institutional and other arrangements for which it makes provision. The third is its potential durability: the probability that the settlement is a robust and lasting one.

Routes towards a Settlement

The cases considered here encompass three broad paths in determining the outcome of conflict. Of these, the first and most traumatic is military victory. Here, the odds are typically stacked in favor of the government, given the enormous resources on which it can draw and the availability of a large network of cross-national support, especially with the ratcheting up of levels of international security cooperation under US leadership after 11 Sept. 2001. The most clear-cut example of such an outcome is the victory of the Sri Lankan armed forces against the LTTE in May 2009. Conversely, an exceptional case of minority "victory" in ensuring its separate statehood (if at an enormous cost) was the creation of what was to become the "Turkish Republic of Northern Cyprus" following Turkish military intervention in 1974. More limited "victories" were won by the Bosnian government (with international assistance), the Spanish government, and the British government in curtailing the freedom of action of their armed rivals, resulting in a strengthening of their bargaining position rather than any kind of ultimate "win." Complete military victories bring their dangers, in that they may create martyrs whose memory may be used to animate later generations, as the Irish poet Yeats reminds us in his poem commemorating the comprehensively defeated nationalist insurrection in Dublin in 1916, whose effect he summarized as "all changed, changed utterly: a terrible beauty is born."[15]

Second, external parties may play a critical role in mediating between the groups in conflict and in arriving at a settlement. Thus, quite apart from intervention by individual powers in the Lebanese conflict, an important role was played by Saudi Arabian leaders and by the Arab League, as well as by Syria, in pressurizing Lebanese politicians into agreement at Ta'if in 1989. Qatari mediators played a similar role later, as Haddad shows, in brokering the Doha agreement in 2008. The role of the British and Irish governments in pushing Northern Ireland's parties towards agreement in Belfast in 1998, with a supplementary agreement in St. Andrews, Scotland, in 2006, is also clear, and President Clinton's representative, Senator George Mitchell, played a central part in steering the negotiations, alongside Canadian and Finnish colleagues. When the Bosnian conflict was brought to an end in 1995, it is significant that the venue was Dayton, Ohio, under forceful US leadership but with Russian and EU participation.

In the case of the three remaining conflicts, there was no single iconic moment like those identified in the agreements just discussed. The South African negotiations took the form of prolonged discussions in the framework of the Convention for a Democratic South Africa (CODESA) in 1991–92, giving way to the Multi-Party Negotiating Forum that eventually agreed on the interim constitution in November 1993, as Guelke shows. Although outside mediators played a role at various times, the crucial actors were the main domestic groups. The Spanish experience was similarly slow and deliberate: the constitution of 1978 paved the way for far-reaching regional autonomy, allowing the regions great latitude in initiating this, but leaving it subject to approval from the center. This mechanism was used notably by Catalonia and the Basque country to extend further their capacity for independent action.[16] In Belgium, as De Winter and Baudewyns show, the process was even more gradual, with a sequence of five major constitutional reforms between 1970 and 2001, steadily hollowing out the political center.

Conflict Resolution Formulas

What general patterns emerge regarding the constitutional settlements arrived at in the cases considered here? The literature on options for ethnic conflict resolution generally emphasizes a broad range of possible strategies.[17] It may, of course, be that the state rids itself of a troublesome minority by agreeing to some kind of boundary change (whether simple adjustment of an existing border or entailing the creation of a new state). But if the territorial integrity of the state is maintained, there are several options. At one extreme is a set of approaches that generally falls outside the bounds of political defensibility, some of which also cross the threshold of moral acceptability: various techniques of "ethnic cleansing," including genocide and population transfer. At the opposite extreme are policies of integration, offering minorities access to power through existing structures, such as political parties, and accommodation, based on the sharing of power (as in consociational government or other such formulas) or the division of power (as in various formulas for territorial and nonterritorial autonomy).[18] In between lies a set of strategies that are neither as brutal as the first nor as generous as the second of these: strategies based on the principle of majority rule, with implications of ethnic hegemony hiding behind advocacy of conventional principles of democracy and possibly accompanied by de facto policies of assimilation.

In the cases considered in this volume, there are clear illustrations of the application of all of these approaches. In Cyprus and Bosnia, policies of "ethnic cleansing" fundamentally redefined the ethnic map. Forced population movement, and genocidal practices in the case of Bosnia, transformed mixed territories into two entities where minorities were very small (as in Bosnia) or almost nonexistent (as in Cyprus). This entirely changed the options for those seeking to devise a settlement based on the new "facts on the ground." What are these options? Here, as in the other cases we have examined, we see settlements based not on a single strategy that excludes others but on multiple strategies, though commonly with one that is predominant.

First, the approach may be based primarily on territorial reorganization. This is the position in Spain, with an elaborate scheme of decentralization of power to "autonomous communities" with clearly defined borders, as Llera has shown. Power sharing may exist at the level of the regions or in the center, but it is typically of brief duration and based on pragmatic short-term electoral considerations rather than on any commitment to institutionalizing such intercommunal deals in the longer term.

Second, as Haddad and Todd suggest, there are cases such as Lebanon and Northern Ireland where this approach is not feasible: with spatially intermingled populations, it is simply impossible to divide the territory between the communities in such a way that each has its own bailiwick, without minorities belonging to other communities. Instead, consociational government lies at the heart of the approach: offices are shared between members of the communities, with the government of Northern Ireland based proportionally on the composition of the assembly, and government offices (and parliamentary seats) in Lebanon allocated on the basis of a fixed formula. In the Lebanese case, this was a singular achievement; the Ta'if Accord of 1989 has been described as "an intriguing case of an internal conflict in a multiethnic state that was resolved not by its partition according to communal lines, as predicted by many observers locally and from afar, but by a renewed formula for integration."[19]

Third, there are cases where territorial and consociational strategies co-exist. In Belgium, the central institutions are a textbook example of consociation, with an equal number of French- and Dutch-speaking government ministers and a communal "alarm bell" procedure in parliament; but this has been accompanied by federal reorganization of the state (and also with an overlapping system of nonterritorial autonomy). In Bosnia we find consociational principles at the center, with a three-person presidency representing the three main ethnic groups, a government with guarantees against domination by any one group, and, again, an ethnic "alarm bell" procedure in parliament. But, in addition, the state itself is divided along quasi-federal lines into two "entities," the Federation of Bosnia-Herzegovina and the Serb Republic, and the former is itself a federation of ten cantons. While Cyprus remains divided, it is noteworthy that the solution proposed in the Annan Plan (2004) envisaged similar arrangements: a power-sharing administration at the center, and a loose confederation of the current northern and southern areas.

Finally, in the two remaining cases neither of the two main strategies of accommodation occupies a prominent position. In South Africa, decades of minority rule, perpetuated by efforts to confine African political rights to territorially incoherent "homelands" and to buy off the Indian and Colored populations with separate representative institutions, helped to discredit both territorial devolution and consociation as appropriate devices for the reformed state. Instead, following a transitional consociational episode, more conventional majority rule-type institutions have been established in the center, with a form of limited federalism linking the provinces. Sri Lanka, too, had episodically flirted with consociational principles up to 1983 and made some gestures towards territorial autonomy.[20] But the general thrust of policy, accentuated after the end of the war, was towards majority rule at the center and tight territorial control from there, as Samarasinghe shows.

Durability of Settlements

To what extent can it be argued that the settlements have brought about a durable solution to interethnic tension in the cases considered in this volume? In answering this, it is worth observing immediately that in many instances the "settlement" is a fluid one, allowing for further evolution. Indeed, it is precisely when settlements are written in stone that they become brittle, lacking the flexibility to allow for adjustment to new realities or changed expectations. Thus, for example, the fixing of confessional ratios in Lebanon's National Pact of 1943 froze political representation in circumstances where the relative size of the groups was gradually but decisively changing, and it took another painfully negotiated pact at the end of a civil war, the Ta'if Accord, to amend this. But there was no mechanism for renegotiating the fixed Greek-Turkish quotas in the Cypriot constitution of 1960, as Joseph points out, and the result was constitutional collapse, communal disorder, and, ultimately, partition. By contrast, the Spanish constitution of 1978 allows autonomous communities to renegotiate their relationship with the state. Similarly, the process of constitutional reformulation is a continuing phenomenon in Belgian politics, with both the disposition of power and the appropriate identification of substate units as the main issues. It is clear, though, that if an agreement is extremely fluid, it does not provide a settlement at all, and leaves open all options, including state breakup.

We may identify two further areas where the settlements are likely to come under pressure. While constitutional pacts may resolve immediate problems, they will not necessarily cut away the circumstances that caused these in the first place. Thus, as Haddad argues, recent deals in Lebanon have bought short-term peace but have not tackled underlying issues. Interethnic competition continues and may even be encouraged by the settlement, as Belloni points out in the case of Bosnia. In any event, both here and in such other cases as Cyprus, Lebanon, and Northern Ireland, the communities may continue to look to (and seek alliances with) different allies outside the state. The settlement may even encourage a form of destabilizing competition between the center and the regions, features to be seen occasionally in Belgium and possibly in Spain.

Other practical concerns may also assert themselves. Paramilitary and other armed groups may not have been disarmed and may still offer at least an implicit threat to those who negotiated the settlements. But, especially if the settlement is of a far-reaching and dramatic kind, it may raise expectations that the new rulers will not be able to satisfy. The Belfast agreement of 1998 offered such a challenge to the Irish nationalist leadership, which had argued that it would open the door to Irish unity, and great expectations regarding economic advance were raised by the advent of majority rule in South Africa. As Guelke shows clearly, though, meeting these expectations, and ensuring improved standards of living especially for the African population, remains a demanding task.

CONCLUSION

The challenge faced by the contemporary state in bridging the gaps between competing ethnic communities is, then, a formidable one. Ethnic diversity need not be translated into interethnic violence, but it all too frequently is; and, when this happens, the difficulty of devising a settlement typically increases. Conflict may be contained within the party system, even where the party system is highly polarized, like the party systems considered here; but there are many cases where it bursts through the limits of party politics, spilling over into intercommunal violence. Structurally, conflicts vary greatly: the number of relevant groups may be just two, or it may be greater; their relative size may be more or less equal, or they may vary greatly; and the basis of division between them may be shallow, or profound. On this will depend the intensity of the conflict, with dyadic relationships between groups of similar size that are culturally remote from each other posing the greatest challenge, at least in principle. In determining the outcome, though, the disposition of political resources between the competing groups has a big role to play, as does their relationship with potential external allies.

One analysis of the Belgian model, which suggested its potential applicability elsewhere, identified four features that are important in the formulation of policy on the management of ethnic tensions: tackling potential flashpoints before trouble breaks out, rather than afterwards; neutralizing the position of kin states; decoupling cultural issues from those about the disposal of material resources; and pursuing incremental change rather than sweeping reform.[21] These are indeed salutary reminders about the care that needs to be taken on the road to interethnic agreement. But do the studies in this volume suggest that there is any particular instrument or package of instruments towards which such agreement should be working? It seems clear from analysis of the eight cases we have considered here that there is no one-size-fits-all formula for ethnic conflict management; neither is it possible to reduce the options to any kind of meaningful ranking. We might nevertheless conclude by asking whether, if we were forced to devise a prescription for the common good, the following might suffice: "integration if possible; federation if expedient; consociation if necessary."

ACKNOWLEDGMENT

I am indebted to Jennifer Todd and Adrian Guelke for comments on an earlier draft.

NOTES

1. It would be futile to try to summarize the vast literature that addresses the issue of terminology in this area, but for a lively discussion, see Walker Connor, "A Nation Is a Nation, Is a State, Is an Ethnic Group, Is a . . .," *Ethnic and Racial Studies*, Vol. 1, No. 4 (1978), pp. 377–400.

2. Bosnia and Herzegovina, *Statistical Yearbook 2008* (Sarajevo: Federal Office of Statistics, 2008), p. 66.

3. Count Paul Teleki and Andrew Rónai, *The Different Types of Ethnic Mixture of Population* (Budapest: "Athenaeum," 1937), p. 28.

4. John Coakley, "National Identity in Northern Ireland: Stability or Change?," *Nations and Nationalism*, Vol. 13, No. 4 (2007), pp. 573–97.

5. In addition, within the White community Afrikaners were significantly less wealthy than the English; Hermann Giliomee, "The Afrikaner Economic Advance," in Heribert Adam and Hermann Giliomee (eds.), *Ethnic Power Mobilized: Can South Africa Change?* (New Haven, CT: Yale University Press, 1979), pp. 145–76, at p. 173.

6. See Tawfic Farah, *Aspects of Consociationalism and Modernization: Lebanon as an Exploratory Test Case* (Lincoln, NE: Middle East Research Group, Inc., 1975), pp. 48–52. A similar confessional allocation was made in central and local government and in the army.

7. On the emergence of the parties, see Michael W. Suleiman, *Political Parties in Lebanon: The Challenge of a Fragmented Political Culture* (Ithaca, NY: Cornell University Press, 1967).

8. See A. Jeyaratnam Wilson, *Politics in Sri Lanka, 1947–1973* (London: Macmillan, 1974); A. Jeyaratnam Wilson, "Sri Lanka: Ethnic Strife and the Politics of Space," in John Coakley (ed.), *The Territorial Management of Ethnic Conflict*, 2nd ed. (London: Frank Cass, 2003), pp. 173–98. For a perceptive comparison with the evolution of the Malaysian party system, see Donald L. Horowitz, "Incentives and Behavior in the Ethnic Politics of Sri Lanka and Malaysia," *Third World Quarterly*, Vol. 11, No. 4 (1989), pp. 18–35.

9. See T. W. Adams, "The First Republic of Cyprus: A Review of an Unworkable Constitution," *Western Political Quarterly*, Vol. 19, No. 3 (1966), pp. 475–90.

10. John Coakley, "Ethnic Competition and the Logic of Party System Transformation," *European Journal of Political Research*, Vol. 47, No. 6 (2008), pp. 766–93.

11. David Chandler, *Bosnia: Faking Democracy after Dayton*, 2nd ed. (London: Pluto Press, 2000), pp. 69–71.

12. John Coakley, "Militant Nationalist Electoral Support: A Measurement Dilemma," *International Journal of Public Opinion Research*, Vol. 20, No. 2 (2008), pp. 224–36.

13. Office of the Coordinator for Counterterrorism, *Country Reports on Terrorism 2008* (Washington, DC: State Department, 2009), pp. 309–10. www.state.gov/documents/organization/122599.pdf [accessed 30 Oct. 2009].

14. US State Department, *Patterns of Global Terrorism 1997: Appendix B: Background Information on Terrorist Groups*, pp. 293–4, 323–4. www.state.gov/www/global/terrorism/1997Report/backg.html [accessed 30 Oct. 2009]; *Country Rports* (2008).

15. William Butler Yeats, "Easter 1916," in *The Collected Poems of W.B. Yeats*, ed. Richard Finneran, 2nd rev. ed. (New York: Scribner, 1996), p. 180.

16. See Michael Keating and Alex Wilson, "Renegotiating the State of Autonomies: Statute Reform and Multi-Level Politics in Spain," *West European Politics*, Vol. 32, No. 3 (2009), pp. 536–58; César Colino, "Constitutional Change Without Constitutional Reform: Spanish Federalism and the Revision of Catalonia's Statute of Autonomy," *Publius: The Journal of Federalism*, Vol. 39, No. 2 (2009), pp. 262–88.

17. For reviews of the options, see Sammy Smooha and Theodor Hanf, "The Diverse Modes of Conflict-Regulation in Deeply Divided Societies," *International Journal of Comparative Sociology*, Vol. 33, Nos. 1–2 (1992), pp. 26–47; John Coakley, "The Resolution of Ethnic Conflict: Towards a Typology," *International Political Science Review*, Vol. 13, No. 4 (1992), pp. 343–58; and John McGarry and Brendan O'Leary, "Introduction: The Macro-Political Regulation of Ethnic Conflict," in John McGarry and Brendan O'Leary (eds.), *The Politics of Ethnic Conflict Regulation: Case Studies of Protracted Ethnic Conflicts* (London: Routledge, 1993), pp. 1–40 and Ulrich Schneckener and Dieter Senghaas, "In Quest of Peaceful Coexistence—Strategies in Regulating Ethnic Conflict," in Farimah Daftary and Stefan Troebst (eds.), *Radical Ethnic Movements in Contemporary Europe* (Oxford, UK: Berghahn, 2003), pp. 165–200. The various types of policy of accommodation are discussed further in John Coakley, "Conclusion: Towards a Solution?," in Coakley, *Territorial Management*, pp. 293–316.

18. On the "integration" option, see Donald L. Horowitz, *Ethnic Groups in Conflict, 2nd ed.* (Berkeley, CA: University of California Press, 2000), pp. 601–52; on consociation, Arend Lijphart, *Democracy in Plural Societies: A Comparative Exploration* (New Haven, CT: Yale University Press, 1977); on federation see, among many other important works, Preston King, *Federalism and Federation* (London: Croom Helm, 1982).

19. Oren Barak, *The Hardships of Consociation, the Perils of Partition: Lebanon, 1943–1990* (Jerusalem: Leonard Davis Institute for International Relations, Hebrew University of Jerusalem, 2000) [Davis occasional papers no. 86], p. 38.

20. Wilson, *Sri Lanka*, pp. 183–4.

21. This is a free interpretation of Richard Lewis, "Lessons from the Belgian Constitution for Multiethnic Societies," in Dzemal Sokolovic and Florian Bieber (eds.), *Reconstructing Multiethnic Societies: The Case of Bosnia-Herzegovina* (Aldershot, UK: Ashgate, 2001), pp. 123–34, at pp. 132–3.

Index

Page numbers in **Bold** represent figures.